PRENTICE HALL PT

Windows® 2000 Cluster Server Guidebook

A GUIDE TO CREATING AND MANAGING A CLUSTER

David Libertone

PH
PTR

Prentice Hall PTR, Upper Saddle River, NJ 07458
www.phptr.com

ISBN 0-13-028469-6

90000

9 780130 284693

PRENTICE HALL PTR MICROSOFT® TECHNOLOGIES SERIES

NETWORKING

- Microsoft Technology: Networking, Concepts, Tools
  Woodard, Gattuccio, Brain

- NT Network Programming Toolkit
  Murphy

- Building COM Applications with Internet Explorer
  Loveman

- Understanding DCOM
  Rubin, Brain

- Web Database Development for Windows Platforms
  Gutierrez

PROGRAMMING

- Windows Shell Programming
  Seely

- Windows Installer Complete
  Easter

- Windows 2000 Web Applications Developer's Guide
  Yager

- Developing Windows Solutions with Office 2000 Components and VBA
  Aitken

- Win 32 System Services:
  The Heart of Windows 95 and Windows NT, Second Edition
  Brain

- Multithreaded Programming with Win32
  Pham, Garg

- Developing Professional Applications for Windows 98 and NT Using MFC, Third Edition
  Brain, Lovette

- Introduction to Windows 98 Programming
  Murray, Pappas

- Windows CE: Application Programming
  Gratten, Brain

- The COM and COM+ Programming Primer
  Gordon

- Understanding and Programming COM+:
  A Practical Guide to Windows 2000 DNA
  Oberg

- Distributed COM Application Development Using Visual C++ 6.0
  Maloney

- Distributed COM Application Development Using Visual Basic 6.0
  Maloney

- The Essence of COM, Third Edition
  Platt

- COM-CORBA Interoperability
  Geraghty, Joyce, Moriarty, Noone

- MFC Programming in C++ with the Standard Template Libraries
  Murray, Pappas

- Introduction to MFC Programming with Visual C++
  Jones

- Visual C++ Templates
  Murray, Pappas

- Visual Basic Object and Component Handbook
  Vogel

- Visual Basic 6: Error Coding and Layering
  Gill

- ADO Programming in Visual Basic 6
  Holzner

- Visual Basic 6: Design, Specification, and Objects
  Hollis

- ASP/MTS/ADSI Web Security
  Harrison

BACKOFFICE

- Designing Enterprise Solutions with Microsoft Technologies
  Kemp, Kemp, Goncalves

- Microsoft Site Server 3.0 Commerce Edition
  Libertone, Scoppa

- Building Microsoft SQL Server 7 Web Sites
  Byrne

- Optimizing SQL Server 7
  Schneider, Goncalves

ADMINISTRATION

- Windows 2000 Cluster Server Guidebook
  Libertone

- Windows 2000 Hardware and Disk Management
  Simmons

- Windows 2000 Server: Management and Control, Third Edition
  Spencer, Goncalves

- Creating Active Directory Infrastructures
  Simmons

- Windows 2000 Registry
  Sanna

- Configuring Windows 2000 Server
  Simmons

- Supporting Windows NT and 2000 Workstation and Server
  Mohr

- Zero Administration Kit for Windows
  McInerney

- Tuning and Sizing NT Server
  Aubley

- Windows NT 4.0 Server Security Guide
  Goncalves

- Windows NT Security
  McInerney

- Windows NT Device Driver Book
  Baker

CERTIFICATION

- Core MCSE: Windows 2000 Edition
  Dell

- Core MCSE
  Dell

- Core MCSE: Networking Essentials
  Keogh

- MCSE: Administering Microsoft SQL Server 7
  Byrne

- MCSE: Implementing and Supporting Microsoft Exchange Server 5.5
  Goncalves

- MCSE: Internetworking with Microsoft TCP/IP
  Ryvkin, Houde, Hoffman

- MCSE: Implementing and Supporting Microsoft Proxy Server 2.0
  Ryvkin, Hoffman

- MCSE: Implementing and Supporting Microsoft SNA Server 4.0
  Mariscal

- MCSE: Implementing and Supporting Microsoft Internet Information Server 4
  Dell

- MCSE: Implementing and Supporting Web Sites Using Microsoft Site Server 3
  Goncalves

- MCSE: Microsoft System Management Server 2
  Jewett

- MCSE: Implementing and Supporting Internet Explorer 5
  Dell

- Core MCSD: Designing and Implementing Desktop Applications with Microsoft Visual Basic 6
  Holzner

- Core MCSD: Designing and Implementing Distributed Applications with Microsoft Visual Basic 6
  Houlette, Klander

- MCSD: Planning and Implementing SQL Server 7
  Vacca

- MCSD: Designing and Implementing Web Sites with Microsoft FrontPage 98
  Karlins

Library of Congress Cataloging-in-Publication Data

Libertone, David.
    Windows 2000 cluster server guidebook/David Libertone.
        p. cm. – (Prentice Hall PTR Microsoft technologies series)
    ISBN 0-13-028469-6
      1. Microsoft Windows 2000 server. 2. Operating systems (Computers) I. Title. II. Series

QA76.76.O63 L514 2000
005.4'4769–dc21   00-039989

Editorial/Production Supervision: *Vincent J. Janoski*
Acquisitions Editor: *Mike Meehan*
Marketing Manager: *Bryan Gambrel*
Manufacturing Buyer: *Maura Goldstaub*
Cover Design Direction: *Jerry Votta*
Interior Series Design: *Gail Cocker-Bogusz*

 © 2000 by UCI Corporation
Prentice-Hall, Inc.
Upper Saddle River, NJ 07458

Prentice Hall books are widely used by corporations and government agencies
for training, marketing, and resale.

The publisher offers discounts on this book when ordered in bulk quantities.
For more information, contact: Corporate Sales Department, Phone: 800-382-3419;
Fax: 201-236-7141; E-mail: corpsales@prenhall.com; or write: Prentice Hall PTR,
Corp. Sales Dept., One Lake Street, Upper Saddle River, NJ 07458.

Printed in the United States of America

10 9 8 7 6 5 4 3 2 1

ISBN   0-13-028469-6

Prentice-Hall International (UK) Limited, *London*
Prentice-Hall of Australia Pty. Limited, *Sydney*
Prentice-Hall Canada Inc., *Toronto*
Prentice-Hall Hispanoamericana, S.A., *Mexico*
Prentice-Hall of India Private Limited, *New Delhi*
Prentice-Hall of Japan, Inc., *Tokyo*
Prentice-Hall Asia Pte. Ltd.
Editora Prentice-Hall do Brasil, Ltda., *Rio de Janeiro*

CONTENTS

A cluster is a group of independent computers that work together to run a common set of applications and provide the image of a single system to the client and application. The computers are physically connected by cables and programmatically connected by cluster software. Computer clusters have been built and used for decades. In fact, in the mid eighties Dave Libertone managed and taught VAX Cluster technologies for Digital Equipment Corporation and it's customers.

Today, as Web-based applications continue to gain importance, it becomes increasingly necessary to host these applications on a flexible platform that provides scalability, reliability, and availability. Clustering technologies can satisfy these needs, providing a solid infrastructure on which to deploy demanding Web applications with confidence.

Microsoft first designed the Cluster service for the Windows NT Server 4.0 operating system. Dave's first book on the subject, *Windows NT Cluster Server Guidebook*, was written to deliver expert guidance for planning, installing, managing, troubleshooting and optimizing Windows NT clusters. This book quickly became a bestseller!

Windows 2000 Advanced and Datacenter Servers provide integrated Cluster Services to deliver higher levels of service and availability. Microsoft Cluster Services technology monitors the health of standard applications and services and can automatically recover mission-critical data and applications from many common types of failure. This remarkable new book, written in Dave's highly readable and instructive style, is a straightforward and practical guide for anyone who wants to exploit and learn these new features to quickly create, manage, and utilize high-availability servers.

About the Book

Several features of Windows 2000 clustering, such as load balancing services designed to enable the even distribution of network traffic across a clustered servers, are introduced early in the book. A step-by-step discussion of Server software installation follows, including a discussion on fiber channel bus, dual NIC configuration, and instructions on how to build a cluster consisting of several computers. A real-world case study of an E-Commerce Web Server demonstrates the implementation of Cluster resources. Detailed sections follow this on implementing Internet Information Server 4.0, SQL Server 7.0, and Exchange Server in a cluster. The remainder of the book contains an expanded section on cluster troubleshooting and detailed information cluster-specific performance issues.

Andrew Scoppa
UCI Corporation
Software Technical Training

The Data Processing Dilemma

There was a movie once about two computer geniuses—the story line itself is not important. In the movie, there is a statement by one of them that can be summarized as follows, "It's not money that controls the world today, it is the data." Think of how true this is. Has an ATM machine not working, a telephone-based banking system not available, or your favorite web site being off-line ever annoyed you? I think the point is clear. We have as a society become very dependent on being on-line. This is not intended to be a social commentary, just a statement of fact. I have worked in the computer industry for 20 years. During that time, I spent five years managing a data center. Systems could be on-line for six months straight, but the one day a system was down always seemed to be the most important day to the clients.

Business infrastructures need to be on-line. The banking industry has the potential to lose millions of dollars even with a very small amount of downtime. Even the smallest business loses revenue when its web site is not available to potential customers. Hospitals need access to patient files. It is not an acceptable option to state, "The system will be up tomorrow."

The goal of every system administrator should be to have stable and capable computers on-line 24 hours a day. This is not an attainable goal. Systems crash. Hardware needs to be repaired and upgraded. But let's approach this another way. Can we configure systems in such a way that the data is either highly available or available seven by twenty-four?

1

Current Potential Solutions

There are various potential solutions to the problem of providing high levels of availability of applications or being fault tolerant. All of the solutions focus on eliminating one or more single points of failure.

UPS

An *uninterruptible power supply* (UPS) provides basic protection against system downtime. If the power fails from the primary power source (most likely the utility company), the UPS provides a few minutes of emergency power until power is restored or can be switched over to a backup power source.

Disk Redundancy

Disk hardware is a major issue when dealing with availability. Speaking from experience, a disk crash can have serious implications both for data availability and data protection. There are various levels of protection from disk failures, and the first one should always be a regular backup schedule. This is not a book on how to be a good system administrator, but one point needs to be made. Every so often, perform a sanity check on your backups by attempting to restore one or more files just to make sure that backups are usable. I have known people that religiously did backups, but when the time came, the backups were unusable.

The next step to increasing the data availability of disks would possibly be to implement either disk mirroring or disk striping with parity. Disk mirroring is just what it sounds. Two disks are exact copies, or mirror images, of each other. The concept is, the operating system sees one drive, such as F:, but there are actually two independent disk partitions that represent the data stored on this drive. The operating system issues disk I/O requests to the F: drive. The disk mirroring mechanism processes the I/O request, and the I/O is issued to one of the physical disks. There are various implementations of disk mirroring, some hardware based and some software based. The hardware version will perform better and put no increased load on the operating system because the work is done at the hardware level but may require different hardware. Software implementations will work with most hardware at the expense of increased operating system activity.

Disk mirroring will only protect against hardware disk failures. If a misbehaving application writes invalid data to a file that corrupts the data, this I/O request will be propagated to both drives, and now there are two bad copies of the data. If a hardware malfunction generates an invalid write, this may be isolated to one mirror member, and the data on the other may be intact.

Disk striping with parity logically merges multiple disks into one. When data is read from or written to the stripe set, it is divided into several sections, and one section is transferred to each disk in the set except one. The data that is written to this disk is information that will allow data to be recreated from one of the disks in the set in the event of a failure. This is known as the parity information. Disk striping with parity generally provides protection in the event of a single disk hardware failure, although some new implementations can handle two disk failures.

Transaction Processing

Transaction processing is the concept of treating a group of subtransactions as one unit. This is common in the database world. For example, if I were to transfer money from my savings account to my checking account, this is really two separate transactions. My bank, however, will want to treat it as one transaction, so that all accounts are accurate. Transaction processing guarantees that all subtransactions or none of the subtransactions within a transaction block are executed. This protects from downtime by not forcing administrators to do restores of files that are considered corrupt because they are out of synch with each other.

There is another level of transaction processing that can occur as the file system level. Disks maintain pointers to directories, which, in turn, maintain pointers to files. If the system were to be interrupted while updating this data, lost files or invalid pointers could exist. This can happen with the FAT file system. Newer file system implementations, such as NTFS on Windows 2000, treat updates to the file system as transactions and therefore provide protection at the disk storage level.

Replication Servers

If 100% availability is required, replicating data to a backup server is an alternative. The replication of data to a backup server introduces additional overhead to the primary server, as it has to push any file update to another system. Also, this method has some potential risk. In most cases, there will be a small amount of latency involved, where a transaction is committed on the primary server and has not yet replicated to the backup server. If a switch to the backup server is made at that time, the possibility of data corruption exists.

Multiprocessors

A multiprocessor is a single computer that has more than one CPU module. The single point of failure of the processor has been removed, and the fact that both processors have direct access to memory means that one processor should have access to any information in memory that the first processor was working with in the case of a failure. Applications may need to be modified to take advantage of moving to another processor in the event of a processor failure. Where multiprocessors excel is in the area of scalability. When a server becomes fully or overutilized, it is much more cost effective to add another processor to a multiprocessor system than to purchase a new more powerful server. Multiprocessor systems also contain redundant power supplies to eliminate another single point of failure. Applications cannot automatically take advantage of the increased processor resource provided by a multiprocessor configuration. Unless a single application is written to be multithreaded, there will be no noticeable performance gain in running the application on a multiprocessor platform. Also, to restart an application in the event of a failure, either the application itself or another software component will need to monitor the application and request to restart it when necessary. The one drawback to a multiprocessor configuration is that to service the system, the whole configuration must be taken off-line, which impacts all users of all the resident applications.

The *symmetric multiprocessing* (SMP) solution is by far the most popular shared hardware architecture today. Whether this is a reflection of the capabilities of multiprocessors or a lack of viable alternatives is the question. The law of diminishing returns begins to apply to most SMP configurations as they move beyond an eight-processor configuration. As the number of processors in a multiprocessor configuration increases, it is not a one-to-one relative increase in the total number of transactions that the system as a whole can process. This diminishing return factor can be accounted for by the overhead introduced as the number of processors in the SMP configuration increases.

The Requirements

Any fault-tolerant and high-availability solution has to support four major features in order to be effective:

- Removal of single points of failure. The solution needs the ability to avoid interruption of services to clients if a hardware or software component fails.
- Performance scalability. The solution needs to be easily expandable without requiring a total replacement of existing hardware to increase processing levels.
- System and resource failover protection. It must be possible for any component resource to be taken over by another cluster member.
- Resource sharing. There must exist the availability to offer resources to clients such as files, printers, and applications.

Microsoft Cluster Solutions

Microsoft currently offers two clustering solutions. First, a *server cluster* is the next version of the MSCS V1.0 product that was released with Windows NT Server 4.0, Enterprise Edition. This type of clustering is geared toward high availability of updateable resources such as an SQL database or a Microsoft Exchange message store. Server clusters are unique as a clustering solution in a couple of ways. First, no proprietary hardware is required. This makes the software an option in almost every possible situation where fault tolerance or high availability is necessary. Second, it digresses from the one prevalent cluster concept where multiple computers in the cluster can access a device at the same time. By following this approach, the server cluster software has less complexity, which implies less overhead.

The second type of clustering is a *network load balancing* (NLB) cluster. As its name implies, this type of cluster offers load balancing of client connections across multiple systems, a feature not offered with a server cluster. The disadvantage of an NLB cluster is that there is no disk sharing. You need to install the application to be shared on each member in the cluster.

Both cluster implementations have advantages, and the technologies can be combined for a complete solution. Use of an NLB cluster in conjunction with a server cluster is discussed in Chapter 8.

What Is a Cluster?

The industry standard definition of a cluster is "Two or more independent computer systems that are addressed and managed as a single system." The cluster concept was originated by Digital Equipment Corporation in the mid-to late-1980s with the introduction of the VAXCluster. The VAX can be classified as a mini-computer. The main idea behind the design of the VAXCluster was "no single point of failure." This meant totally parallel hardware with multiple CPUs, disks, and disk controllers. The network controllers were redundant by the fact that each computer had a separate Ethernet connection. Redundant hardware was not a requirement to run a VAXCluster but was necessary to be able to allow any component hardware failure without affecting the services offered by the cluster as a whole. See Figure 2-1 for a sample VAXCluster design.

The main bus of the cluster was a device known as a star coupler. The star coupler accepts connections from processors and special controller units. Notice in the diagram that there is no redundant star coupler. The star coupler is a passive device without a power supply. It can be considered a patch panel or passive hub.

The specialized controller units are known as *hierarchical storage controllers* (HSCs). The HSC handles disk and tape drive I/O. To provide disk redundancy, the VAXCluster supports what is known as volume shadowing. This is a mirroring product that keeps the data on two disk drives the same. Any writing of data is performed to both droves, but data reads only need to be done to one drive, since they contain the same information. By connecting

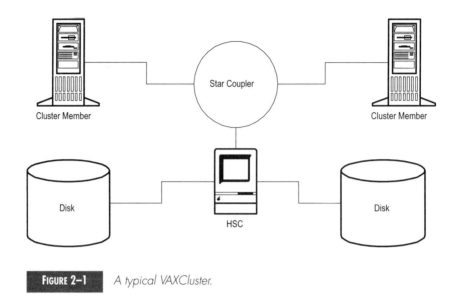

FIGURE 2-1   *A typical VAXCluster.*

one member of the shadow set to a different HSC, there is now redundancy at the disk and controller level. Since all processors in the VAXCluster have access to the HSCs via the star coupler, there is not a single point of failure in the hardware. Still to be solved, however, is software failover. For example, let's assume that a process is running on VAX A and is serving as some sort of daemon. If VAX A were to crash, the software needs to be smart enough to realize this and start the process daemon running on another member of the cluster.

There are four basic components to the functionality of a cluster. First is the removal of any single point of failure. A user connection should never run the risk of being dropped due to a failure of any cluster hardware or software component. Second, the cluster should provide scalability. Rather than having to replace computers with more expensive and faster computers, the cluster should allow for the introduction of more processing power without sacrificing the processors that are already in place. Third, the cluster needs to provide for resource failover between processors. If a directory is currently being accessed through one cluster member and that cluster member goes off-line, the directory resource should be made available on another cluster member. Last, the cluster needs to provide sharing of resources such as disks and printers.

Clustering Solutions

Active/Passive

In an active/passive clustering solution, a standby server monitors a continuous signal from the active server. The standby server remains in a backup, passive mode until it recognizes that the active server has failed. It then comes on-line and takes control of the cluster. When the primary server comes back on-line, manual intervention may be necessary by the administrator to revert the systems to their original state. Depending on the implementation, the cluster may have to go off-line to return to its primary configuration.

Active/Active

In an active/active configuration, all servers in the cluster can run applications and act as backup servers to the other cluster members. There is no concept of a primary or standby server. All servers can dynamically assume either role.

Cluster Models

Cluster implementations can be placed into one of two categories. The cluster can be a shared resource cluster. This means that a resource such as a file can be physically accessed by more than one cluster member simultaneously. The term "physical" here implies a computer issuing an I/O request on a disk controller. The other cluster implementation is referred to as a shared nothing cluster. In this implementation, only one computer can access a disk. Both implementations have advantages and disadvantages.

Shared Resource Cluster Model

As was stated earlier, in a shared resource cluster, multiple cluster members are allowed independent access to the same resource. The most common example to use is a file. See Figure 2-2. Let's assume the cluster consists of two computers, NODE A and NODE B. Let's also assume that processes and both members want to open the same file named LOTTO.NUM. First, it is necessary to understand what happens when an application program opens a file. When the application requests to open the file, it specifies the level of access it needs, such as read or read/write. It also states what level of sharing it will allow on a file. This is also something like read or read/write. This information is kept in memory in a structure known as a lock block. Let's look at a couple of examples.

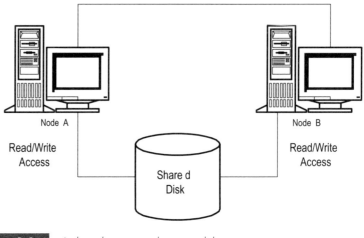

Node A

Node B

Read/Write
Access

Read/Write
Access

Share d
Disk

FIGURE 2-2   *A shared resource cluster model.*

For our first example, we will only use one computer. Suppose USER A runs an application that opens a file for read access and allows no shared access. A lock block is created in memory with this information. Now, USER B runs another application that needs to open the same file. When the application USER B is running attempts to open the file, the lock block is checked, and it is determined that access to the file is denied because USER A specified no shared access. The message that commonly would be displayed by the application is "Access denied" or "Error 5."

For our second example, we will still work with only one computer. Now, USER A runs an application that opens the file for read access and allows shared read access. Now USER B runs an application that wants to open the file for read access and allows no shared access. Even though USER A has allowed the access that USER B desires, the application that USER B is running will fail because it specifies no shared access and USER A already has the file open. If the operating system allowed USER B to open the file, the application would be running under the assumption that no other process has the file open, when in fact USER A has it open.

All the previous examples have simply dealt with how locking works on a single computer. For the next example, let's assume there is now a two-member cluster consisting of NODE A and NODE B. Now, USER A from NODE A opens a file for read access and allows no shared access. A lock block is created in memory. Now, USER B from NODE B attempts to open the same file. The problem is, there is no lock block resident in memory on NODE B. There needs to be a method of supplying information to NODE B that the file is already open and the lock block that needs to be checked is on

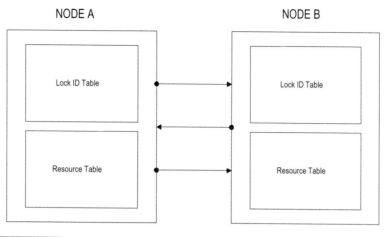

NODE A   NODE B

FIGURE 2–3   *Distributed lock manager traffic.*

NODE A. There needs to be an operating system component to manager file access among the various computers.

Distributed Lock Manager

The distributed lock manager is the software that coordinates resource access between cluster members. Generally, a distributed lock manager consists of two structures. See Figure 2-3. First is a table that points to all the lock blocks that currently reside on the system. This structure is referred to as a lock ID table. The second structure is a table of resources and what cluster member the lock for the resource can be located on. This structure is known as a resource table. The two tables are used to implement distributed locking as follows. A process on NODE A requests a lock on a resource. The local computer examines the resource table to locate the computer that should manage the lock. A request for access is then sent to the computer that is managing the lock based on the information from the resource table, in this case, NODE B. The computer maintaining the lock generates a positive or negative acknowledgment to the lock request, which is then delivered to the requesting process.

There are two major disadvantages to running a distributed lock manager. The first one is the complexity of distributing the lock database and making sure it is accurate among all processors using the distributed lock manager. Locks are constantly being validated by the operating system. The traffic generated to this lock request and acknowledgment could overload an already busy network. This assumes that the lock messages are transported over the standard network media. This is not always the case. Some cluster implementations allow the administrator to designate a path for this type of traffic. Also, what happens when a computer participating in the distributed locking mechanism goes off-line? Any lock blocks that were owned by this computer could now have invalid references on other members. The distributed lock manager has to be able to handle this by recognizing that the owning computer is not reachable and create a new lock block on one of the remaining members. This all needs to occur before user processing can continue. Whenever a member exits a cluster, the cluster temporarily suspends all noncritical processing. What is happening is that the cluster is doing work like failing resources over to other members, and also, if a distributed lock manager is being used, all the lock blocks that were owned by the exiting computer must be moved to another member. But how can lock blocks be relocated when the computer that owned the lock block has crashed? What really happens is that the remaining members must process their entire resource table, and any references to the member that has gone off-line will be reestablished on one of the remaining members, not necessarily on the member with the entry in the resource table. The distributed lock manager allows participating members to be given priority values that determine the percentage of the distributed locks they should manage. This allows the administrator to use more powerful processors effectively. This process of the cluster suspending activity while it relocates various resources and structures is known as cluster transition. Cluster transitions can take anywhere from five seconds to several minutes depending on the number and type of resources that were owned by the departing computer. This brings us to an important point. Since cluster transitions are a known and accepted characteristic of a cluster, they may not be the best platform to implement a real-time, critical application. For example, if a computer were controlling metal pieces that were getting stamped on an assembly line, what happens to the assembly line during cluster transition? Does the arm stamping the metal stop? Does the whole assembly line stop? Here is an even more critical environment. Should a cluster control a nuclear power plant? Obviously, cluster transitions would be unacceptable in that type of environment. Clusters offer many benefits, but they are not the solution to every problem.

The second disadvantage of running a distributed lock manager is in the area of operating system caching. Accessing the disk is one of the most expensive operations with regard to overall performance. To reduce the amount of time spent on disk activity, operating systems will maintain one or more caches. Caches are chunks of memory used to temporarily store various information on the disk such as directory entries and the actual file data. In the case of a distributed lock manager, multiple systems can be accessing files. Each system will have its own caches. The lock manager is responsible for making sure that all systems are looking at valid data. For example, two computers NODE A and NODE B could be accessing a file and have the same data records in memory. If NODE A updates one of these records, the distrib-

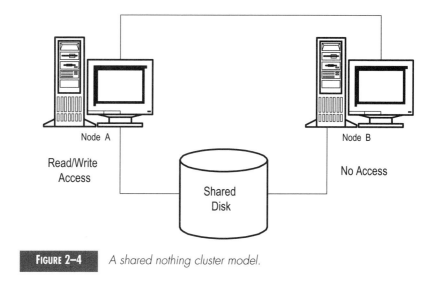

FIGURE 2–4   *A shared nothing cluster model.*

uted lock manager must update the information in the data cache on NODE B. Again, if this is happening constantly, extra messaging traffic is being introduced onto the network.

The distributed lock manager hides the fact that an application is running in a cluster environment at the expense of a larger, busier operating system. A distributed lock manager allows access to files to be coordinated through the native file system. No additional code needs to be generated for an application to perform I/O. An application would only need to be cluster aware if it were necessary to create a shared resource of a type other than a file. Also, a distributed lock manager allows for easy scalability and load balancing.

The main arguments for a distributed lock manager are the scalability it provides and the ability to load balance a single application. As the demands on the cluster grow, additional CPUs and disks can easily be added. Since the same file can be accessed by multiple computers, users can be spread among the processors so as not to overload one processor while another sits idle.

Shared Nothing Cluster Model

The alternative to a shared resource cluster model is a shared nothing cluster model (Figure 2-4). As its name implies, in this implementation resources are not simultaneously shared between the cluster members. In this model, each node of the cluster will own a subset of the hardware resources that the cluster consists of. As a result, only one node can own and access a given resource at one time.

There are advantages and disadvantages to the shared nothing cluster model. The advantage to this model is that it avoids the overhead associated with a distributed lock manager. This makes the cluster software smaller and less complex.

Disadvantages of the shared nothing model include load balancing and resource failover. Since only one cluster member can access a resource, it is not possible to spread the processing load for a given resource across the cluster members. There is no capability to perform dynamic load balancing. The only load balancing possible is known as static load balancing. Here, it is the responsibility of the administrator to spread the different applications across the cluster members to balance the user-processing load of each system. This leads to another issue. A disk is a resource and can therefore only be accessed by one cluster member. To be able to support cluster-based applications running on each cluster member, it is necessary to have multiple physical disks, or multiple RAID sets, so that each cluster member can "own" the disk that contains the application resources the cluster node is running.

The second disadvantage is in the area of resource failover. In a shared resource model, a resource can be accessed by a cluster member without the issue of which cluster member "owns" the resource. Therefore, if one cluster member becomes unavailable, the resource is still available, usually immediately through another cluster member. In the shared nothing model, the cluster node must own the resource to offer the resource to clients. It is therefore necessary to move resource ownership between cluster members. This is called resource failover. When a resource moves between cluster members, there will be a temporary stoppage in user processing while the resource is being relocated to another cluster member. Also, the client may be required to reestablish its connection to the resource. The exact requirements of the client will be specific to the resource being used.

The Quorum Resource

When a cluster member is booted, it must determine whether the cluster to which it belongs is already running. If it is, then the booting cluster member simply joins the existing cluster. If the cluster is not running, then the booting cluster member must establish the cluster as an entity on the network. The danger occurs when two or more cluster members are restarting at the same time. Administrators will not generally do this; it is most often caused by a power outage. When the computers restart, a situation could occur where all the booting members do not detect a cluster and decide to form a new cluster. This is referred to as a partitioned cluster. All proper synchronization to resource access is lost, whether this is a shared resource or shared nothing cluster. Data would most likely be corrupted in a short period of time as computers are independently modifying files and allocating disk space.

Various methods have been devised to avoid this situation, and they generally involve some use of a quorum resource. The definition of quorum is "majority." One implementation of a cluster and quorum involves allocating votes to various cluster members. Real democratic! A quorum value is calculated from all the outstanding votes. If the current members of the cluster own more than a "quorum" number of votes, the cluster is allowed to function. Otherwise, the cluster transitions into a paused state until more cluster members rejoin. The problem with this implementation is that the entire cluster could be paused when there are numerous servers up and running.

Microsoft Server Clusters solve the partitioned cluster problem by using one of the features of a shared nothing cluster model. One disk is selected as a quorum resource. Since only one computer can access a disk in a shared nothing cluster, the rule is as follows. When a cluster member is booting, if it owns the quorum disk, create a new cluster. If the cluster member is booting and does not own the quorum disk, it must join an existing cluster. If the computer that owns the quorum resource were to fail, the resource will be relocated to another cluster member, and when the failed cluster member restarts, it will join the existing cluster.

To avoid any potential problems, it has been recommended that the boot delay times on the Microsoft Cluster Server members be modified so that they are not the same. This will give one member enough time to allocate the quorum resource in the event of a power failure.

Microsoft Cluster software uses the quorum disk to store what is referred to as the quorum log. The quorum log stores changes that have been made to the cluster configuration, such as a group or resource being added. A log is necessary to store the changes if one of the cluster members is off-line at the time configuration changes are made. When a cluster member boots, it checks the quorum log for any changes and updates its registry information.

An Architectural Overview of Microsoft Cluster Software

The Microsoft Cluster software has two primary components. One is the Cluster Service (Figure 2-5). As its name implies, this program runs as a Windows 2000 service. The Cluster Service carries out six or seven very distinct and separate tasks. Each component of the Cluster Service is known as a manager. Every manager runs as one or more threads within the context of the Cluster Service process. While these components work behind the scene, it is useful to know their functionality, because the cluster logging mechanism records the component making the log entry.

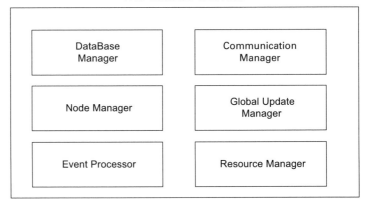

The Cluster Service

DataBase Manager

Communication Manager

Node Manager

Global Update Manager

Event Processor

Resource Manager

FIGURE 2–5   *Components of the Cluster Service.*

The Cluster Service on a node can be in one of three possible states. These states are different from the Windows 2000 service states. They are the status of the service from the Cluster Server software's perspective.

- Off-line
  If the state is off-line, the node is not a functioning member of the cluster. The node may not be started, the Cluster Service may have failed during startup, or the Cluster Service may not have been configured to start.
- On-line
  If the state is on-line, the node is a functioning cluster member. It is participating in group and resource ownership and is generating or responding to heartbeats.
- Paused
  In a paused state, the node is also a functioning cluster member. The difference between this state and the on-line state is that a paused node cannot own any groups or resources. The purpose of the paused state is to provide the ability to upgrade applications without interfering with cluster activity. A paused cluster member can be rebooted without severely impacting the cluster because there are no groups and resources to failover. Cluster transition times would be minimal in this case.

The Database Manager

The database manager is responsible for maintaining the cluster database. The cluster database contains information such as the cluster name, resource types, groups, and resources. The cluster database is stored in the registry of each cluster member. The registry key for cluster-related data is HKEY_LOCAL_MACHINE\Cluster.

The database managers on each cluster member coordinate with each other to maintain consistent cluster configuration information. It is also the responsibility of the database manager to supervise changes to the cluster database. For example, multiple cluster members cannot modify a resource's properties simultaneously.

The Event Processor

The event processor is responsible for the Cluster Service initialization process and any cleanup that needs to occur when a cluster member exits. To implement this control, the event processor implements two substates for the Cluster Service. These states are internal to the Cluster Service and are not viewable from the operating system level via the graphical interface.

- Initializing

   The Cluster Service is in the process of starting. After the event processor puts the Cluster Service into this state, it calls the node manager to continue the initialization process.

- Exiting

   The Cluster Service is in the process of cleaning up before exiting.

The event processor acts as a dispatcher. It is an interface between an application and the Cluster Service. For example, a cluster-aware application may request all available cluster resources to be enumerated, or listed. This could occur when an application needs to create a new cluster resource and is verifying that any dependent resources already exist. The application makes the request to the cluster via an API call. These API calls are discussed in detail in a later chapter. The request is accepted by the event processor and is handed off to the appropriate module of the cluster software

The Node Manager

The node manager is responsible for tracking the status of other cluster members. If a cluster member goes off-line, it is necessary to relocate any resources that were owned by the failed member. The node manager tracks the status of cluster members by listening for "heartbeats." A heartbeat is defined as a message that is sent regularly by the Cluster Service between nodes to detect node failures. The heartbeat functions more like a PING. The first computer to boot into the cluster assumes the responsibility for generating the heartbeats. As other members join the cluster, the first node starts sending heartbeats to them. If the secondary computers fail to respond to a heartbeat, the cluster considers the member off-line and starts moving any resources that it owned. The heartbeat messages are generated every one-half second. This is not necessarily a large amount of traffic, but the capability exists to send all cluster communications traffic on an isolated network segment. This is discussed in the chapter on building a cluster.

The node manager is also involved when a computer is forming or joining a cluster. As a cluster member is initializing the Cluster Service, it goes through several "state" transitions in the context of being a cluster member. These states are totally separate from the Cluster Service states and are not visible outside the Cluster Service. The possible states include:

- Member Search

  The node is attempting to locate an on-line cluster member. This is used to determine if a cluster already exists and can be used to join the cluster.

- Quorum Disk Search

  The node is attempting to locate a quorum disk with which it can synchronize its cluster configuration from the registry to form a cluster.

- Dormant

  The node has been unable to find an on-line cluster member or a quorum disk. If neither of these components can be located, the member cannot form or join a cluster and goes into a "sleeping" state.

- Forming

  The node could not locate an on-line cluster, but it was able to locate the quorum disk and is in the process of creating a cluster.

- Joining

  The node has discovered an on-line cluster member and is doing the negotiation to join the cluster. If the negotiation is not successful, The node manager returns a failure message to the event processor.

One interesting situation is this. If the network connection between the cluster members fails, each cluster member will act as if it were the only cluster member and will want to take control of all resources. The problem is solved using the quorum resource. If communications between cluster members fails, the node with control of the quorum resource brings all resources on-line. Nodes that do not own the quorum resource will take all their resources off-line.

The Communications Manager

The communications manager functions as a low-level transport mechanism for all other Cluster Service components to communicate between nodes. Most if not all of the other managers use the communications manager as their underlying message delivery mechanism. For example, the communications manager is responsible for:

- heartbeats
- resource group push and pull
- resource state transitions
- cluster connection requests, such as with the Cluster Administrator utility
- nodes joining or exiting the cluster

This component is also known as the Cluster network driver.

The Global Update Manager

The global update manager also functions as a dispatcher. It provides a mechanism for other Cluster Service components to initiate and manage updates. For example, an administrator has the capability through the cluster administrator to change the state of a resource or group between on-line and off-line. All cluster members need to be notified of the change in resource or group status. The global update manager performs this notification process.

The Resource Manager

The resource manager is responsible for all control interaction with resources. This includes bringing a resource on-line, taking a resource off-line, and performing failovers of resources to other cluster members. The resource manager depends on information from other managers such as the node manager and one or more resource monitors for cluster, node, group, and resource status.

FAILOVER

The resource manager is responsible for moving resources among cluster members to keep the resource on-line as much as possible. One event the resource manager handles is when a cluster member goes off-line. In this case, the resource manager will relocate all cluster resources onto any remaining cluster members as long as the remaining cluster member has been identified as a possible owner of the resource. For example, there may be a very CPU-intensive cluster resource. The decision needs to be made whether this resource should be moved and started on another cluster member in the event of a system failure. Do any remaining cluster members have enough available processor time to support the new application without severely impacting the clients they are already servicing? This is a hardware capacity planning decision that needs to be made.

The next situation is when an application fails and the cluster member is still active. The cluster provides two options here. See Figure 2-6. First, the

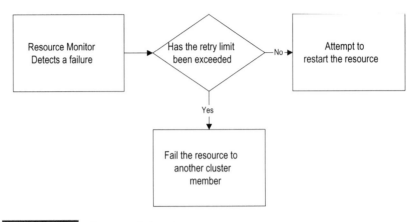

FIGURE 2–6   *Resource failure detection.*

application can be restarted on the same processor. Obviously this provides the fastest recovery if the application can restart successfully. Eventually, after a definable number of restarts, the resource is moved to another cluster member. There may be situations where it makes more sense to fail over the resource immediately as in cases where it may be acceptable to be off-line for five seconds but not ten. By immediately failing the resource over, downtime could possibly be minimized. This is very application and installation specific and would require on-site testing to determine the best possible approach.

FAILBACK

Failback is the process of moving resources back to the original cluster member that owned the resource. Failback can only occur after a failover of a resource. Failback can be disabled to avoid resources being moved at inconvenient times. The cluster administrator can then manually move the resource back to the original cluster member at some point. Also, failback can be configured to only occur during certain hours of the day, such as midnight until 6 A.M. This allows resources to be automatically returned to their original cluster member at a time when the impact to clients should be less.

Resource Monitors

The resource monitor is the second major component of the Cluster software. Resource monitors and dynamic link libraries (DLLs), reside between the Cluster Service and a resource. They handle any communication between the Cluster Service and the resource. A DLL is basically a set of routines or functions. A term used throughout this book and in the Microsoft Cluster software documentation is "cluster-aware." A "cluster-aware" application has been written to handle the possibility of running in a clustered environment. Cluster-aware applications make use of the cluster API. The cluster API is a collection of functions implemented by the cluster software that can be used by a cluster-aware application to manage the cluster. This includes adding new resources, checking to see what resources exist, and bringing a resource on-line. For example, assume an application runs on the cluster that serves multiple database to clients. With the standard resource types supplied by the Cluster software, the database server application would need to be the resource. Remember that this is a shared nothing model. Since a resource can only be running on one cluster member at a time, only one cluster member can function as the database server. If the database were defined as a new resource type, however, now the component that is allocated to a given cluster member is a specific database. The database server software could now run on multiple cluster members, each offering different databases to the clients. As a general rule, when an application is no longer the resource, an instance of the application can be running simultaneously on different nodes, each with its own set of resources. The cluster API is discussed in much more detail in Chapter 7.

The resource monitor runs as a process of the operating system. One resource monitor can support one or more resources. Resource monitors are created by the Cluster Service as resources are brought on-line. The default for the Cluster Service is to control as many resources as possible in one resource monitor. This consumes as few system resources as possible. Situations could arise where a poorly written application causes the resource monitor to hang. Any other resources under the control of the same resource monitor could possibly become inaccessible by the Cluster Service. To work around this problem, a resource can be configured to run in a separate resource monitor. This should only be used when there is a misbehaving application, or when there is not a shortage of system resources such as memory.

Resource monitors track the on-line/off-line state of resources. If a resource state changes, the resource monitor does not take any action of its own. Instead, it notifies the resource manager that will take the appropriate action of restarting the resource or initiating a failover of the resource to another cluster member.

Every resource monitor contains a "poller" thread. These threads are used to detect resource failures. There are two polling intervals used by the thread. They are:

- *LooksAlive* interval

  This is a quick check by the Resource Monitor to determine whether a resource is still running.

- *IsAlive* interval

  A more detailed check is made to verify the state of the resource. Polling occurs at this interval whether the resource is on-line or off-line. This allows for automatic recovery if a resource is able to correct the problems that were stopping it from responding to the LooksAlive poll.

If the resource monitor fails to receive a response from the LooksAlive message, the IsAlive check is performed. If the resource monitor does not receive a response to the LooksAlive check, the monitor notifies the resource manager that the resource has failed. The resource manager then decides whether to restart the resource or perform a failover to another cluster member.

Virtual Server

A virtual server is the logical equivalent of a file or application server. There is no physical component in the Microsoft Cluster Service that represents a virtual server; it is made up of two separate resources, a unique network name and a unique TCP/IP address. A resource is associated with a virtual server by linking it with the network name and TCP/IP address. At any point in time, different virtual servers can be "owned" by different cluster members. The virtual server entity can also be moved from one cluster member to another in the event of a system failure. Since the virtual server appears exactly like a physical server to clients, it is not necessary for the user to learn anything new to use clustered resources. In fact, they do not even need to know that the system they are using is a cluster. The client will use the network name assigned to the virtual server just like they would normally use a computer name. For example, if a user runs applications from a server named ADMIN-SERVER before a cluster is implemented, the administrator can create a network name of ADMINSERVER on the cluster, limiting the impact to the client. The administrator could take this one step further. Whereas in a standard configuration there is a limit of one computer name per server, in a clustered environment that limitation no longer exists. The administrator can create user-friendly network names for virtual servers that are easy for clients to remember and use.

Building a Cluster

The process of installing the necessary hardware and software to run a Microsoft Server Cluster requires a good foundation of knowledge in both Windows 2000 and disk hardware configuration. The disk hardware and how it is configured have a major impact on the functionality that can be provided by the clustering component of Windows 2000. Regarding disk configuration, it is necessary that devices and cabling be configured in such a way that chances are it will be very new, even though you may have been working with similar hardware for years. The knowledge of Windows 2000 can be as rudimentary as how to create a user account;, but realize that if problems occur during the installation process, the more experience you have with Windows 2000, the better.

The installation process is initiated by first identifying the hardware and software configurations that will support Microsoft Server Clusters. The hardware configuration is a more complicated task than the software configuration in implementing a successful installation.

Designing a Cluster

Before cluster hardware is acquired and software loaded, it is useful to do some planning to guarantee that the Cluster Service is implemented in the best method possible to achieve the desired results. Generally, implementing a cluster achieves a goal such as:

- to provide redundancy in the event of a system failure
- to offload some of the activity of a file server
- to offload a server-based application such as SQL Server

Implementing a cluster can attain all of these goals, but hardware configurations will vary slightly with each goal.

During the design phase for cluster hardware, it is very important to pay special attention to the disk configuration. The reason for this is probably the most important rule to remember when working with Microsoft's clustering software:

Important Note   One member of the cluster physically owns a disk. No other cluster member has any access to the disk unless through the network or provided by third-party software.

Therefore, if the goal is to load balance file and application server load among the Server Cluster members, it will be necessary to have more than one physical disk on the shared I/O bus, whether it is a fiber channel hub or a SCSI bus. With a multidisk configuration, it will be possible to allocate resources among the cluster members. See Figure 3-1.

When determining the processor size and memory necessary for a cluster member, the worst possible scenario should be used. Make the assumption that, at some point in time, all resources will be running on one server. Is the one processor powerful enough to handle the entire application load? Is the server's network bandwidth adequate? Realize that the situation is temporary. If one server cannot handle the total expected load, how much degradation in performance will your client base and management accept?

Hardware Requirements

The hardware requirements can be broken down into two categories. First, since the Cluster Service is a component of Windows 2000 Advanced Server, it is necessary to comply with the hardware requirements for the operating system. Second, the cluster software has some unique requirements in the area of peripheral device configuration.

Disk fault tolerance is not a hardware requirement but more of a design issue and needs to be discussed. The majority of resources the cluster can manage will involve some level of disk access. The cluster is designed to eliminate certain single points of failure such as memory and processor. It does not address the disk as a failure point mainly because there are already numerous fault tolerant disk implementations to choose from. One of the more popular solutions is the use of redundant array of inexpensive disks

(RAID). Although Windows 2000 has the capability to implement RAID at a software level, this feature is not supported by the Cluster Service. It will be necessary to implement the hardware RAID solution. Remember that the over-all configuration is only as reliable as its weakest component. Any cluster designed with the goal of maximum uptime and on-line availability in mind will need some level of hardware RAID included.

Windows 2000 Advanced Server — Hardware Requirements

Before we list the requirements to install Windows 2000 Advanced Server, realize that these numbers are the minimum and do not take into account any application-level activity such as running SQL Server or Microsoft Exchange. The general requirements published to support Windows 2000 Advanced Server are:

- The processor must be at least a 133-MHz Pentium.
- Each server must have at least 64MB of RAM.
- The Windows 2000 Advanced Server operating system uses approximately 800MB of disk space.
- Other hardware requirements specific to a cluster are listed in the next section.

If possible, perform some capacity planning from whatever data is available about the applications that are going to run on the cluster. For example, the plan may be to balance the applications across the cluster members, and this situation may leave 20–30MB of RAM available on each cluster member. It is beneficial to plan for the worst possible case. What will happen to the proces-sor load if one of the cluster members is down and the other has to take over its application load along with supporting its own applications? Will the remaining cluster member provide adequate response times to the client base? Different applications have widely varying requirements for the basic system resources of memory and processor. Sadly, information to help capacity plan in this manner is generally not available, so most of the time we have to depend on our previous experience with software products or just load up the system and see how it runs!

Windows 2000 Cluster Service Hardware Requirements

The Windows 2000 Cluster Service currently is supported in a two-computer hardware configuration. Both computers must comply with the Windows 2000 Advanced Server hardware compatibility list. As usual, this list can be interpreted as the hardware that Microsoft has certified will work and that they will support. Just because your hardware does not appear on the com-patibility list does not mean that it definitely will not work. My advice would be to perform a software installation on the hardware in question. Chances are good that you will be successful.

The following outlines the hardware requirements for each computer in the cluster:

- The system must have a minimum of two disk controllers. It is not necessary that the controllers be of the same type. For example, using the on-board IDE controller and a SCSI controller is acceptable.
- Either a SCSI or fiber channel adapter to access the shared disks.
- At least one external disk on either the SCSI or fiber channel bus.
- One or more network adapters; two are recommended.

In addition to the above requirements, it is also strongly suggested that similar hardware be used on all cluster members, at least with regard to the disk controllers and network adapters.

DISK CONTROLLERS

A valid cluster configuration requires that each cluster member contain more than one disk controller. Of these controllers, one must be a SCSI adapter or fiber channel interface to service the disks that will be shared by the cluster members. One reason for the two adapters is to hide the disk that contains the Windows 2000 installation. Windows 2000 cannot be installed on a disk that is connected to the shared I/O controller. However, this is not completely true: Windows 2000 Advanced Server will install, but when it comes time to install the Cluster Service, the device and controller that Windows 2000 is resident on will not be available drives for the Cluster Service software installation. So, basically one disk controller is required for the Windows 2000 Advanced Server installation, and a second disk controller, which must be SCSI or fiber channel, will be required for Cluster Service operations.

SCSI BUS AND DEVICE CONFIGURATION

To properly configure the SCSI devices and controllers for operation in a cluster, it is necessary to understand some of the basics of SCSI operation. Every SCSI bus can be viewed as a single cable that is terminated at both ends. See Figure 3-1. Some SCSI controllers provide an option for internal termination so that the SCSI cable can be plugged directly into the back of the computer. This is a nice and clean configuration for a stand-alone server but can cause problems in a cluster environment. First, if the SCSI bus ever loses termination, it is likely that all devices on the bus will be unreachable. In a clustered environment, one of the features is the ability to take a computer down for maintenance without affecting clients and the resources they use. If a cluster member is providing internal termination to a SCSI bus, and the SCSI bus is unplugged from the computer because the computer is going to be upgraded, the bus has now lost termination and all devices would be unavailable. Second, not all SCSI devices have the ability to provide termination without

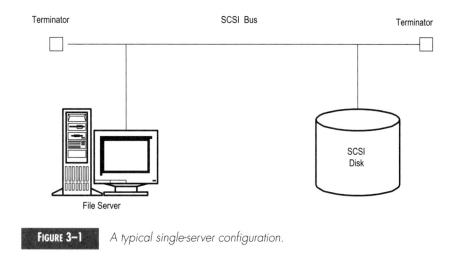

| FIGURE 3–1 | A typical single-server configuration. |

power to the card. In this case, a single point of failure now exists: the power supply. A better configuration is to use either a SCSI Y cable or a trilink connector. Either of these options allows the SCSI bus to be terminated outside the Server Cluster members. Now, the SCSI bus can be disconnected from one or more cluster members without affecting the physical termination of the bus. These cables are not available from all cable vendors and will take some explanation when attempting to order them. One supplier is Digital Equipment Corporation.

All devices on a SCSI bus require a unique SCSI id. This includes the SCSI controller and all peripherals on the bus. By default, most SCSI controllers are configured to use SCSI id 7. Since the SCSI bus connects to more than one SCSI controller, one of the controller SCSI id values must be changed. See Figure 3-2. This is done via the setup utility supplied with the SCSI controller card and can vary slightly between vendors. Furthermore, it is documented in the Cluster Server release notes that the controllers in the two cluster members must use SCSI ids 6 and 7 to ensure proper bus arbitration. If other SCSI ids are used, timeouts on the SCSI bus could occur, leading to errors in the Cluster Service.

Some SCSI controllers generate a bus reset at boot time. Normally it would be a good idea to clear the bus before booting, but in the situation of a cluster, resetting the bus could again cause errors in the Cluster Server software. Use devices that do not generate a bus reset or at least provide the ability to turn off the feature in the BIOS of the controller.

Devices on a SCSI bus use one of two available transmission methods, single-ended or differential. Single-ended transmission establishes a signal connection using two leads, one data and the other ground. This method is more susceptible to noise problems, and all cable distance rules must be

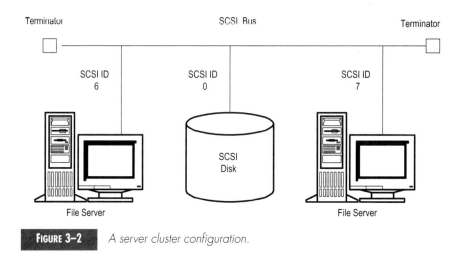

Terminator · SCSI Bus · Terminator

SCSI ID 6 · SCSI ID 0 · SCSI ID 7

SCSI Disk

File Server · File Server

FIGURE 3-2   *A server cluster configuration.*

strictly followed. Differential transmissions establish a signal connection where neither lead is at ground. This is a more stable configuration. It allows for longer cables and faster bus speeds. All devices on the same SCSI bus need to use the same transmission method. If it is necessary to mix the transmission methods on the same bus, it will be necessary to use a signal converter. Signal converters convert single-ended SCSI signals to differential SCSI signals. Mixing transmission methods on the same bus without a signal converter can severely damage hardware.

The requirement that the SCSI disk be an external disk is more of a recommendation than a strict requirement. Internal SCSI disks can use two cables just like an external disk, but the cable is slightly different. It is a flat ribbon-like cable. An internal SCSI disk can be used as a cluster disk, but it is not recommended. First, it is possible to run the ribbon cable between two computers, but this can be messy. There is no connection point on the back of the computer to use. The second, and more critical reason, for not using internal drives is that they draw their power from the computer power supply. Even if the controller were cabled properly to another cluster member, turning off power to the computer will spin the disk down. This violates the goal of having the capability to allow access to resources independent of whether a specific cluster member is available. It would not be possible to remove the computer from the shared SCSI bus without impacting users and access to resources.

The requirement for one or more network adapters is because cluster communications occurs over the network. Although the amount of extra traffic generated due to cluster communications is not excessive, Server Clusters provide the ability to isolate the traffic on a separate segment. A short piece of thin wire Ethernet is very useful here because no hub is necessary.

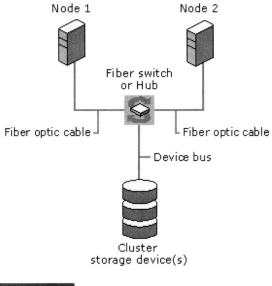

Node 1   Node 2

Fiber switch
or Hub

Fiber optic cable ⌐   ⌐ Fiber optic cable

⌐ Device bus

Cluster
storage device(s)

FIGURE 3–3   *Typical fiber channel configuration.*

This next statement is very important. DO NOT connect the shared SCSI bus to both computers at the same time until at least one has the Cluster Server software installed. It is the Cluster Server software that restricts both computers from accessing the disk simultaneously. Failure to follow this rule can easily corrupt the integrity of the disk, as both computers will be independently accessing the drive and maintaining their own file caches.

FIBER CHANNEL HARDWARE CONFIGURATION

There are some advantages to using a fiber channel connection to service the disks that will be shared in the cluster. Since the connection between the controller card in the computer and the fiber channel hub is a fiber-optic connection, the length that this cable can be is much greater. See Figure 3-3. We're talking around two kilometers for the fiber connection as opposed to approximately three meters for the SCSI bus. Obviously, the fiber connection allows us to distance our cluster members, perhaps into different buildings. The second advantage of the fiber channel is there are no ids that need to be manually assigned. Assignment is an automated process.

Software Requirements

Windows 2000 Advanced Server

Windows 2000 Advanced Server is one version of the entire Windows 2000 operating system suite. The goal is to be an all-inclusive product suite for enterprise environments. Two features of the Advanced Server version that we will focus on are:

- Server Clusters—This is the standard cluster model that carries over from Windows NT 4.0, where the cluster is implemented through specific hardware configurations. This model is designed for failure redundancy.
- Network Load Balancing Clusters—This cluster model uses TCP/IP ports to spread the connections to a given application across multiple servers.

INSTALLING WINDOWS 2000 ADVANCED SERVER

If systems are being upgraded from Windows NT 4.0, their role as a domain controller or member server has already been decided, because whether or not a system can function as a domain controller cannot be modified during an upgrade. If the cluster members are being loaded new, then some decisions need to be made about the role the cluster member will assume on the network. It is obvious that the cluster members will perform the tasks of a file, application, and print server. The basic rule has usually been not to have the same computer perform the tasks of a domain controller and a file and application server. For best performance, applications such as SQL Server are not recommended to be installed on a domain controller. There are two supported configurations for Windows 2000 Advanced Server within a cluster. The possible configurations are:

- Both computers can be member servers. This means they will not assume the burden of client logon validation and account database synchronization. Both nodes must be members of the same domain.
- Both computers can be domain controllers in an existing domain.

The most efficient configuration is to use the domain controller configuration in a domain that consists of only the cluster members. This alleviates the domain controller load of logon validation support and also avoids any file permission issues that could arise from member servers maintaining their own account database. In order to allow users access to the cluster resources, a trust relationship will need to be established with the domain that contains the enterprise account database.

Upgrading to Windows 2000 on Cluster Nodes

Two factors complicate the process of upgrading to Windows 2000 Advanced Server on cluster nodes. First, although the nodes are physically distinct, they cooperate to provide services to clients. You cannot make upgrade plans for one node without considering the impact on the other node. Second, you probably use clustering because the cluster nodes provide critical services to your enterprise. Taking those off-line during an operating system upgrade temporarily prevents client access to important information.

You can eliminate the downtime of your cluster and minimize administrative complexity by performing a *rolling upgrade* of the operating system. In a rolling upgrade, you sequentially upgrade the operating system on each node, making sure that one node is always available to handle client requests.

Overview of Rolling Upgrades

A rolling upgrade has three steps. You must have at least two nodes in your cluster to perform a rolling upgrade. In this example, they are named *NODE A* and *NODE B*. It is assumed that both NODES A and B are running Windows NT Server 4.0, Enterprise Edition with the following software:

- Microsoft Cluster Server.
- If the cluster has an Internet Information Services (IIS) resource, it must be an IIS version 4 resource.
- The latest released Service Pack (Service Pack 4 or greater) for Windows NT Server 4.0, Enterprise Edition.

Another assumption at this point is that both cluster members are active.

STEP 1

Pause NODE A, letting NODE B manage all cluster resource groups while NODE A is upgraded to Windows 2000 Advanced Server

STEP 2

When the upgrade to NODE A is complete, have it rejoin the cluster. Now, pause NODE B and perform the upgrade to Windows 2000 Advanced Server on NODE B.

STEP 3

NODE B can now rejoin the cluster. At this point, you can return to a normal active/active cluster configuration

There are two major advantages to a rolling upgrade. First, there is minimal interruption of service to clients. (However, server response time may decrease during the phases in which one node handles the work of the entire cluster.) Second, you do not have to recreate your cluster configuration. The configuration remains intact during the upgrade process.

Installing the Cluster Service

Preliminary Steps

Before the Cluster Service can be installed, there are a few tasks that need to be performed. First, verify that the drive letters for the shared SCSI disks are the same on both servers. Even though you may be able to boot both systems and view the shared disks before the Cluster Service is installed, it is not recommended. Boot one system first and verify the drive letter for each disk. Also, verify that the disks are configured as basic, not dynamic, disks.

TIP To verify the disk configuration, select Programs, Administrative Tools, Computer Management, and Disk Management.

Assign drive letters for the shared disks and any other devices such as CD-ROM drives. It may be wise to assign drive letters that are not consecutive with the local disks. For example, you might start assigning drive letters at M: for the shared devices. This leaves room for future local drive additions and the ability to keep local drive letters contiguous. If the shared drives are not viewable when one machine is powered off, this may be due to internal termination being used from the SCSI adapter, and the adapter cannot provide the termination with the power off. To work around this, boot the second computer, but at the boot menu press the up or down arrow. This will stop the boot process at this point. Now check the drive letters on the first computer and make any desired changes. Now reverse roles and configure the drive letters on the second computer to be exactly the same, at least for the shared SCSI devices. It is not required, but it may be useful to have all partitions with the same drive letter assignments whether or not they are shared. The Cluster Service only supports the NTFS format on shared disks, so perform a format from one of the computers either in Disk Administrator or from a command prompt. If there is preexisting data that needs to be preserved on the drives, the drive can be converted to NTFS instead of performing a format, which will erase existing data. Open a command prompt window and issue the command "CONVERT *drive*:/FS:NTFS", where *drive* is the drive letter to be converted. The switch "/FS::NTFS" is necessary even though there are currently no other options. If there are files open on the drive, the conversion

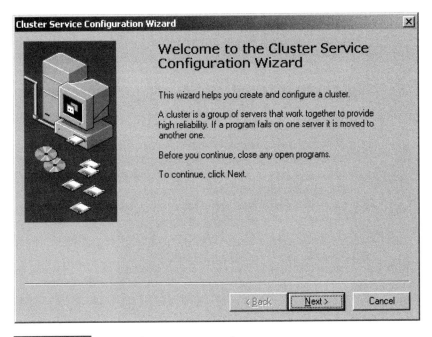

FIGURE 3–4   *Main Cluster Service installation page.*

process cannot take place immediately but will be performed automatically during the next reboot of the system.

The Cluster Service runs under the context of an account that can be specified. The installation process requires that an account and password already created for this purpose.

TIP   To create an account, select Programs, Administrative Tools, and Computer Management. To assign rights, select Programs, Administrative Tools, and Local Security Policy.

The account used will need the right to log on as a service, but the installation program grants the privilege automatically. However, if the privilege were to be manually revoked at a later time, the Cluster Service would fail to start. Make sure that there are no restrictions enabled on the account that require password changes and the option to force the password to be changed at next logon. Since this account will not be used interactively, this would again cause the Cluster Service to fail at startup.

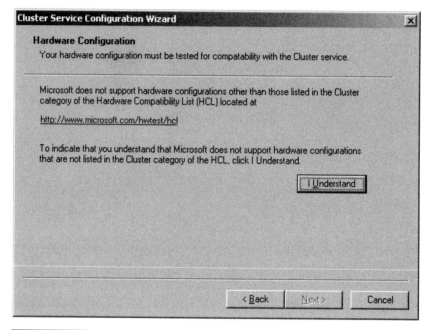

FIGURE 3–5   *Hardware compatibility acknowledgement page.*

INSTALLING THE SOFTWARE—FIRST CLUSTER MEMBER

Now that the preliminary steps have been completed, the installation of the Cluster Service can be performed. To start the installation process, select Programs, Administrative Tools, and Configure Your Server. See Figure 3-4.

Windows 2000 cannot update files that are currently open. With files such as DLLs, it may not be obvious what application has it open. The safest thing to do is to shut down all unnecessary applications during the Cluster Service installation.

There are published hardware compatibility lists for both Windows 2000 Advanced Server and the Cluster Service products. Confirm that the Cluster Service is being installed on compatible hardware by selecting the "I Agree" button. See Figure 3-5. The safest method is to only use hardware that is listed. My experience with hardware compatibility lists has been that most hardware that is not listed will work, but there is no guarantee. Most of the hardware issues associated with the Cluster Service deal with the SCSI controllers and adapters. If possible, use the same model SCSI controller in all cluster members. If this is not possible, at least make sure that the controllers use the same transmission method as discussed earlier in the chapter. Also, only use controllers with the same data path size. Do not mix 8-bit, 16-bit, and 32-bit controllers.

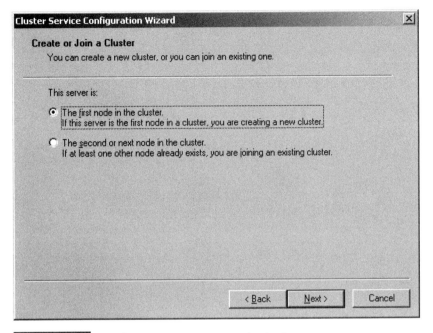

FIGURE 3-6   *Node type (primary or secondary) selection page.*

It is necessary to declare whether this Cluster Service installation should create a new cluster or participate in an already formed cluster. Which option should be chosen here (Figure 3-6) depends on whether this is the installation of the first cluster member or secondary cluster members. Since this is the installation of the first cluster member, the option to form a new cluster should be selected. If this were an installation of a secondary cluster member, the option to join an existing cluster would be used. The options to join an existing cluster and to install Cluster Administrator only are discussed in more detail later.

If the computer receiving the first node installation is not a domain controller for its domain, a domain controller must be running and available in order for the Cluster Service installation to complete successfully.

Enter the name of the cluster to be created if this is the installation of the first cluster member (Figure 3-7). If this is a secondary cluster member, enter the name of the cluster to join. Also, in the case of a secondary member installation, the initial cluster member must be up and Cluster Service must be running.

The only restriction on the cluster name is that it needs to follow typical NetBIOS naming conventions. It cannot be longer than 15 characters, and the name must not already exist on the network. The installation process attempts

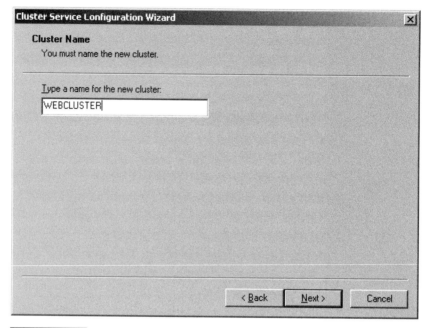

FIGURE 3–7   *Specifying the cluster name.*

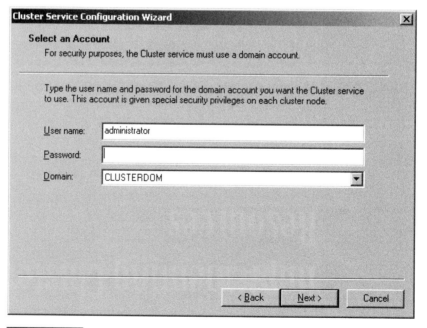

FIGURE 3–8   *Supplying the service account credentials – Primary node.*

to determine whether the name supplied already exists as a NetBIOS name on the network. The normal NetBIOS name resolution methods are used, including WINS and broadcast.

Enter the username and password that has been designated for the Cluster Service account (Figure 3-8). As was stated earlier, the account does not need any special privileges when it is created. The installation process modifies the account to have the necessary rights and permissions. Because the installation process needs to modify the account permissions, a domain controller for the domain to which the cluster member belongs must be on-line during the installation process. This is because all account database changes are applied to a domain controller for a domain, then these changes are propagated to any other domain controllers. Also, if the service account does not reside in the local domain account database but rather resides in a trusted domain database, a domain controller for the trusted domain must be accessible during the installation process. This is not a recommended procedure, because the account information will need to be verified every time a cluster member is booted. The recommended configuration is to have the cluster members be domain controllers in a separate domain and to set up any necessary trusts to allow access to the cluster resources.

It is necessary to have at least one shared disk. If there is not, the installation cannot continue. By default, all SCSI disks on SCSI buses other than the bus that contains the Windows 2000 installation will appear in this screen (Figure 3-9). The Cluster Service has no method of determining which SCSI disks are on shared controllers and which disks are not. The only assumption the Cluster Service makes is that no disk on the same bus with the disk containing the Windows 2000 installation can be a cluster-shared disk. Make sure that any SCSI disks that are not going to be on a shared SCSI bus do not appear in the Shared Cluster Disks window.

It is not possible to have one partition treated as a shared cluster disk and the other partition to not be shared. Also, the Cluster Service only supports NTFS-formatted drives. If devices are on the shared SCSI bus but are not allowed to be a cluster shared disk, check the disk format and, if necessary, format or convert the disk to the NTFS format.

The second disk specification required by the Cluster Service installation is the location of the quorum resource. Any disk previously selected to be a cluster shared disk can store the quorum resource. Select the disk that will store the quorum resource (Figure 3-10). The quorum resource is designed to keep the cluster members from booting up and forming separate, independent clusters. If it becomes necessary, the disk designated as the quorum disk can be changed later through the Cluster Administrator utility. The use of the quorum resource is discussed in detail in Chapter 2.

At this point, the installation program will detect all network adapters on the computer (Figure 3-11). It is useful in a cluster configuration to have more than one network adapter. One adapter could be used solely for the cluster

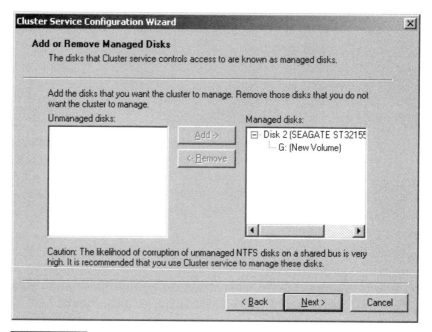

FIGURE 3–9   *Selecting disks to share in the cluster.*

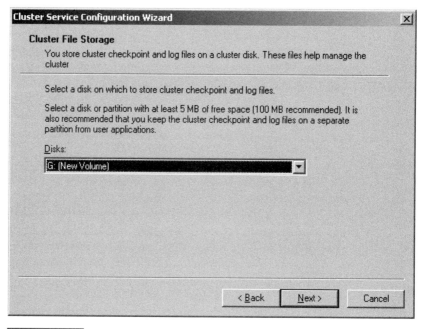

FIGURE 3–10   *Selecting the location for the quorum files.*

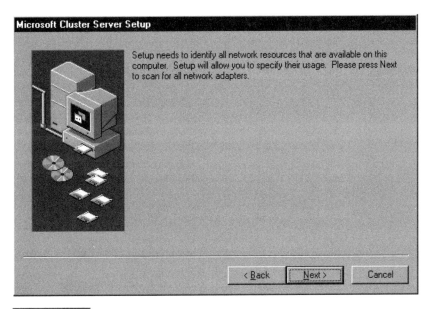

Network adapter search.

communications traffic. This could be a totally isolated network segment and eliminates extra traffic on your company network.

After the network adapter detection process has completed, the installation process allows each adapter to be configured. For each network adapter detected, assign a descriptive name (Figure 3-12). Also, the software allows each adapter to be designated as to what type of traffic it can carry. First, make sure the box "Enable this network for cluster use" is checked. Select the option "Internal cluster communications only" if the adapter is connected to a separate network with the intention of isolating the underlying cluster traffic. Select the option "Client access only" to not allow the cluster to send internal heartbeats and messages via this network. And select the option "All communications" to allow all traffic. This would be the case if there is only a single network adapter in the cluster member.

If there are multiple network adapters with cluster communications allowed, at this point the installation will allow those adapters to be prioritized (Figure 3-13). For example, there may be two network adapters, both with cluster communications allowed but only one with client access allowed. To do this, select "All communications" on one adapter and "Internal cluster communications only" on the other. If both networks are available, it makes sense to split the load by having the cluster traffic use the adapter designated for internal cluster communications only if the network is available. This can be accomplished by ordering the networks, the top being given the highest

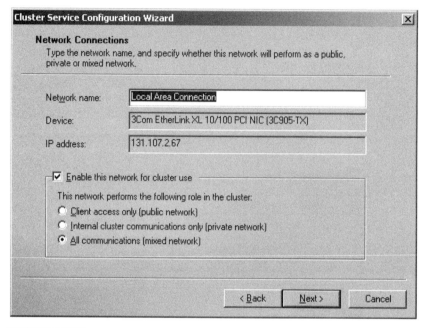

FIGURE 3–12   *Network adapter configuration.*

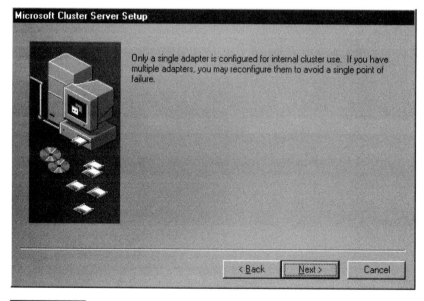

FIGURE 3–13   *Prioritizing network adapter use.*

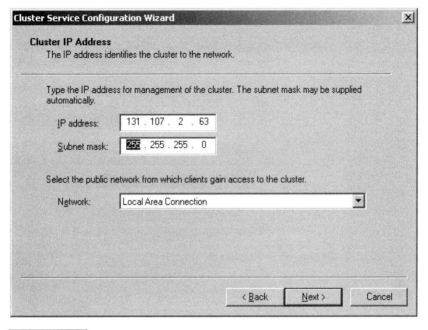

FIGURE 3-14   *TCP/IP Configuration.*

priority, in the order the networks should be used for internal cluster communications.

It is necessary to assign a static TCP/IP address and subnet mask to the cluster (Figure 3-14). This becomes the Cluster IP address resource and is one method of referencing the cluster. The cluster IP address resource should not be used by clients connecting to cluster resources because there is no guarantee that the same cluster member will own both the cluster IP address resource and the resource the client is attempting to access. This address can be used by administrators to connect to and manage a cluster with the Cluster Administrator utility.

At this point, all necessary information has been supplied to the installation program. Select "Finish" to complete the installation. See Figure 3-15.

If the installation is successful, it is necessary to reboot the system to start the Cluster Service (Figure 3-16). To verify the installation after the computer reboots, start the Cluster Administrator utility in the Administrative tools group. If a timeout occurs, wait a few seconds and try again. The Cluster Server software starts in the background and sometimes is not completely running when the desktop is displayed.

Another check for a successful installation is to verify that the "Cluster" key has been created in the HKEY_LOCAL_MACHINE section of the registry.

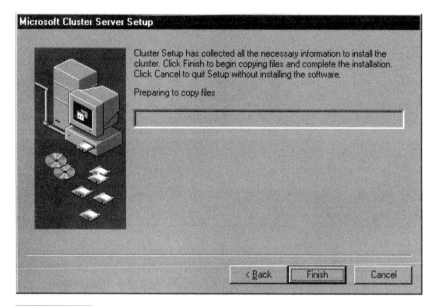

FIGURE 3–15   *Completing the installation.*

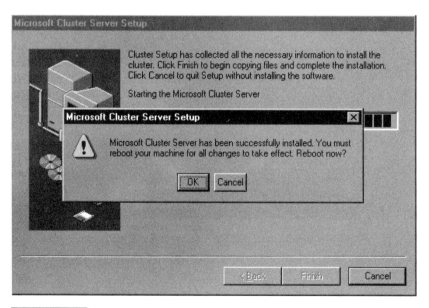

FIGURE 3–16   *Completing the installation, continued.*

INSTALLING THE SOFTWARE — THE SECOND NODE

Installation of secondary nodes in the cluster is a very simple process, with limited input required from the administrator. As with the first node, the hurdle is getting the SCSI controller and devices configured properly. Remember the basic rule that both computers should not be booted until at least one has the Cluster Server software installed. Once one system is a functioning cluster member, it will lock the disk from access by the other planned cluster member until the Cluster Server software is loaded successfully.

As mentioned previously in the section on preliminary steps, the disk drive letter assignments to the devices on the shared SCSI bus should be verified. It is necessary that the drive letters be the same on both cluster members. If not, shut down the computer running the Cluster Server to make the devices available to the new potential cluster member. Run Disk Administrator and configure the drive letters to be the same as on the first node.

At this point, the installation of the second node can be started. Be sure to reboot the existing cluster member. This may require that the second node be shut down to release the SCSI devices. If the boot process stalls at the SCSI device detection then displays the message "Device timeout," the second node will need to be shut down to release the devices to the existing cluster member. Once both cluster members are rebooted, the Cluster Service can be installed on the secondary member by using the Configure Your Server tool in Administrative Tools. Screens that are the same as the primary cluster node have been left out of this discussion. Select the option "The second or next node in the cluster. See Figure 3-17.

Enter the name of the cluster (Figure 3-18). At this point, the first node in the cluster needs to be on-line. If the first node is not the primary domain controller of the domain the computers are members of, it also must be online. If either server is not available, the Cluster Service installation will fail.

After completing the screen requesting the location for the cluster software, the password to the Cluster Service account is requested. See Figure 3-19. Notice that both the username and password fields are greyed. The username and password used for the Cluster Service must be exactly the same on both nodes. As a security check, the installation requires the password to be entered. In the situation where both cluster members are domain controllers, the account used for the Cluster Service has already been granted the right to log on as a service. If the cluster nodes are member servers, it is a good idea for the administrator to make sure the account has been granted the proper privileges

Removing the Cluster Service

If it ever becomes necessary to permanently remove a node from the cluster, it is accomplished as follows:

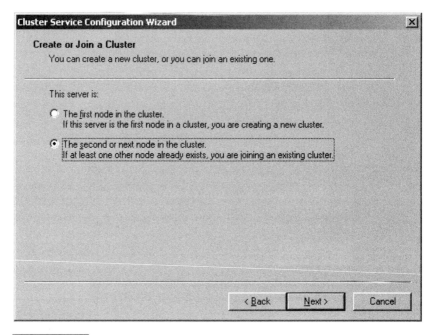

FIGURE 3–17   *Specifying the type of installation, second node.*

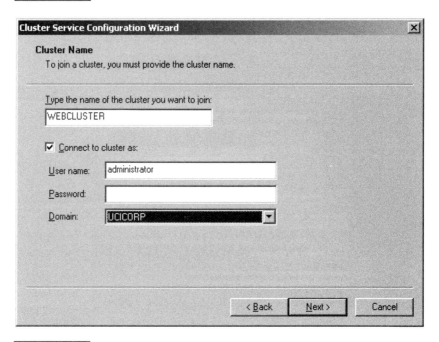

FIGURE 3–18   *Specifying the cluster name.*

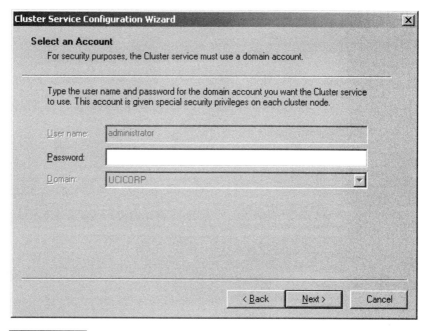

FIGURE 3-19 *Supplying service account credentials, second node.*

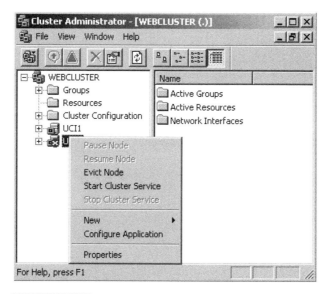

FIGURE 3-20 *Evicting a node from the cluster.*

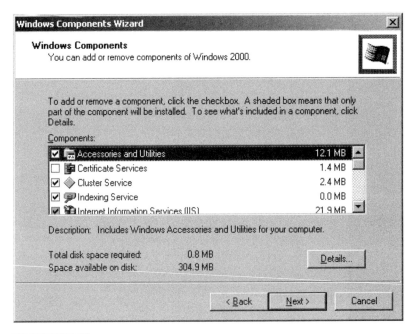

FIGURE 3–21   *Deinstalling the Cluster Service.*

- Move all resources to the remaining cluster member. If a cluster member is being replaced, it is not possible to install the new node until the old one is removed. By moving all resources to the remaining cluster member, the interruption, or cluster transition time, of the users will be minimized.
- Use Cluster Administrator to evict the node being removed.
- Deinstall the software on the node.

EVICTING THE REMOVED NODE

The first step in removing the Cluster Service should be to move any groups and resources owned by the node that is being removed to the node that will remain a cluster member. This can be done via Cluster Administrator (Figure 3-20). When the software is deinstalled on the cluster member, it does not remove itself from the cluster configuration database. This is accomplished by evicting the node from the cluster. This is performed in Cluster Administrator.

DEINSTALLING THE SOFTWARE

The Cluster Service does not have its own uninstall option, but it does install with InstallShield, which allows software to be removed via a standard application. To remove the Cluster Server software, use the option "Add/Remove Programs" from Control Panel. A screen will appear with the list of installed software that can be removed with this method. See Figure 3-21.

Clear the checkbox for "Cluster Service". The software should be removed. If the software is being removed with plans to immediately reinstall, perhaps as a troubleshooting option, be sure to reboot at this point before attempting to reinstall the software.

Implementing Cluster Resources

*O*nce the cluster is built, the administrator can begin the process of configuration. This includes placing resources such as applications, shared directories, and printers in the cluster to take advantage of the fault tolerance the cluster can provide. Many cluster components need to be created, such as TCP/IP addresses and network names. It will take some planning to implement the cluster resources in a method that includes both of the cluster features of load balancing and fault tolerance. For example, in a non-cluster implementation, a shared directory is available depending on the current status of the file server. In a cluster, a shared directory should be available depending on the overall status of the cluster. If the cluster is on-line, the resource has the capability of being on-line. A resource should still be available to clients as long as one member of the cluster is operational. This is a loose definition of fault tolerance. Clients' access to their data or application should not be dependent on a cluster member computer encountering a hardware or software "fault." In a properly configured cluster, it will be transparent to the clients what cluster member is serving their request. The administrator implements this by configuring the resource and all the necessary parameters on the cluster. The goal of this chapter is to discuss the various resources that can be offered to clients as cluster resources and the necessary steps to properly configure them.

To implement cluster resources, the administrator needs to:

1. plan and create groups
2. configure the resource
3. define failover and failback policies for both the group and resource

Group Objects

Groups Defined

A group is a collection of dependent or related resources that are to be managed as a single entity. A group typically contains all the necessary resources to run a specific application. You will find that very few resources are independent. Most rely on other resources for part of the functionality a resource represents. For example, a file share resource allows a directory to be accessed over the network by using the standard NetBIOS method of mapping a drive with a "net use" command. At a lower level, the disk that stores the directory being offered by the file share is also a resource. It is futile to attempt to share a directory on a disk if the computer does not "own" the disk. Since this is a "shared nothing" cluster model, we must remember that Cluster resources are only accessible by one member. A group and all of the resources in the group will be "owned" by the same cluster member. Therefore, the basic purpose of a group is to make sure that resources stay together in order to maintain their intended functionality.

Standard Cluster Groups

There are two groups created during the installation process, the Cluster Group and Disk Group 1. The Cluster Group contains the Cluster Name and Cluster IP Address. The specifics regarding these resources will be discussed later in this chapter. The Disk Group 1 resource group contains the disk devices selected for cluster access. See Figure 4-1.

The group Disk Group 1 is selected in the left pane, and its member resources are displayed in the right pane. Notice there are two disks displayed, G: and H:. Since disk ownership by a cluster member is at the physical level, if a single disk is partitioned into multiple logical drives, the drives will always be resident on the same cluster member. If the system were to allow these resources to be separately managed, one resource could fail over to another cluster member and become inaccessible. Another important note is that disks should not be repartitioned once they are cluster resources. In reality, the disks can be repartitioned, but be careful of drive letter changes affecting certain types of resources such as a file share or print server.

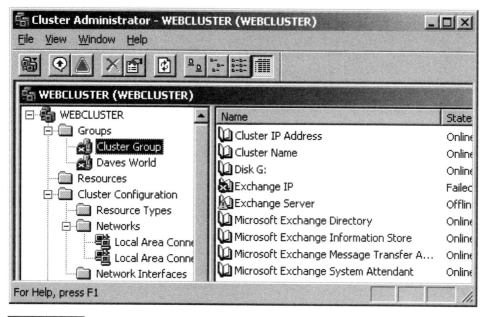

FIGURE 4-1

Planning Groups

The applications contained in the clusters' groups represent the majority of the workload to the cluster members. For this reason, it is very important to perform some planning at this stage.

1. Since a group will generally provide underlying resource support for one or more applications, list all the applications that are to be installed on the cluster members. The total resources, such as memory and processor for the total cluster, need to be greater than the total required by the application list created plus the resources consumed by the Windows 2000 operating system.

2. Determine which applications can be configured to use the Cluster Service failover feature. The requirements for an application to be capable of using the failover feature of the cluster are:
   - The application must support TCP/IP as a transport protocol.
   - The application must be capable of specifying a location for data storage outside the Windows 2000 installation directory structure. This sometimes becomes an issue with operating system components, as they tend to store files in the Windows 2000 root directory tree. For the application to fail over properly, the application must be able to use one of the shared SCSI devices to store all relevant information.

3. List all the resources that can be implemented that are not generally associated with an application, For example, this will include print spoolers and file share resources. The actual operating system print spooler or server service does not move between cluster members; it is a resource that supports print spooling and file sharing that fails between cluster nodes. These resources, while not specific applications, still impact the system resources consumed by a cluster member. For example, a print spooler resource will consume memory to format and buffer the print job and generate disk I/O as it fetches the print job from the disk. A file share resource also introduces disk I/O and will consume memory.

4. List all known dependencies for a given resource. This information will be covered for each resource later in this chapter. For example, a file share resource uses a NetBIOS name and a directory. The NetBIOS name is a network name resource, and the disk that holds the directory is a physical disk resource. For a quick summary of resources and their dependencies, see Appendix A. Two guidelines here are:
   - A resource and all its dependencies must be in the same group.
   - A resource can only be in one group. For cxample, if several applications require the same disk resource, they must be in the same group.

Creating Groups

All resources need to be placed in a group at the time they are created. The first step is to create the groups to hold the resources. The default CLUSTER group could be used, but this is not recommended. In addition, it is not recommended to use the cluster name and IP address as resource dependencies, but we will discuss this in the section on resources.

HOW MANY GROUPS?

This is not as difficult a question as you may think. The logic, with a few exceptions, is as follows:

1. Since a resource can only be used by one cluster member at a time (shared nothing cluster model definition), we can assume that a disk on the shared bus will be "mounted" by one of the cluster members. Any resources using that disk need to follow the disk to the same cluster member to guarantee the resource is functional. Therefore, we only need to create one group per shared disk and place all the resources that use the disk in the same group.

2. There may be situations where you want more groups than disks. For example, I could store an executable in the same directory on a local, not shared, disk on all cluster members. I could then share the directory as a cluster resource. Since this resource is not using a shared disk, it does not need to be placed in a group with a disk.

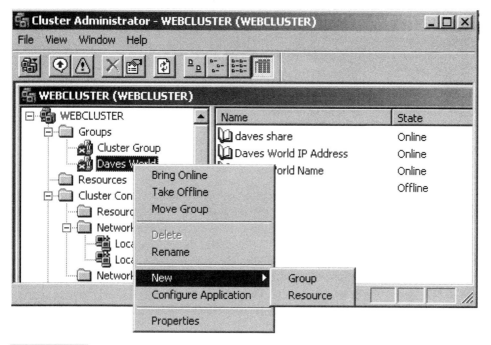

FIGURE 4-2

The question of how many groups to create was really answered during the cluster hardware-planning phase, but it also impacts the group planning. If load balancing is a primary objective, then multiple physical disks must be part of the cluster hardware configuration, and all disks cannot be members of the same fault-tolerant disk set. By definition, load balancing implies that all cluster members will be doing some level of work. Remember, in the shared nothing cluster implementation, only one cluster member has access to a cluster disk. For cluster members to simultaneously offer resources to clients, each cluster member must be able to own at least one disk. This means that there must be at least as many independent disk devices as there are cluster members. Next, each of these disk resources must be placed in separate groups. The cluster software offers the ability to influence which group should be owned by which cluster member when all members and resources are available. This is known as "preferred ownership."

To create a new group, simply right click the mouse somewhere in the Cluster Administrator utility and select New – Group. See Figure 4-2. The New Group screen appears. Enter a name and description for the new group. Be as descriptive as possible to help when managing the cluster at a later date. See Figure 4-3.

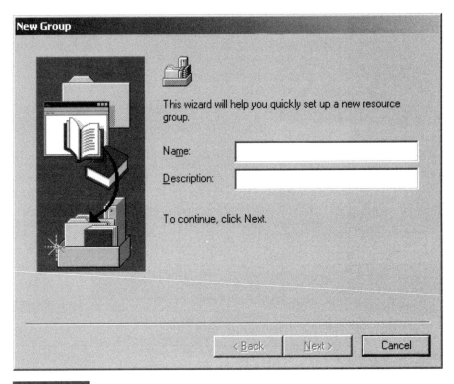

FIGURE 4-3

Optionally, preferred owners can be defined for the group. A *preferred owner* is a cluster member that should become the owner of the group when multiple cluster members are on-line. This is how it is possible to do some balancing of the total workload of a cluster. Let's assume there are two cluster members, NODE A and NODE B. Let's also assume that there are two applications called App1 and App2. To balance the load between the cluster members, create two groups, App Group 1 and App Group 2. Now place the App1 resource in the App Group 1 group and make NODE A the preferred owner. Place the App2 resource in the App Group 2 group and make NODE B the preferred owner. Now, if both members of the cluster are on-line, App1 and App2 are split between the cluster members. If NODE A or NODE B goes off-line, the other node takes ownership of the group as long as it is listed as a *possible owner* for the resource. This is slightly confusing. Possible owners are defined at the resource level. Preferred owners are defined for the group. When the off-line node rejoins the cluster, it will take back ownership of any groups in which the node is the highest ranked preferred owner. It is possible to have multiple preferred owners. Use the Move Up and Move Down buttons to specify their relative priority status. See Figure 4-4. Click Finish to complete

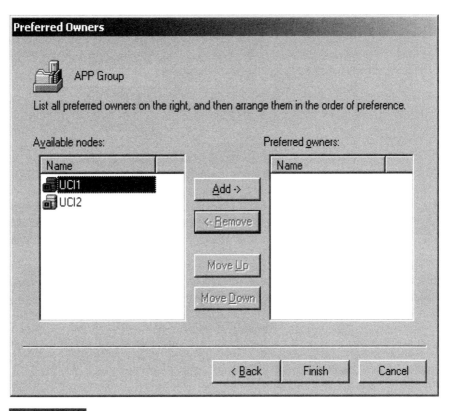

Preferred Owners

APP Group

List all preferred owners on the right, and then arrange them in the order of preference.

Available nodes:

Name	
UCI1	
UCI2	

Add ->

<- Remove

Move Up

Move Down

Preferred owners:

Name	

< Back   Finish   Cancel

FIGURE 4—4

the creation of the group. In the main Cluster Administrator window, the group will appear with a yellow symbol next to it. This is tagging the group as being off-line.

Working with Groups

In the normal operation of the cluster, groups require very little maintenance. There are situations, however, when hardware or software maintenance needs to be performed. A primary benefit of a cluster is that it virtualizes a server, making it transparent to users what actual computer in the cluster they are working on. They connect to the cluster for resources, not for a specific computer. But what happens if maintenance needs to be performed or the administrator wishes to do a hardware upgrade? One method of handling this is to just unplug the cluster member for maintenance and let all the resources fail over to the other cluster members!

FIGURE 4–5

The only problem with this is the slight delay while the cluster attempts to first restart the resource, decide it is not able to restart the resource, then move the resource to another cluster member. This is known as *cluster transition*.

Rather than letting the cluster detect the failure, it is a smoother operation to manually move the group away from the cluster member that is going off-line for maintenance to a remaining cluster member. To do this, right mouse click on the group or groups in question and select the Move Group option. See Figure 4-5.

Entire groups can be brought on-line or taken off-line. An example is an administrator wanting to take a group off-line when a software upgrade to a resource in the group is going to be applied. The administrator can take the group off-line. The resources in the group will then be unavailable to clients. The software can be upgraded, and the resource can be brought back on-line. When a request is made to bring a group on-line, all resources in the group are brought on-line. If one or more resources cannot be brought on-line for some reason, the group still brings on-line any resources it can. Likewise, groups can be taken off-line. When a group is requested to go off-line, all resources will also be taken off-line. For instance, I have accidentally requested the group with the quorum disk be taken off-line, and the software took off-line all the resources except the quorum disk.

In the situation where it is necessary to pull a member out of the cluster for maintenance, all groups should be moved to another cluster member. Select the Move Group option. It would be nice (but it is not possible) to use the control (Ctrl) or Shift keyboard keys to select multiple groups at a time to be moved. There is also a Pause Node option, by right mouse clicking on the cluster member itself, but all this does is to stop any new activity from being moved to that member. All groups still need to be manually moved to another member of the cluster.

SETTING GROUP PROPERTIES

Two important features of groups are the failover and failback functions. *Failover* occurs when a resource becomes unavailable on the cluster member that is the current owner. The group containing the resource is moved to another cluster member that has been configured as a potential owner of the resource in question. In that respect, failover is associated more with resource settings, which we will discuss later. As far as a group is concerned, there are two parameters that deal with failover. Examine Figure 4-6.

The Threshold parameter is the number of times the group is allowed to fail over to another cluster member. The Period is the number of hours to monitor for the threshold number of times a failover of a group has occurred. For example, the default threshold is 10, and the default period is 6 hours. If a group is constantly bouncing between cluster members, the group will not be moved on the eleventh failover trigger, as long as all the failovers occurred in a period of less than 6 hours. The assumption is that one or more of the group resources is not behaving properly, and it is better to leave the group where it is than affect the properly behaving resources of the cluster by introducing more cluster transitions.

Failback is the function of moving a group back to the original cluster member. Failback only occurs once a failover has already taken place. See Figure 4-7. Failback can be prevented. This option is useful if the cluster is constantly servicing requests for the resources of the group in question. Any time a group is moved from one cluster member to another, a delay is experienced. This delay is again a cluster transition. For a period of 5–20 seconds, the cluster will be unresponsive. This time period is directly affected by the cluster configuration, the number of connected users, and the specifics of the applications running on the cluster. To avoid users experiencing this delay, failback can be delayed or disabled. If failback is disabled, it is the responsibility of the administrator to manually move the group back to the original cluster member at a convenient time, perhaps when there is little or no activity on the cluster. Otherwise, failback can be enabled. To avoid cluster transitions during normal working hours, failback can be configured to only occur between certain hours of the day. For example, setting the failback hours

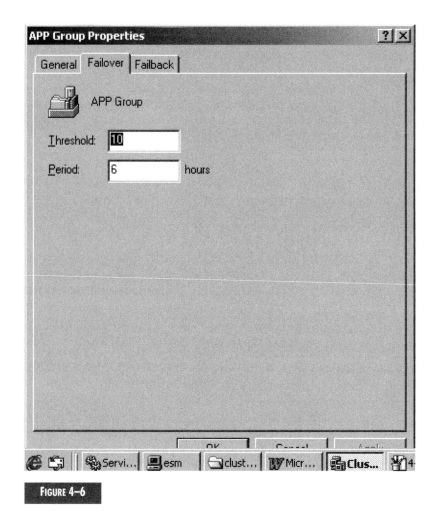

FIGURE 4–6

between 0 and 6 would postpone all failback operations until the period of midnight to 6 A.M.; again, hopefully when there is less activity on the cluster.

Resource Objects

Resources Defined

A resource is defined as a physical or logical entity managed by a cluster node such as a file or printer. A resource provides a service to clients in a client/ server environment. The Cluster Service organizes resources by type. Several

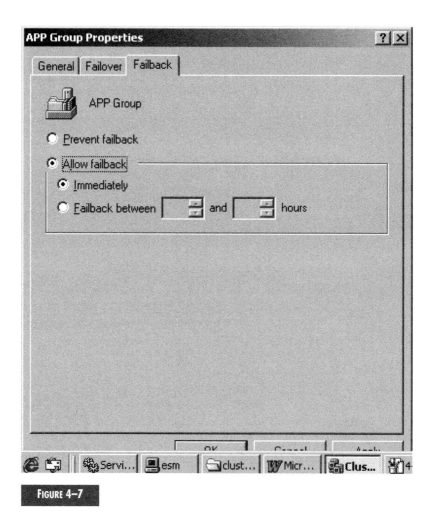

FIGURE 4–7

resource types are supported. In addition to files and printers, some core Windows 2000 services and Internet Information Server virtual servers are very useful resource types. Resources are implemented by providing a resource dynamic link library (DLL) that has the capability of communicating with resource monitors and the Cluster Service.

Resources can have dependencies. A dependency can be described as follows. If resource A is dependent on resource B, then if resource B is unavailable, resource A will not attempt to start. Resources are members of groups, and when a group fails over to another cluster member, all resources move with it. Resources can only define dependencies on other resources in their same group. Since dependent resources must be members of the same group, the Cluster Service is guaranteed that the resources will be available to the same cluster member. When planning resources and groups, dependency is a very important concept. To allow for fault tolerance, a resource such as a file share must be a member of a group with the shared cluster disk that contains the directory it shares. To allow for load balancing, there must be separate groups to allow one or more groups to be on each cluster member. The most critical resources are the shared I/O devices. Since the disk resource can only be in one group, in order to have applications running on the different cluster members, there needs to be more than one physical disk. There is one slight variation to this: If the application is installed on a local disk of each cluster member, a disk resource does not need to be included as a dependency, and the entire dilemma of needing a shared disk per group is avoided.

Standard Cluster Resources

A number of resources are defined at the time the Cluster Service is installed, for example, the Cluster IP Address, Cluster Name, and Cluster Disk resource. They are members of the Cluster group and should not be modified. A detailed description of these resources and their characteristics will not be done at this time. However, individual resources will be discussed throughout this chapter.

Working with Resources

The various types of resources will require different parameters to be supplied during the configuration process. For example, a file share resource will need the disk and directory it is sharing, but an IP address resource will need the TCP/IP address and subnet mask that it represents. Because of this, a discussion on resource properties will be made for each type of resource. There is one group of settings that is consistent among all resources. The common settings will be found in the Advanced page of the Properties screen, and we will discuss these shortly. Working with resources after they are created is more of a standard procedure, and that will be discussed now.

To manage a resource that is already defined on the cluster, locate the re-source in the Cluster Administrator utility and right mouse click on it. A menu appears. See Figure 4-8.

If any options are grayed out or unavailable, it is most likely because the action would be redundant. For example, if a resource is already on-line, it makes no sense to select the Bring Online option.

THE BRING ONLINE OPTION

The option to bring a resource on-line first checks for resource dependencies. Any dependent resources that are not on-line are triggered by the Cluster Service to be put on-line. Only when all dependent resource are on-line will the

FIGURE 4-8

Cluster Service bring the target resource on-line. For example, assume there is a network name resource APPSERVER that has a dependency on an IP address resource called APP IPADDRESS, and both are off-line. If the Bring Online option is selected for the APPSERVER resource, the Cluster Service must first bring the APP IPADDRESS resource on-line. If the IP address resource cannot be brought on-line for some reason, such as after encountering a duplicate TCP/IP address on the network, the network name resource of APPSERVER will also not be brought on-line.

THE TAKE OFFLINE OPTION

The second option, Take Offline, basically works the opposite of the Bring Online option. Again using the example of the network name resource of APPSERVER and the IP address resource of APP IPADDRESS, now assume that both resources are on-line. If the APPSERVER resource is selected and the Take Offline option is selected, the APPSERVER resource is taken off-line. If the IP address resource is taken off-line while both resources are on-line, the Cluster Service will also take the network name resource of APPSERVER off-line because one of its dependent resources has gone off-line. There is no warning by the Cluster Service; the resources are just taken off-line. In the

Cluster Administrator utility, a yellow warning symbol next to the resource is the only notification of what resources are off-line. The basic rules are:

- When a resource is taken off-line, any resources that are dependent on the resource being taken off-line must also go off-line.
- When a resource is brought on-line, any resources that it is dependent on must be brought on-line first.

The Initiate Failure Option

The next option is Initiate Failure. It may seem strange to include an option that forces a resource to fail that has been added to the cluster! However, this provides the perfect method of testing what happens to a resource if it does fail instead of waiting for a failure to occur while the resource is in production. To determine what happens when the Initiate Failure option is selected, it is necessary to examine the configuration settings for the resource.

Common Resource Properties

By selecting Properties from the menu, it is possible to view the policies regarding what actions the Cluster Service is configured to perform should the resource be classified as "failed." These settings can be examined by selecting the Advanced property page from the resource Properties page. See Figure 4-9. The first option defines whether the resource should be automatically restarted after a failure has occurred. It is convenient that a resource can be restarted without any administrator intervention except in the case of a resource that is negatively impacting the performance or integrity of the operating system. In this case, it may be better not to have the resource auto-restart, The resource automatically starting and stopping can make trouble-shooting even more difficult than it already is. In this case, the resource should be manually taken off-line.

If the resource is configured to automatically restart, the checkbox Affect the group determines whether the resource and the group it is a member of should be moved to another cluster member after a certain number of failures. Threshold defines the number of failures, and Period is the duration of time to monitor for the configured number of failures.

The default is three failures for the Threshold and 900 seconds or 15 minutes for the Period setting. When the resource fails for the fourth time within 15 minutes, the resource will be moved to another cluster member. If there is not another cluster member that can take over the resource, the resource goes into a "failed" state and can only be brought back on-line manually. When a resource is brought back on-line, the failure count is not cleared. For example, if a resource has failed four times and has gone into a "failed" state, if one more failure occurs within the 15-minute window after

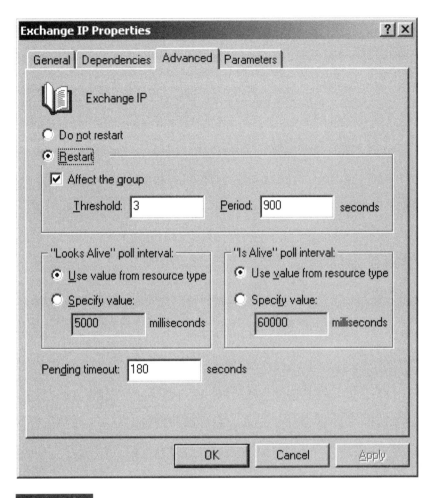

FIGURE 4–9

the administrator manually brings the resource on-line, the resource again goes into a "failed" state.

The next two settings are the Looks Alive and Is Alive timers. The Looks Alive timer is how often the Cluster Service checks to see whether the resource has had activity. This is a very cursory check to see if a resource appears to be on-line. The Is Alive timer is a more thorough check to see if a resource is on-line. When a resource is off-line, the Is Alive polling still occurs, so that if the resource goes back on-line without intervention, the Cluster Service will be notified and the resource status updated.

The Pending timeout defines how long a resource can be in an Online Pending state. If a request is made to bring a resource on-line, this timer allows the request to fail rather than to continue indefinitely with attempting to bring the resource up.

THE CHANGE GROUP OPTION

The next option from the main Cluster Administrator window is Change Group. Even with the best planning, there will be situations where a resource needs to be moved from one group to another. When a resource is moved to another group, the Cluster Service also moves any dependent resources. It must also move any resources that have dependencies on any resources being relocated to the new group. For example, assume there is a file share resource and a print spooler, both with dependencies on the same physical disk resource. If the file share is moved to another group, it is obvious that the disk resource must also be moved. If these two resources were moved, the print spooler resource would not work. In this case, the Cluster Service also moves the print spooler resource. Moving one resource to another group could start a chain reaction and move every resource out of the initial group. It would be simpler just to add the new resource to the existing group. An easy method to move a resource between groups is drag-and-drop. Highlight the resource in the right Cluster Administrator window and, while holding the mouse button down, drag it to the target group in the left window.

The Delete option is simple, but it can also do more than expected. When this option is selected, the software will also delete any resources that have dependencies with the resource being deleted. It at least asks the administrator to confirm this action. The proper sequence to delete a resource is to first remove any dependencies on the resource, then delete it. This option can be useful just to find what resources have dependencies on the resource being deleted.

THE PROPERTIES OPTION

The Properties option is used to change the current configuration of the resource, such as dependencies, possible owners, and resource specific parameters. The Properties screen has already been discussed in the previous pages.

The IP Address Resource

What Is an IP Address Resource?

An IP address resource is defined as a 32-bit number in dotted decimal notation that represents an Internet Protocol (IP) address and is supported as a cluster resource by a resource DLL provided in the Cluster Service. For example, it is possible to create an IP address resource on the cluster and assign it the address 192.17.1.10. Resources can move somewhat seamlessly between cluster members. Therefore, it is possible to ping the assigned address and get a positive response no matter which member in the cluster currently owns the address resource. The IP address resource is probably the most important resource from a functional perspective. It allows us to create the basis for a *virtual server*. A virtual server is a logical representation of a computer. We generally think of accessing computers in terms of either TCP/IP addresses or computer names. Computer names are nothing more than user-friendly representations of TCP/IP addresses. The IP address resource is a core resource that many other resources depend on.

A Short Discussion on TCP/IP

If a network device supports TCP/IP as a protocol, a unique TCP/IP address is allocated to it. The underlying functionality of TCP/IP addressing and subnetting requires a lengthy discussion, so we are not going to go into it here. There are many books on the subject.

All network devices contain an on-board address referred to as a MAC, hardware, or Ethernet address. When one computer requests a TCP/IP connection to another host, that request may be made by computer name or by TCP/IP address. Network communications at a low level only works with hardware addresses. When a computer name or TCP/IP address is used, some translation has to occur. For our example, assume that the connection request from one computer to another is generated using a computer name. In this case, two levels of translation need to occur. First, the computer name needs to be translated to a TCP/IP address. There are various methods of performing this translation, including Domain Name Server (DNS), Windows Internet Name Server (WINS), and files such as HOSTS and LMHOSTS. Once the computer name is translated to a TCP/IP address, the next translation can occur. The TCP/IP address must be converted to a hardware address. This is done via a mechanism known as address resolution protocol (ARP). ARP broadcasts on the local segment requesting the computer that owns the TCP/IP address in question to respond with its hardware address. To speed up the process, ARP maintains an ARP cache. This cache holds recently resolved TCP/IP addresses and their corresponding hardware addresses. Once the computer that initiated the request has a hardware address of the target system, network communications can commence.

When an IP address resource is created on a cluster, a moving target has been introduced into the IP address resolution mechanism. A client makes a request to connect to the cluster via some IP address. Of our two nodes in the cluster, assume NODE A responds to the request. At this point, the hardware address for NODE A is written to the ARP cache in the client for future lookups. Now, NODE A goes down, and the IP address resource fails over to

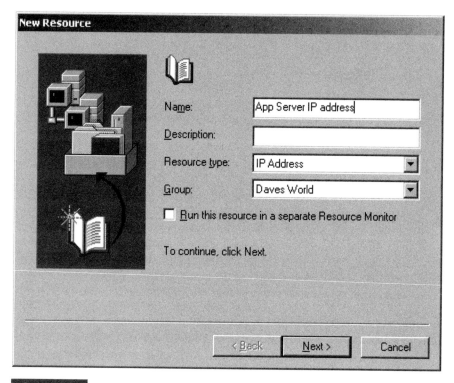

FIGURE 4–10

NODE B. Here is the problem: NODE B has a different hardware address. If our client were to make a request, it seems logical that a connection failure would occur.

This problem is solved by following the recommendations outlined in request for comment (RFC) 826. RFCs are the documentation for how TCP/IP works. RFC 826 states that all systems receiving an ARP request must update their IP address to hardware address mapping for the source of the request. Because ARP requests contain both the IP address and the hardware address of the source of the request, it is possible to update the address mappings stored in the ARP cache.

As part of the TCP/IP registration process, the Windows 2000 TCP/IP driver broadcasts an ARP request on its subnet. This request is made to determine TCP/IP address conflicts on the local segment. When this ARP request is generated, Windows 2000 specifies the IP address being registered to be the source of the request. Therefore, all systems on the subnet will update their ARP cache with the new information. The result is that the registering computer becomes the new owner of the address. When an IP address resource is

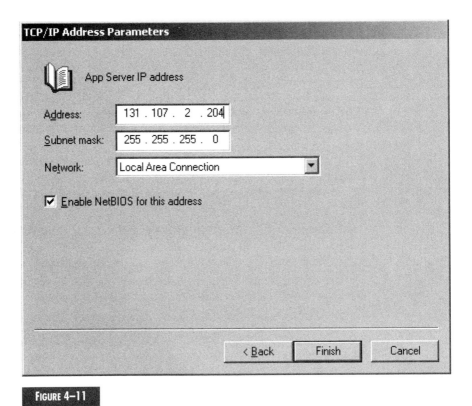

FIGURE 4–11

being brought on-line, the cluster member that now owns the resource will broadcast an ARP request. This request forces all computers on the subnet to update their ARP cache. This results in computers now being able to access the new cluster member via the same TCP/IP address in case of a failover. This solves one of the resolution steps. Host name to IP address resolution is discussed in the section on network name resources.

Creating an IP Address Resource

To create an IP address resource, right mouse click in the Cluster Administrator utility and select New – Resource. Supply a descriptive name and description, and be sure to select a Resource type of "IP Address." See Figure 4-10.

Include all possible owners of the resource and define any dependencies. There are no required dependencies for an IP address resource. It is not necessary to remember what resources require what dependencies. The software will not let you create a resource without supplying the required dependencies. To help, a chart of resources and their dependencies has been included in Appendix A.

The final screen is the TCP/IP Address Parameters screen. See Figure 4-11. Supply the TCP/IP address and subnet mask that the resource should represent. Do not enter an arbitrary address. If you are not the administrator of TCP/IP addresses on your network, request a valid address and subnet mask from the network administrator. Entering an invalid address could make the cluster member or the entire network unreachable. In the Network option, select which network to associate with the IP address. Selecting the wrong network to associate with the TCP/IP address could cause just as much trouble on your network as supplying an invalid address and subnet mask.

To verify the functionality of an IP address resource, there are a couple of different tests that can be performed. One is simply to use the Ping utility from a non-cluster member computer. Another check that can be performed by the administrator is to issue the command *ipconfig* from the cluster member that currently owns the resource. This command is issued from a command prompt window and will return data similar to what is shown in Figure 4-12. Notice that there are four different TCP/IP addresses associated with the single network adapter. These addresses include the standard address assigned in the operating system network properties, the Cluster IP Address assigned at the time the Cluster Service software was installed, and two IP address resources. One last piece of information is the output from the *route print* command in Figure 4-12. This command displays the routing table information for TCP/IP. Notice all four addresses have a gateway of 127.0.0.1, which is a local loopback address. The routing table is updated automatically when an IP address resource is started.

The Cluster IP Address Resource

The Cluster IP Address resource is defined at the time the Cluster Service is installed. It is an IP address resource and does not have any special functionality. The intent of the Cluster IP Address resource is that it be used to connect to the Cluster for administrative purposes through the Cluster Administrator utility.

The Network Name Resource

Network Names Defined

A network name is defined as a friendly name for a device that exists on a network. It is an alphanumeric string associated with a specific network

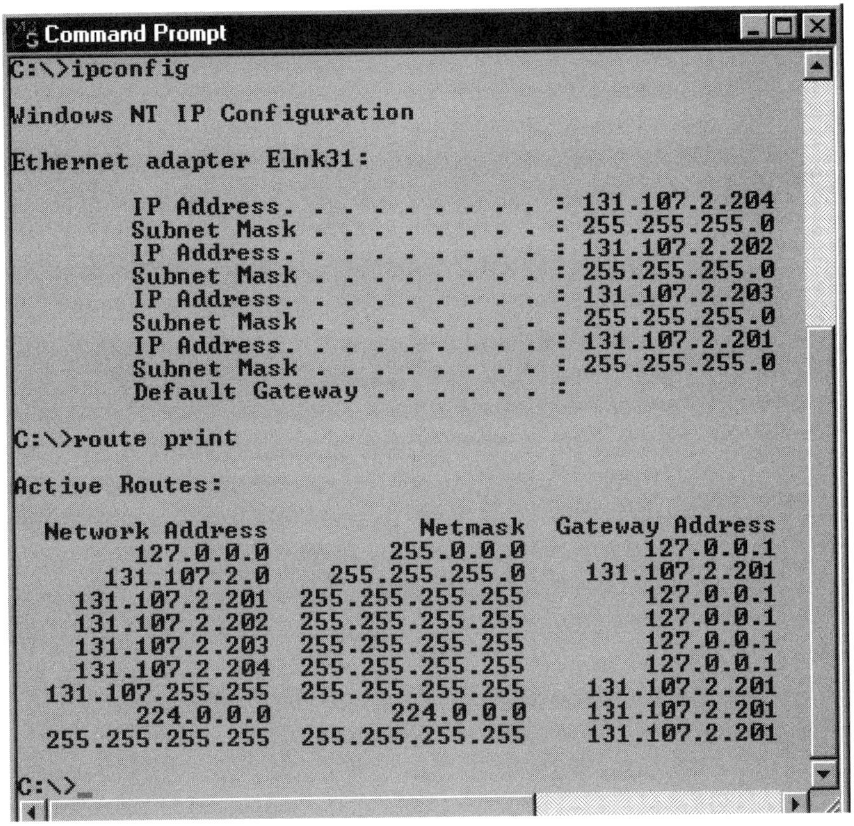

```
Command Prompt                                          _ □ X
C:\>ipconfig

Windows NT IP Configuration

Ethernet adapter Elnk31:

        IP Address. . . . . . . . . : 131.107.2.204
        Subnet Mask . . . . . . . . : 255.255.255.0
        IP Address. . . . . . . . . : 131.107.2.202
        Subnet Mask . . . . . . . . : 255.255.255.0
        IP Address. . . . . . . . . : 131.107.2.203
        Subnet Mask . . . . . . . . : 255.255.255.0
        IP Address. . . . . . . . . : 131.107.2.201
        Subnet Mask . . . . . . . . : 255.255.255.0
        Default Gateway . . . . . . :

C:\>route print

Active Routes:

   Network Address          Netmask    Gateway Address
         127.0.0.0        255.0.0.0          127.0.0.1
       131.107.2.0    255.255.255.0      131.107.2.201
     131.107.2.201  255.255.255.255          127.0.0.1
     131.107.2.202  255.255.255.255          127.0.0.1
     131.107.2.203  255.255.255.255          127.0.0.1
     131.107.2.204  255.255.255.255          127.0.0.1
   131.107.255.255  255.255.255.255      131.107.2.201
         224.0.0.0        224.0.0.0      131.107.2.201
   255.255.255.255  255.255.255.255      131.107.2.201

C:\>_
```

FIGURE 4–12   *Verifying an IP Address resource.*

address. For example, it is probably much easier for a user to remember that a database is accessible via the name WIDGETDATA as opposed to remembering the address 194.73.18.162. Since network names are not necessary to establish a network connection, they can be classified as an optional resource, but in reality, everyone uses them because of the convenience the mechanism provides to the user. Some may argue that Universal Naming Convention (UNC) names, names in the format of \\server\share, require a network name. This was true in early versions of Windows NT, but now, using a TCP/IP address in the server field works.

Creating a Network Name Resource

Use the standard procedure to start the processing of creating a new resource, and select a Resource type of "Network Name." See Figure 4-13.

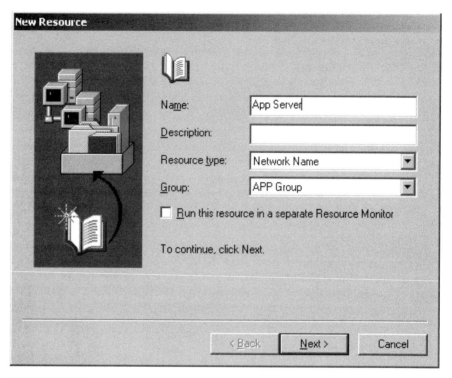

New Resource

Name: |App Server|

Description: | |

Resource type: |Network Name ▼|

Group: |APP Group ▼|

☐ Run this resource in a separate Resource Monitor

To continue, click Next.

< Back | Next > | Cancel

FIGURE 4-13   *Creating a Network Name resource.*

Since a network name resource is a character representation of a TCP/IP address, an IP address resource is a necessary dependency. This is the only dependency required. If you do not see the IP address resource you created, it is probably not in the same group being used for the network name resource. See Figure 4-14.

There is only one parameter to supply for a network name resource: the character string to associate with the IP address resource. The parameter must follow the standard conventions for NetBIOS names, such as limiting the string to 15 characters. See Figure 4-15.

Now that there is a network name that represents a TCP/IP address, there is one problem that needs to be resolved. The mechanism of TCP/IP address resolution provided by ARP only resolves TCP/IP addresses to physical addresses. Given a network name, there needs to be a resolution of that name to an address. Various mechanisms exist to perform this task, such as WINS, DNS, LMHOSTS, HOSTS, and a broadcast message requesting name resolution. This last method will only work if the client is on the same physical network segment as is the cluster. The LMHOSTS and HOSTS files are text

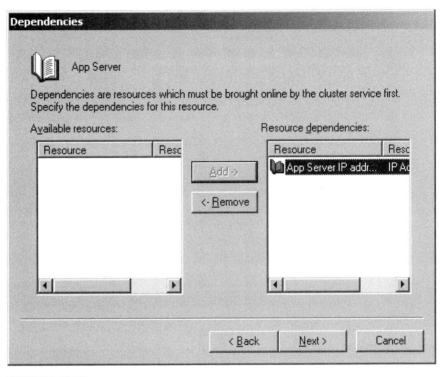

FIGURE 4–14   *Defining resource dependencies.*

files that contain network name and TCP/IP address entries. Is there a potential problem using these files with hardcoded entries for resolution, since the name resource has the potential to move between cluster members? The answer is "No" because the IP address resource moves with the network name. For example, assume an IP address resource of 190.35.172.15 has been created, and a network name resource of WIDGETSVR is dependent on this resource. Making an entry in a HOSTS file connecting these two components will be valid because the cluster member that owns the IP address resource will also own the network name. The only disadvantage of using such files as HOSTS or LMHOSTS is that they are resident on the client. If there are 500 clients, there is a lot of maintenance. Some administrators have implemented code in a login script that gets executed when the user logs in: It copies a HOSTS file from a central server to the local client. This works and is a great way to make sure that all clients have the same information.

The best solution currently available is to have the cluster members configured with WINS server addresses. To summarize, WINS is software that runs on Windows 2000 that maintains a database of TCP/IP addresses and

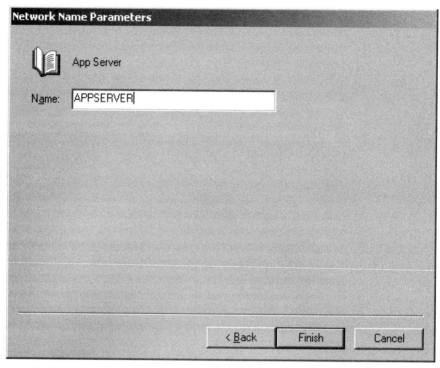

FIGURE 4–15   *Supplying the network name.*

NetBIOS names. It is very similar to DNS except for one very important feature: The WINS name registration mechanism is dynamic. With Windows 2000, it is possible to have entries dynamically registered into a DNS database. This feature is actually implemented by DHCP, which you will not be using for your cluster resources. WINS servers depend on their clients to register and deregister the name and TCP/IP address they are using. This originally was designed to support DHCP but also allows network name resources to be registered for later translation by clients. When a cluster member brings a network name resource on-line, the network name and TCP/IP address are registered with the WINS server defined in its TCP/IP properties.

THE CLUSTER NAME RESOURCE

The Cluster Name resource is a standard network name resource. It is similar to the Cluster IP Address resource in that the intended use for the Cluster Name is for remote management. The Cluster Name resource is dependent on the Cluster IP Address.

The File Share Resource

What Is a File Share?

A file share resource is a standard NetBIOS-based shared directory offered to users by the cluster. Clients connect to file share resources just as they would to any other directory share, by using the *My Network Places* tool or a "net use" command. An example of using a file share resource is when the goal is to provide the maximum on-line availability for an application or database. Think of a file share as nothing more than a directory, except instead of residing on the client computer, it resides on the cluster. The client may need to establish a network connection to the cluster to use the files in the file share, but it will be transparent to the client which cluster member is actually providing access to the resource. The file share resource does not implement this transparency. The association of a file share resource with a network name resource provides the flexibility for a file share to move between cluster members and have little or no impact on a client.

CREATING A FILE SHARE RESOURCE

To create a file share resource, right mouse click somewhere within the Cluster Administrator window and select New – Resource. If the group is selected before right mouse clicking, the resource is automatically associated with that group. This is not a necessity, as during the resource definition the owning group can be specified.

Enter a resource name and description and select a Resource type of "File Share." Be as descriptive as possible with the name and description. The option Run this resource in a separate Resource Monitor should usually only be selected if a resource is not behaving properly. Each resource monitor represents a process. When the resource monitor process is launched, the specific DLL is loaded to support that type of resource. There are standard dynamic link libraries that ship with the Cluster Service that support all the available resource types. Also, vendors have the capability to develop their own resource DLLs. Each resource monitor will consume system resources. See Figure 4-16.

Next, specify which nodes in the cluster are allowed to potentially own the file share resource. If various members of the cluster will support the file share, some planning should be done. The file share resource associates with a specific disk and directory. The Cluster Service treats the disk as a separate resource. It is the responsibility of the Cluster Administrator to guarantee that the disk and file share resources will always be owned by the same cluster member. To guarantee that the resources reside on the same cluster member, they must placed in the same group. Remember, groups, not individual resources, are moved during a failover. See Figure 4-17.

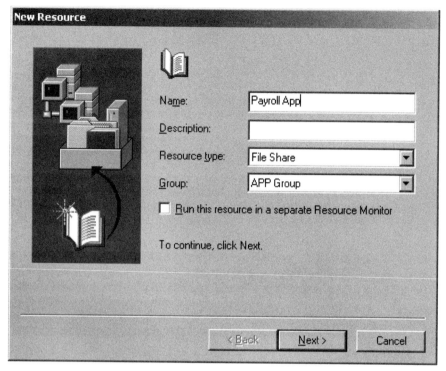

FIGURE 4-16   *Creating a File Share resource.*

Also, it does not make sense to attempt to bring a file share resource on-line if the shared disk that the file share resides on is off-line. To stop this from happening, the administrator can define a dependency between the file share resource and the disk resource. It seems logical that the disk would be a required dependency, but it is not. We will see the reason for this shortly.

Other optional resource dependencies include network name and IP address resources. It is not necessary to define both network name and IP address resource dependencies. The network name has to have a dependency of an IP address resource. When a resource is requested to be brought on-line, the Cluster Service must also bring on-line any dependent resources. This has a cascading effect. If the file share resource is dependent on a network name, which we know is dependent on an IP address, simply requesting to bring the file share on-line will automatically request that the network name and IP address be brought on-line as well.

The File Share Parameters page defines the characteristics of the network share point. See Figure 4-18. In the Share name box, enter the name that is to be offered on the network. This is the name that users will reference with a UNC name to map a network drive. The path field contains the physi-

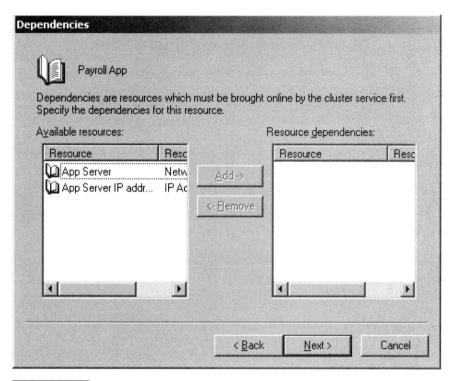

FIGURE 4-17   *Defining resource dependencies.*

cal device and directory that the file share represents. This can be either a local device or a shared SCSI device. One point about the path: The software does not verify whether the device and directory are valid. That test is not made until the resource is brought on-line. Then, the resource simply fails if the path is invalid.

Then one only gets a failure and no message on the screen. I also attempted to use a network drive in the path. The resource failed when an attempt was made to bring it on-line. I do not know exactly how this could have been used. Since it did not work, I did not pursue it further.

The User Limit defines the number of simultaneous users that can be connected to the resource. This controls the number of NetBIOS sessions that are allowed against the resource. The Permissions button allows the administrator to build an access control list defining allowed and disallowed users and groups.

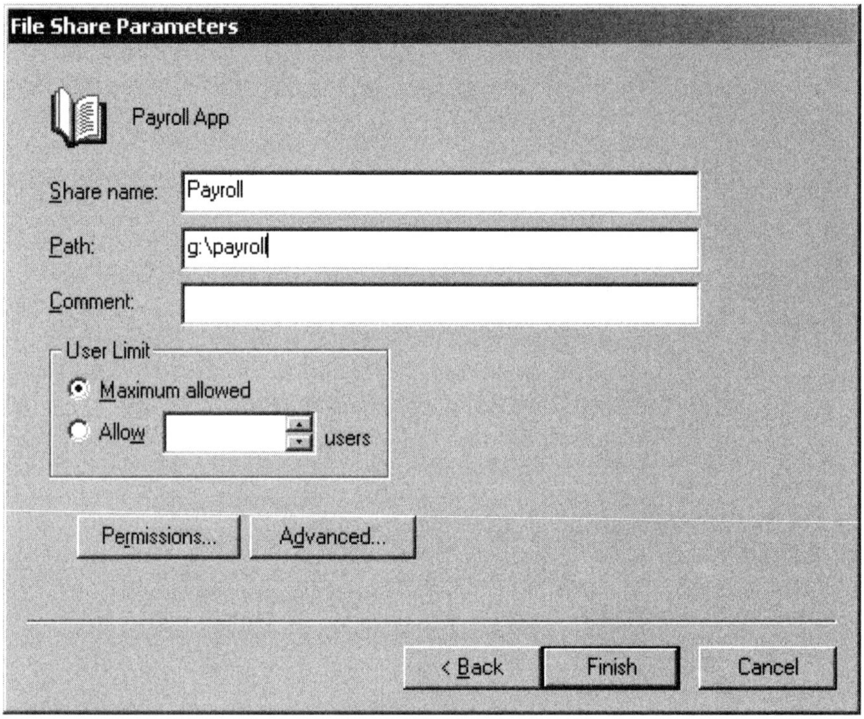

File Share Parameters

    Payroll App

Share name: Payroll

Path: g:\payroll

Comment:

┌ User Limit ─────────────────────
│ ◉ Maximum allowed
│ ○ Allow [   ] ▲▼ users
└──────────────────────────────────

[Permissions...]   [Advanced...]

[< Back] [Finish] [Cancel]

FIGURE 4–18 *Supplying File Share resource properties.*

Creating Multiple File Shares with One Resource

Every cluster resource that is created has a performance impact. The Cluster Service must periodically poll all resources to determine if they have failed. Because of this, you may notice that your cluster's performance decreases as you increase the number of resources that it manages.

If you want to use a cluster to create a high availability file server that will have hundreds of file shares, you should consider managing those file shares with a single file share resource. You can do this if the folders on the network that you want to share are all subfolders of a common folder. For example, if you use your file server to support hundreds of users, and each user has a private home folder that is a subfolder of the Users folder, you can manage individual file shares for each user by using a single file share resource. You also have the option to hide the file shares that you create for each user.

The combo file share option permits a file share resource to share subdirectories. Subfolders of a combo file share are shared using the subfolder name. You cannot specify a name for a subfolder share. The only way to change a subfolder share name is to change the subfolder name. Changing the name of a shared subfolder will break the share. The subfolder share will be unavailable for the time specified by the file share resource Is Alive poll interval. The subfolder will be shared again the next time the file share resource Is Alive poll is called.

USING A FILE SHARE RESOURCE

Users request a connection to a file share resource just like any other shared directory on the network. If the *My Network Places* tool is used, on-line network name resources will appear as standard computer names. From a command prompt, the *NET VIEW* *network_name* and *NET USE x:* *network_name\share_name* work as usual. One thing that may be slightly confusing is that a file share resource may appear under multiple network names. For example, let's go back to our NODE 1 and NODE 2 example. Assume the cluster name is WIDGETWORLD. Also assume that we have created a file share dependent on the network name WIDGETAPPS and that the cluster name, network name, and file share are all owned by NODE 2. Our file share, WIDGETAPPS, will show as an available shared resource under all three names in the *My Network Places* tool. Why? Because all three network names are internally associated with the MAC address of the network card in the NODE 2 computer. The argument is whether to create network names for all file share resources or to let the users map via the cluster name. There is no guarantee that the cluster name and network name to be used for the file share resource will always be owned by the same cluster member unless they are located in the same group. It is also suggested to not use the cluster group for any add-on resources other than what was placed in the group during the Cluster Service installation. To limit the number of network names that users need to remember, a preferred option may be to create a file share that is associated with an application root directory. The actual applications can then reside in subdirectories. Users only need to remember one network name. A disadvantage to this method is that the same cluster member must offer all applications. The load will not be balanced. If the goal is to spread the processor activity, then multiple groups, file shares, and network names will need to be defined. Any load balancing has to be done at the group level.

What Happens During a Failover

Up to this point, we have discussed how to implement a file share resource. But what really happens when a user is in the middle of an update through a file share resource and a resource failover occurs? The answer is, "It depends." It is the responsibility of the application to handle the network interruption or relocation to another cluster member. If a network drive is mapped, and a failover occurs, the drive connection will be automatically reestablished by the network client software. Where it gets messy is when a file was opened on the file share. A file handle represents an open file. File handles are stored in memory. When a resource is moved to another cluster member, none of the client state, such as file handles, goes with the resource. It is up to the application that the client is running to recognize that the file handle is gone and to reopen the file. This reestablishment of the client state is something that cluster-aware applications need to perform.

The test I made was a simple one of mapping a drive and opening a file with the Edit program. After the file was opened, a resource failure was initiated by right mouse clicking on the resource and this time selecting Initiate Failure. After the failure completed and the file share resource was back on-line, an attempt to save the file by using the File – Save option failed. Upon examination using the Computer Management tool, the NetBIOS session that was created to support the network drive no longer appeared. Attempting to save the file with the File – Save As option was successful as long as the network drive letter that was mapped was selected. The fact that the second attempt to save the file worked is because network drive connections will be reestablished automatically when they are used. This is sometimes referred to as a persistent connection.

CREATING A FILE SHARE RESOURCE TO A LOCAL DISK

When a file share resource is defined, a device and directory path is configured. With regard to file access, there are really only two major levels of access: read and read/write. In a situation where read/write access is allowed to the file share, the device and directory associated with the resource should be located on one of the shared disks. We do not want a situation where there are multiple data files being updated. There is no easy way to keep the files accurate. The issue here is that if the file share resource needs to be located on a shared SCSI disk, only the cluster member that currently owns the disk is able to offer the file share. In this situation, a dependency of the disk resource on the file share would be a proper configuration. The problem with this is that there is no way to load balance client requests simultaneously among the cluster members because the disk resource is only available through one member at a time.

In a situation where the access to the data is going to be read-only, synchronizing changes to the data is not an issue because no changes are occurring. If the device and directory supplied for the file share resource is a local path available on all cluster members, such as C:\APPS, then multiple file shares could be created, and now there is the capability of doing some static load balancing. Static load balancing means that the administrator would need to configure the client connections in such a way as to balance the users across the different file share resources. Now if one of the cluster members goes off-line, the file share resource that was resident will fail over to another cluster member. Since the path is local to all cluster members, clients will see no disruption in service. At this point, we have now loaded the one cluster member with more work, but it is only temporary, until the other cluster member goes back on-line. The network load-balancing version of a cluster provides the same base functionality. This type of cluster is discussed in Chapter 8.

The Print Spooler Resource

Print Spooler Resource Defined

The print spooler resource is defined as one or more printer queues that provide access to network-based printers. This resource gives a method to centrally manage print queues rather than creating and maintaining print queues on every client computer. Functionally, the print spooler resource is similar to the file share resource. One difference, however, is that there is no limit on the number of file share resources that can be created, whereas only one print spooler resource can be defined. This is not the same as only allowing one print queue. One spool process is created, and that spool process can support multiple printers.

Creating a Print Spooler Resource

Resources up to this point have been mostly self-contained: You create the resource, and it is available to the client via the cluster. This is not true with a print spooler resource. Once a print spooler resource is created, the administrator has to carry out the task of creating print queues that use the cluster spooler. The creation of the print spooler resource will be discussed first. As usual, the first step is to invoke the New Resource wizard by right mouse clicking in the Cluster Administrator utility and selecting New – Resource. Select a Resource type of "Print Spooler." The print spooler resource will need a disk and directory to be able to spool jobs. Therefore, it requires a disk dependency. Make sure the owning group for the print spool resource contains at least one disk resource. See Figure 4-19. Along with a disk dependency, the print spooler resource requires a network name. This will be the name for clients to use. Since there is a network name dependency, an implied IP address dependency exists. See Figure 4-20.

There are only a few parameters required for a print spooler resource. See Figure 4-21. First is the spool folder. This is the disk and directory to use as jobs are spooled. Spooling is basically an intermediate holding area for a print job between the user application and the physical printer. It is intended to allow the user to continue to work, since their application does not need to wait until the print job completes. It is not necessary to create the spool folder

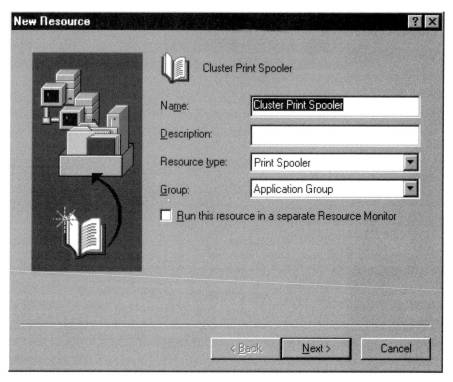

FIGURE 4-19 *Creating a Print Spooler resource.*

in advance. If the directory does not exist, the Cluster Service will create it. One point of interest here is that the Cluster Service does not give any notification that the device and directory supplied are invalid. When the spooler resource is started and the supplied spool folder location is invalid, the resource is started using a directory in the Windows 2000 system directory structure. The second parameter is the job completion timeout. Job completion timeout controls how long a document can take to travel from the cluster member with the print spool resource to the physical printer. If this timer expires, the printer stops trying to print the document.

At this point, we now have a cluster-wide print spooler. If the network name is viewed with *My Network Places*, it would not yet display any available printers. The output can be slightly confusing here. If there are locally defined printers, they will display here when a network name resource is browsed on the network. This is because the network name resolves to a TCP/IP address, and the *My Network Places* tool simply displays all shared resources available via that address. To have printer resources that can fail

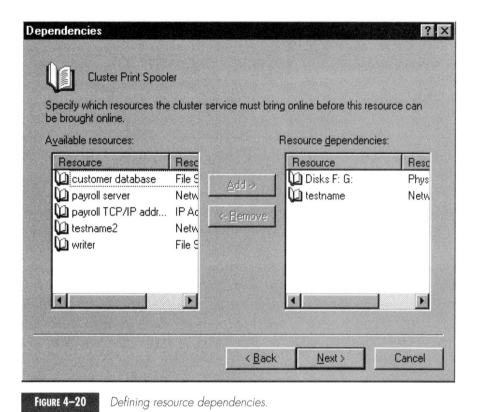

FIGURE 4–20   *Defining resource dependencies.*

over between cluster members, it is necessary to define new printers via the method discussed next.

Configuring Cluster Print Devices

CREATING PORTS

Even though a cluster-wide print spooler is supported, there is no cluster-wide method of configuring and mapping ports such as LPT1 and various LPR ports so that all members are aware of the port mappings. Currently, all print device configurations and all device drivers must be manually configured on all nodes in the cluster. This is not a complex task, but there are very specific steps that need to be followed.

First, all printer ports must be defined on each member of the cluster that will support the print spooler resource. To initiate this process, select Start – Settings – Printers. Next invoke the Add Printer Wizard. Make sure the "Local Printer" option is selected. The goal is to define any ports that are

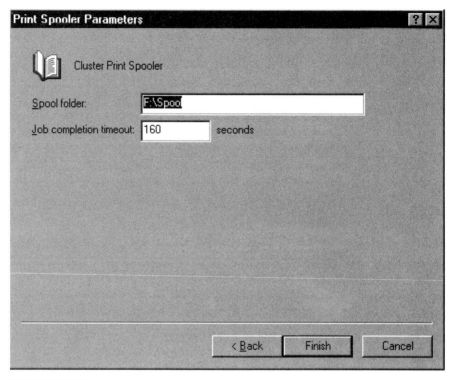

FIGURE 4–21   *Supplying Print Spooler resource properties.*

going to be used for cluster-wide printing. See Figure 4-22. All ports used for the cluster printer should be network ports such as LPR ports. Do not use physical ports such as LPT1. If the print spooler were to fail over to another cluster member, the printing device would be inaccessible by the current owner of the print spooler resource, and any print processing to that device would fail.

The LPR software actually consists of two components: a client and a server. The client utilities are LPR, which allows a client to submit a print job, and LPQ, which allows the client to view a print queue. The server side is known as the TCP/IP Printing Service and can be viewed in the Services tool in the Administrative Tools group. This software component is not loaded by default. If "LPR Port" does not show as an available option when adding a printer port, this is a sign that the TCP/IP printing service has not been loaded. See Figure 4-23. To load the service, activate the Network properties screen, select the Services tab, and add "Microsoft TCP/IP Printing." Select LPR Port and New Port. The Add LPR compatible printer screen appears as displayed in Figure 4-24.

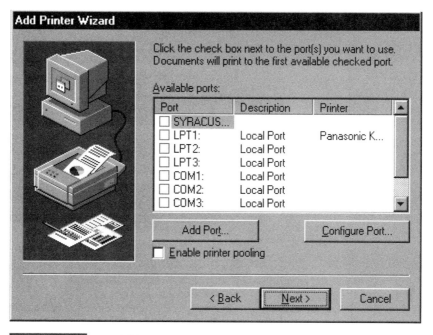

FIGURE 4–22   *Available printer ports.*

Enter the TCP/IP address or the host name of the computer that is providing the print queue. This can be either a TCP/IP address of a computer running an LPR service or the TCP/IP address of a network-connected printer, such as a printer with an HP JetDirect card. The Name of printer field is optional and would only be used if the host of the printer has the capability to assign names to the printer it manages. One example would be a UNIX-served printer. Clients would use a printer resource offered by the cluster, and the totally transparent print request would be routed to the UNIX server. This is beneficial because it allows the administrator to control all client access through the cluster and not have to configure clients to have direct access to other systems on the network, such as a UNIX server, which may require additional software to be installed on the client.

Once the port information has been defined, do not continue with the printer creation. Canceling the print creation process does not affect the ports that have been configured. They are permanently defined unless the administrator manually removes them.

LOADING PRINTER DRIVERS

The next step in the printer configuration process is to load printer drivers on each cluster member that will support the print spooler resource. There is no

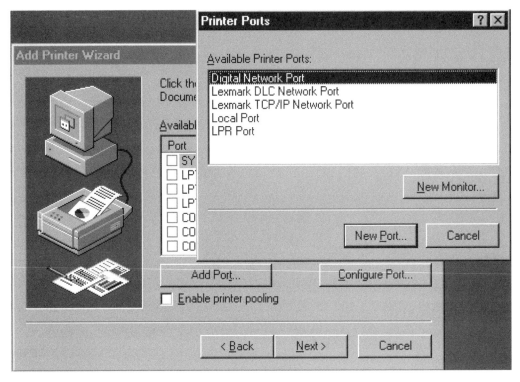

FIGURE 4–23   *Creating a new printer port.*

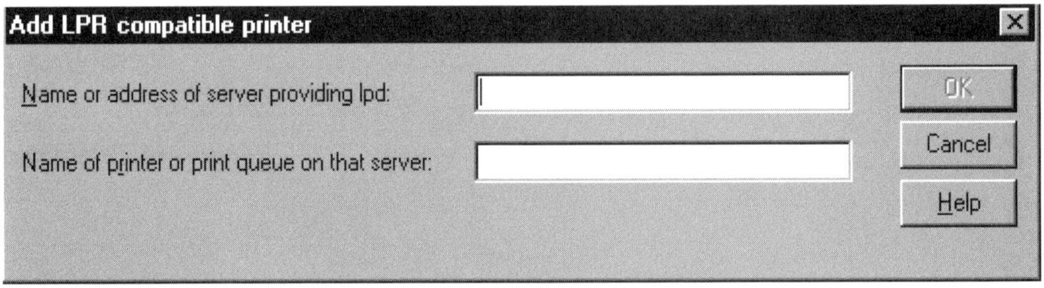

FIGURE 4–24   *Creating a new LPR printer port.*

clean way to do this, so the method used is to step through the screens in the Add Printer Wizard and create a printer. This has the effect of loading the necessary printer drivers. Select any available port; the printer is just temporary. It is not necessary to share the printer or print a test page because as soon as

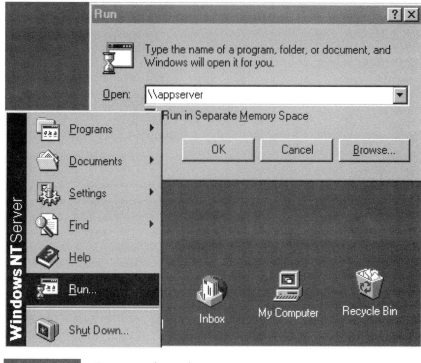

FIGURE 4–25   *Creating a clustered printer.*

the printer is created, it can be deleted. The printer drivers are not deleted along with the printer. Make sure to load all necessary printer drivers on each cluster member. Now that the printer ports are created and the printer drivers loaded, the actual process of creating cluster-based printers can take place.

INSTALLING CLUSTER PRINTERS

The final step is to create the printer as a shared resource of the network name that was associated with the print spooler resource. If the printer is created by invoking the Add Printer Wizard on one of the cluster members, the resource would be associated with that cluster member and not with the virtual server. To have the printer resource be "owned" by the virtual server, it is necessary to run the Add Printer Wizard under the context of that virtual server. Since it is not a physical computer that can be logged on to, it is necessary to perform this task over the network. From the Start menu, select Run and enter the text "*virtual_server*," where *virtual_server* is the network name resource created for the print spooler. See Figure 4-25. A window will display the shared resources for this network name. One of the resources is the Printers folder. From this folder, the Add Printer Wizard can be executed and the printer created in the appropriate context. Since we are now working in the context of the network name defined by the cluster, this step only needs to be performed once, not once per cluster member as in the previous steps. When creating the printers, make sure to use the appropriate ports and printer drivers.

The Generic Service Resource

What Is a Service?

A *service* is a powerful feature of the Windows 2000 operating system. It is basically an application running in the background, not associated with the desktop window and user. In the UNIX world, a service is very similar to a *daemon*. The operating system makes extensive use of services to support the low-level functions that it provides. One example of a service is the Server service. This application is responsible for accepting NetBIOS-based connection requests from clients. The list of configured services can be viewed through the Services tool. See Figure 4-26.

Before discussing how to configure a service to run in a cluster, it is important to understand how a service is implemented by the operating system. A service is an application program that is written following very specific rules. Approximately 80–90% of a service program is very standard. Because a large portion of a service application is standard, it is fairly simple to have a program sometimes referred to as a *wrapper*. In this case, the wrapper program takes an existing application, wraps it with the necessary service code, and allows it to run as a service. This will not work for all applications, but it is a nice feature for those applications it will support.

A service can run as a separate process or as a thread in the context of the primary Services process. The primary difference is that every process has unique security information, or access token, whereas a thread inherits the access token of the process to which it belongs. It is important to realize that the standard Windows 2000 security mechanism applies to services when they attempt to access an operating system resource. Windows 2000 security can be summarized as follows. The access token of the process, or thread, must match a granted access in the access control list of the resource. The Services tool provides the option to define the user context to use when creating the service process. Double-click on the service to be configured, and the screen in Figure 4-27 appears.

Enter the username and password in the fields provided. The password supplied is actually stored in the registry in association with the service parameters, so if the password on the account is ever changed in the user account database, the properties of the service will need to be updated.

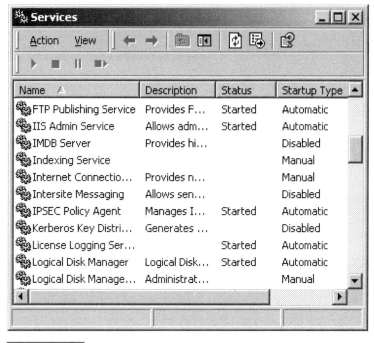

FIGURE 4-26   *Viewing installed services.*

Applications sometimes store information in the registry. Registry information can be replicated between cluster members. This takes the burden away from the application developer or system administrator. The replication process ensures that every cluster member computer has up-to-date registry information. In addition to the application-specific information in the registry, the operating system also stores all of the necessary information to start the service. To view this information, use the REGEDT32 utility provided with Windows NT. Some administrators prefer the utility REGEDIT. Both ship with Windows 2000. The REGEDIT utility has a couple of nice features. First, it represents the registry as one large structure as opposed to five or six separate structures such as REGEDT32. It also allows searches on components other than key names, which is a big drawback to REGEDT32. The one feature that the REGEDIT utility is missing is that it does not contain any security menu. Access control lists are supported on registry objects just like any other object. This is because the REGEDIT utility originated in Windows 95 where less emphasis is placed on security. The registry path is:

HKEY_LOCAL_MACHINE\SYSTEM\CurrentControlSet\Services

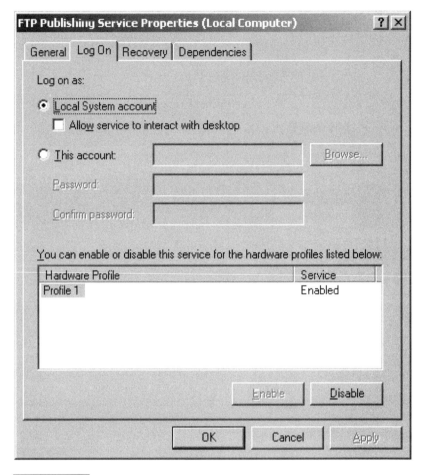

FIGURE 4-27   *Supplying service logon credentials.*

to view service-related properties. Under this registry location is a separate key entry for every service installed in the operating system.

Service Resource in Microsoft Cluster Server

A service resource object in a cluster is a service that has been installed on all members in the cluster. The service may or may not be in a running state on all members. There are situations where an application runs in the context of a service. Microsoft SQL Server is a good example. Two services, SQLSERVER and SQLEXECUTIVE, mainly support SQL Server functionality. Specifics on how to manage SQL Server are discussed in a later chapter. Associating a

Cluster Service resource with a Windows 2000 service allows for failover of the service to occur. When a cluster member goes off-line, and that cluster member owns a service resource, the Cluster Service will move the service resource to another member in the cluster. Realize that this function involves a process or thread being terminated on one system and a similar process or thread being recreated on the new owning cluster member. Any object handles will become invalid and need to be corrected by the application.

Configuring a Generic Service Resource

To configure a service to run as a cluster resource, the following tasks need to be carried out:

- Create or designate the group the service resource will be a member of.
- Provide the text name of the service. This is the text displayed from the Services program in Control Panel.
- Define any necessary registry replication.

Invoke the New Resource wizard and complete each of the screens that follow (Figures 4-28 – 4-35).

As illustrated in Figure 4-28, enter a text name and description for the resource. Take advantage of the name and description fields. For example, 6 months from now, if an administrator were to examine Cluster Administrator, would he or she more likely remove a resource called APP1 or a one called Customer Database? Take the time to generate useful names at this point and avoid potential problems later.

The checkbox Run this resource in a separate Resource Monitor was probably originally designed specifically for two types of resources: generic services and generic applications. Because both of these resource types will allow many different programs to run as a resource, the risk of introducing a poorly behaving resource to the cluster increases. To protect the other cluster resources from being interfered with, consider running these resources in separate resource monitors. The decision whether to run the resource on a separate resource monitor requires the application in question to be tested in a cluster environment. Make sure to test failover for the resource.

As usual, specify the possible owners of the resource and any resource dependencies.

Enter the Service name. See Figure 4-29. This is the text string that is displayed by the Services program in Control Panel. The text is specified when the service is installed and is simply an entry in the registry.

Enter any startup parameters. These will be application specific and must be documented by the programmer. A startup parameter is data that is passed to the program when it starts. The application then uses that data to

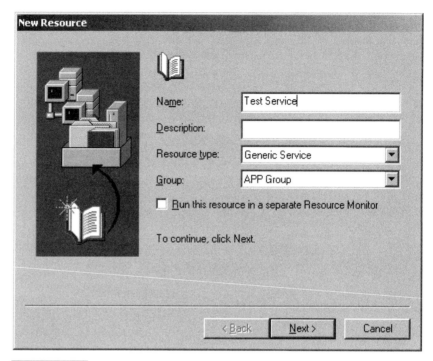

FIGURE 4–28   *Creating a Generic Service resource.*

decide what tasks it needs to perform. For example, an application such as a security monitor may need to be supplied for the disk and/or directory.

Another method of providing data to a service application that programmers can use is to store data in the registry. See Figure 4-30. Since each cluster member has a unique registry, it will be necessary to replicate the registry data between cluster members. In this screen, supply the root, or starting point, for the registry information that needs to be replicated. For example, if a service named *FileMon* has been installed, and a registry key named FileMon has been created in the HKEY_LOCAL_MACHINE\SOFTWARE section of the registry, the root registry key to be entered would be:

HKEY_LOCAL_MACHINE\SOFTWARE\FileMon.

This would replicate any data in the *FileMon* key and any subkeys.

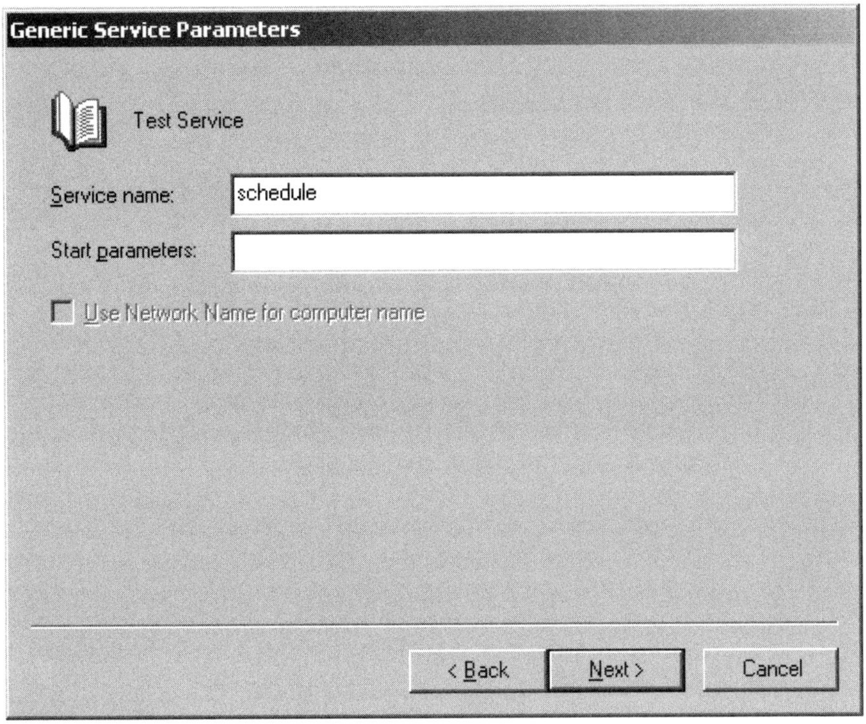

FIGURE 4–29   *Supplying service resource properties.*

The Generic Application Resource

Generic Application Resource Defined

The generic application resource allows a program to run as a resource. Conceptually it is very similar to a generic service resource, except that it does not require all the extra code in the program to interact with the service control manager. The generic application resource can be useful when the administrator wants to guarantee that a program will always be running. For example, assume that a disk defragmentation utility offers the ability to perform work while the computer is in normal operation. A generic application resource can be created with the appropriate command to start the disk software. This guarantees that if the software is stopped or terminates for some reason, it will be restarted automatically by the Cluster Server software. Notice that this is not taking advantage of any load balancing or fault tolerance, but is simply using the auto-restart capability of a resource. To continue with the example,

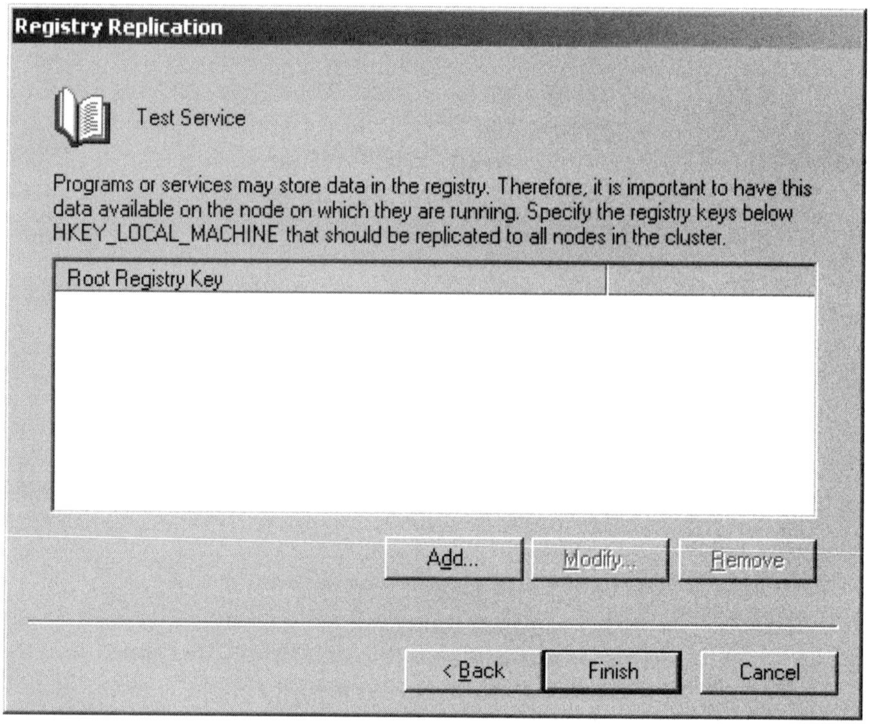

FIGURE 4-30   *Defining registry key replication.*

a generic application resource should be created for each cluster member to execute the disk maintenance software on all systems. Obviously, in this example there is no need to configure any failover. Another example of an application that works well here would be a program that performs security monitoring. A security program does not provide any benefit if it is not running. With the monitor defined as a generic application, the Cluster Server software will always attempt to restart the program if it fails.

The program associated with the generic application resource is required to be a program that runs indefinitely. It should not complete. If the program were to complete, the Cluster Server software would assume the resource has failed and needs to be restarted. After the failure threshold for the resource has been reached, the resource would be moved to other cluster members (if the resource configuration allows) and would eventually be taken off-line due to the large number of failures being detected.

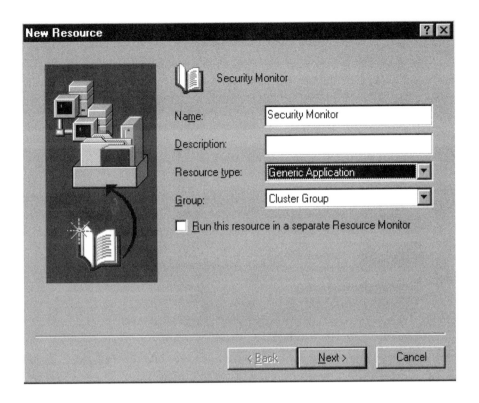

FIGURE 4–31   *Creating a Generic Application resource.*

Creating a Generic Application Resource

To create a generic application resource, invoke the New Resource wizard and select a Resource type of "Generic Application" (Figure 4-31).

Place the resource in the group that holds any dependent resources it will require. For example, if the generic application resource runs an executable on one of the shared SCSI disks, then the physical disk resource associated with the SCSI device should be a dependency. Do not rely on the Cluster Service to determine resource dependencies. The Cluster Administrator tool will allow a generic application resource, or any resource, to be associated with a directory or executable without requiring that the physical disk resource containing the directory or executable be a dependent resource. The Cluster Service only enforces a type of dependency, such as a network name resource dependency on an IP address resource.

Since the generic application is a file-level resource, it may seem reasonable that a disk resource is required, but this is not the case. Similar to the file

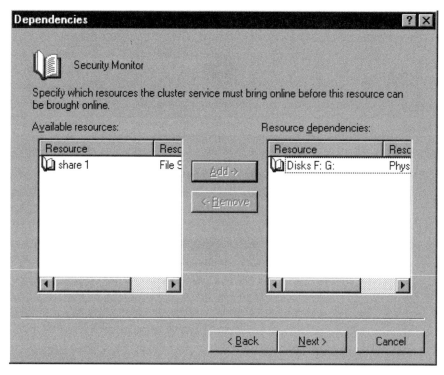

FIGURE 4-32   *Defining resource dependencies.*

share resource, the generic application resource can reside on a local disk of the cluster member. This is useful when an application has been installed on all the cluster members and is bound to a specific directory, such as under the Windows 2000 root directory. Most likely, a generic application will be configured with a physical disk dependency. See Figure 4-32.

Because the generic application resource does not require a disk resource, load balancing, by application, can be achieved without having to dedicate important disk resources to a specific application. For example, in a cluster configuration consisting of one SCSI disk RAID array, all disk resources will be owned by one cluster member or the other since the RAID array needs to be treated as a single resource. This forces one of the cluster members into a passive mode because it does not have any disk resources. By using generic application resources that are configured to use executables on the local disks, the passive cluster member can now be put to work.

If the generic application is located on a local member disk, remember to install the application in the same directory for each cluster member that is a potential owner of the resource.

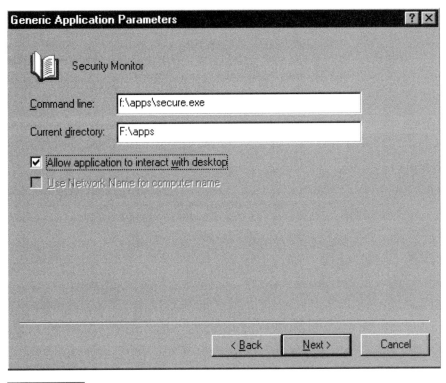

FIGURE 4-33   *Supplying Generic Application resource properties.*

Enter the command line that invokes the program to be executed (Figure 4-33). The current directory is the default directory the application will run under. This means that if the application requests access to any files, the current directory will be searched first.

The checkbox Allow application to interact with desktop allows or disallows the application to open a window to display its output. If an application normally opens a window, and this box is not checked, the resource does not fail. It will be running as a background process. To verify whether this mistake has been made, the Processes tab of the Task Manager utility can be used. The Task Manager utility can be invoked by right mouse clicking on an open area in the Taskbar.

Many applications are using the registry as a storage location for small amounts of data such as configuration information for how many simultaneous clients the application should support. Since the registry is computer-specific data, the portion of the registry that the application uses needs to be copied to other cluster members in case the application were to fail over to another cluster member at some point. If the generic application resource

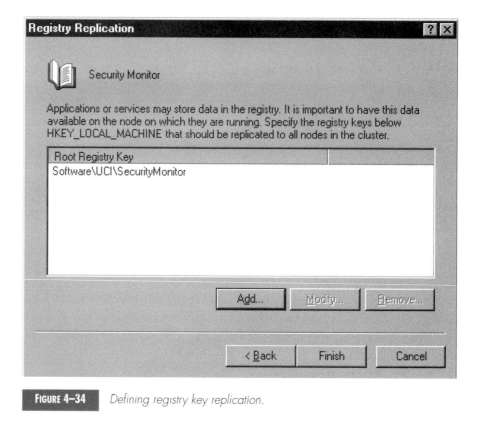

FIGURE 4-34   *Defining registry key replication.*

uses the registry to store information, specify the registry path used by the application. See Figure 4-34.

The Physical Disk Resource

The Physical Disk Resource Defined

The physical disk resource is defined as a fiber- or SCSI-attached disk used for shared folders or storage. At least one physical disk resource is defined at installation time. This is a requirement because the quorum resource must be stored on a physical disk resource. The quorum resource is discussed in Chapter 2. The physical disk resource is linked to physical disk hardware, not to logical disk partitions.

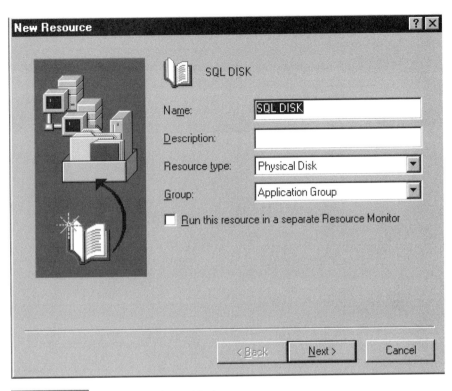

FIGURE 4-35   *Creating a Physical Disk resource.*

Creating a Physical Disk Resource

Creating a new physical disk resource is a straightforward task. The only work that must be performed before adding the physical disk resource is to connect the hardware, create one or more disk partitions with the Disk Administrator utility, and format the partitions as NT File System (NTFS). The Cluster Service only supports NTFS-formatted drives. When the new disk is connected to the shared bus, remember to assign a unique ID to the device if you are using a SCSI bus. How this is done is disk specific, usually accomplished by configuring one or more jumpers, toggle switches, or a thumbwheel. Once this work is done, invoke the New Resource wizard and select a Resource type of "Physical Disk." See Figure 4-35. The only parameter is the disk device itself, which is selected from a pull-down menu. At this point, the disk is available as a shared cluster device.

To verify which cluster member currently owns a disk resource, the Cluster Administrator utility can be used. When troubleshooting, it may be beneficial to determine whether the Windows 2000 operating system on a

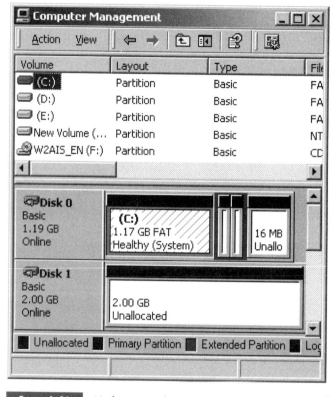

FIGURE 4–36   *Verifying Windows 2000 disk configuration.*

given cluster member has control of a disk resource. The best utility to do this is the Computer Management tool. See Figure 4-36.

The IIS Server Instance Resource

THE IIS SERVER INSTANCE DEFINED

By default, each domain name, such as *www.ucicorp.com*, represents a unique computer on the Internet. It is possible to take a single computer and make it appear as multiple servers, such as *schedule.ucicorp.com and regis-tration.ucicorp.com*,. These secondary domain names are virtual servers defined within Microsoft Internet Information Server (IIS). The advantage of this is that multiple, independent web sites can be offered from a single computer. It is efficient from an administrative perspective to only manage one physical web server. Also, with security and the web being such a major concern, the fewer physical servers a site has on the Internet, the less likely they are to be the target of a hacker. A virtual server is nothing more than a TCP/IP address bound to the network adapter and an entry in a DNS that associates the TCP/IP address with a domain name. There are various methods for host name resolution, but only two of those methods work with fully qualified domain names (FQDNs). An FQDN is a name in the format *www.uci-corp.com*. The two methods for resolving this type of name are DNS or a HOSTS file. Both of these methods require manual updates and maintenance by the network administrator, although rumors of a dynamic DNS with a future version of Windows NT are common. Install these virtual servers as cluster resources, and the result is web servers that can be served by any cluster member. This is especially important to companies that depend on the Internet for their revenues, for example, by taking orders via one or more web pages.

In addition to virtual servers, the IISsoftware also supports virtual directories. A *virtual directory* is a directory that one of the three services, WWW, FTP, or GOPHER can use to publish data. These directories can be scattered across various disks and even be network drives, but the client will be presented with one "virtual" directory tree, with the home directory being the root and each virtual directory addressed as if it were a subdirectory of the home directory. Physical subdirectories of these virtual directories are also available to the client.

Creating an IIS Server Instance Resource

Before an IIS virtual server resource is defined, verify that the IISsoftware is loaded. From the desktop Start menu, select Programs, and there should be an option of Microsoft Internet Server. If there is not, install the Internet Server software either by selecting the icon on the desktop labeled Install Internet Information Server or by running the program Inetstp that is found in the Inetsrv directory under the appropriate directory, such as I386, on the Windows 2000 Advanced Server distribution media. Once the Internet Server software is loaded, it is useful to examine some of the settings before defining virtual directory resources (Figure 4.37). Invoke the Internet Service Manager program from the Internet Server Group. Display the properties for the Default Web site. This is a virtual server according to IIS. It has its own top-level directory and virtual directories under it.

In the case of an IIS server resource, the web site will have a unique TCP/IP address. This is represented by the IP address resource dependency. To provide a friendly URL name to the TCP/IP address, such as *www.uci-corp.com*, it is necessary to configure one of the host name resolution methods that Windows 2000 provides. Of the methods available, the most useful ones are DNS, WINS, or a HOSTS file. DNS (domain name server) has been an industry standard for many years in the TCP/IP environment. It involves manually making an entry in a database that will reside on one or more

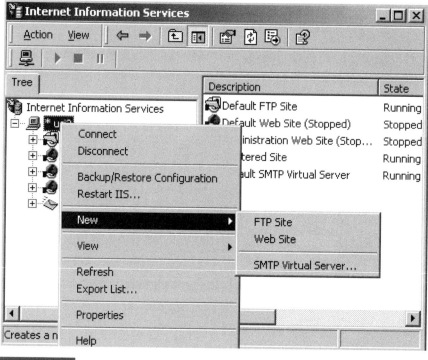

FIGURE 4-37   *Viewing IIS configuration.*

domain name servers. A lookup request is generated by client software known as a resolver. The Internet, with regard to domain names, can be viewed as a large tree structure, each branch consisting of subdomains from a parent domain, such as COM or GOV. When a client resolver request occurs, many internal requests may need to be made to traverse the domain tree being referenced. This may seem cumbersome, but the response time is remarkably short when it is understood what is actually happening.

Another method of host name resolution is WINS (Windows Internet Naming Service). As its name implies, WINS is only available on Microsoft operating systems. One advantage of WINS is that it is dynamic. Clients register their names and addresses at boot time. This is useful if a method such as DHCP is being used to allocate addresses. One disadvantage of WINS is its inability to understand fully qualified domain names such as *www.hampton-beach.com*. In a situation where a fully qualified domain name is being resolved, WINS only looks up the string up to the first period, in this case, *www*. This could obviously give erroneous results, as there are www hosts in many domains.

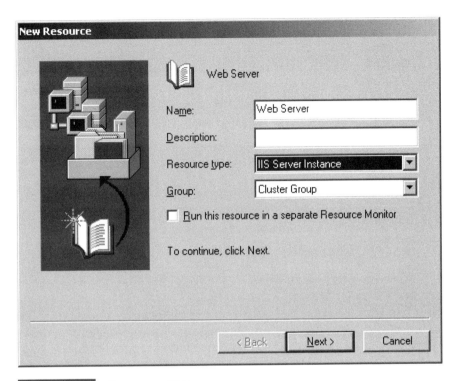

FIGURE 4-38   *Creating an IIS Server resource.*

The last option is to maintain a HOSTS file. The issue with a HOSTS file is that it resides on the client computer. In a network of 5000 clients, it would be impractical to manage such a large number of files. One interesting workaround is accomplished using a login script. A login script is a file that is executed every time a client logs onto the network. A line can be placed in the login script to download a HOSTS file from some central location on the network. Now only one file is maintained, but all clients will have the information resident on their computers.

No matter which method is used, the only task of the administrator is to make the entry in the database associating the TCP/IP address with the appropriate domain name. Since host name resolution deals with translating a name to a TCP/IP address, it is transparent at this level which member in a cluster owns the resource. Where it becomes an important issue is at the level of TCP/IP address resolution, where TCP/IP addresses are mapped to Ethernet or MAC addresses. How this is accomplished in the cluster is discussed in detail in the section on IP address resources.

To create an IIS Server resource, first create a directory on one of the cluster shared disks. It is necessary to place this directory on the shared disk

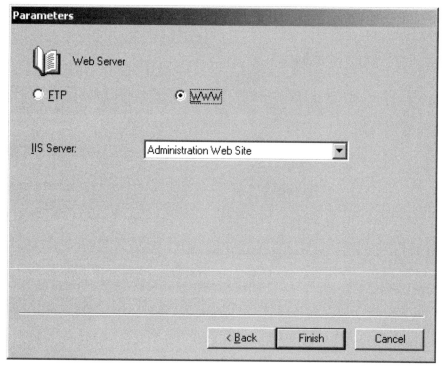

FIGURE 4–39   *Supplying IIS Server resource properties.*

for failover to work properly. Next, create an IP address resource that will function as the address of the virtual server. The IIS Server resource has a dependency of an IP address resource. Now, the virtual server resource can be created. Invoke the New Resource wizard and select a Resource type of "IIS Server Instance." See Figure 4-38. As was mentioned earlier, a dependency on an IP address resource is required. Also, it makes sense that if the resource uses a directory on one of the shared SCSI disks, there should also be a disk dependency defined, although one is not required. This is mostly likely for the same reason that a file share resource does not have a disk dependency. If the data is to be read-only, separate copies could be placed on local disks of the cluster members as long as the path names were consistent, for example, D:\webdata. It would then be necessary to implement some process to guarantee that all copies of the data in question were the same. Not having the disk dependency can be useful when trying to force some level of load balancing on the cluster.

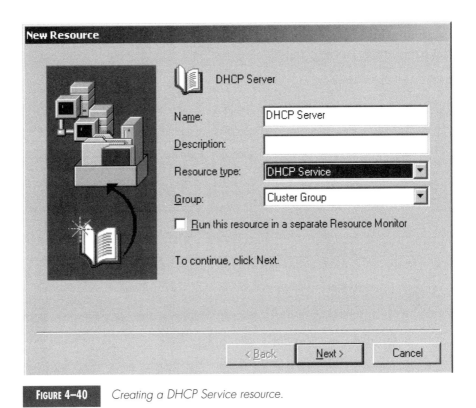

FIGURE 4-40   *Creating a DHCP Service resource.*

The Parameters screen accepts the details for the virtual server. See Figure 4-39. First, specify whether the directory should be an FTP or WWW directory. Next, select the IIS virtual server to associate this resource with.

The DHCP Server Resource

New with the Cluster Service for Windows 2000, Dynamic Host Configuration Protocol_(DHCP) is a supported resource. It is very straightforward to create. The DHCP software must be loaded on the cluster member before attempting to create the resource. Create a new Resource type of "DHCP Service." See Figure 4-40. The resource has three dependencies: a disk, an IP address, and a network name. The only configuration parameters for the resource are directories for the database, auditing, and a backup path. See Figure 4-41.

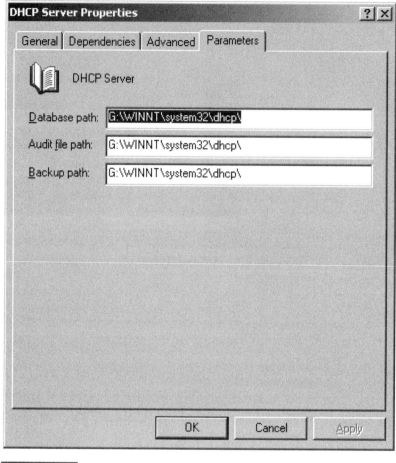

FIGURE 4–41   *Creating a DHCP Service resource (continued).*

The Distributed Transaction Coordinator Resource

The Distributed Transaction Coordinator Defined

Distributed transactions are transactions that update data on two or more systems. The primary problem with distributed transactions is protecting the integrity of the data on the various computers from corruption due to network or system failures while processing the transaction. The possibility exists of a transaction being completed on one participating system but not on another. There needs to be a method of guaranteeing that either the entire transaction

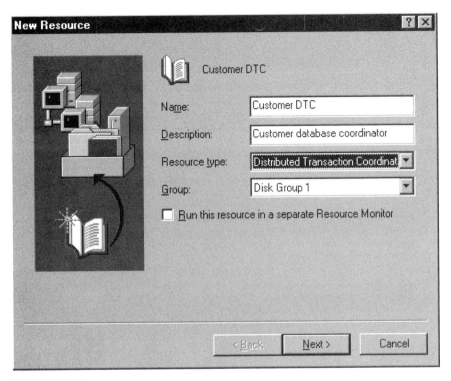

FIGURE 4-42   Creating a DTC resource.

is processed or no part of the transaction is processed. The transaction needs to be "atomic." This problem is resolved by using the Microsoft Distributed Transaction Coordinator. There are various components that work together to provide the functionality of distributed transactions.

Resource Managers

A resource manager is the software that actually manages the data that transactions are being applied to. For example, SQL Server is a resource manager. When a resource manager starts, it contacts its local transaction manager to declare the resource manager's existence. It then waits for execution requests from applications. When a request arrives, the resource manager contacts the transaction manager and enlists in the transaction. By enlisting in the transaction, the resource manager will be notified by the transaction manager when the transaction commits or aborts.

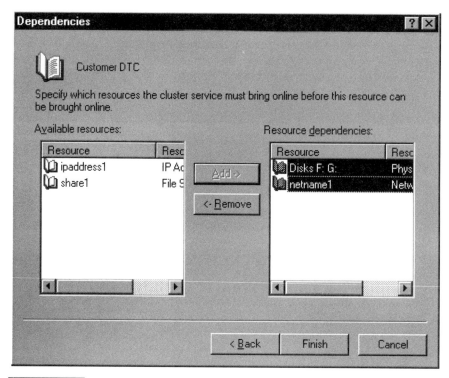

FIGURE 4–43   *Defining resource dependencies.*

Transaction Managers

A transaction manager is responsible for controlling transactions by performing the following tasks:

- Create transaction objects at the request of applications
- Accept requests by resource managers to join a transaction
- Track the status of the transaction among the resource managers and either commit or abort the transaction

Every system will have a local transaction manager. When a transaction involves multiple computers, the transaction manager communicates with the other transaction managers involved to coordinate the activity.

The transaction manager uses a method known as a two-phase commit when requested to commit a transaction. In phase one, the transaction manager requests that all resource managers involved in a transaction prepare the transaction. Depending on the results of phase one, the transaction manager requests that all the resource managers either commit or abort the transaction.

CREATING A DISTRIBUTED TRANSACTION COORDINATOR RESOURCE

The Cluster Server software supports the distributed transaction coordinator as a cluster resource. The failure of a distributed transaction coordinator resource can have a wide-ranging impact. If one transaction coordinator were to fail, the entire transaction would need to be aborted, which could impact numerous other servers and clients. For this reason, running this resource in a separate resource monitor will provide another layer of protection by isolating the resource from potential problems due to another resource using the same monitor. See Figure 4-42.

The distributed transaction coordinator keeps a log on disk. This log is a sequential file that records transaction events. For this reason, a transaction coordinator resource requires a disk dependency. See Figure 4-43.

A network name dependency is required, since transaction coordinators communicate with each other on the network as transactions are being processed. The network name resource supplied as a dependent resource should also be the name registered in the SQL Enterprise Manager to perform configuration of the coordinator.

Cluster Management

By this time, a functional cluster is running, and smoothly, of course. The challenge and excitement of something new has most likely begun to wear off. But building the cluster is only one piece of supplying clients with a high degree of application availability and fault tolerance. The cluster is now in production, and the goal is to keep it there.

Cluster management tasks can be divided into three categories. The first is the normal administrative tasks such as performing hardware upgrades, software updates, and backups. The second task is performance monitoring, and the third is troubleshooting. These may overlap somewhat. For example, one of the troubleshooting steps may include doing some performance monitoring.

Some standard procedures that your organization follows may need to be modified slightly to take advantage of the features that the cluster provides. For example, a documented software installation policy may require that it be performed during off-peak hours due to the possibility of system corruption or failure. Since the cluster concept eliminates the server as a single point of failure, software installs and updates can possibly be performed during normal business hours. Another policy that will probably need some revision will be the backup procedures. This will be discussed in detail later.

The Cluster Administrator Utility

The Cluster Administrator utility is the primary tool for the system administrator to manage a cluster. The tool is installed on any system that has the Cluster Service installed. It is also possible to install just the Cluster Administrator tool on a desktop to perform remote cluster management. Any system running Windows 2000 Server or Advanced Server, Windows NT Server 4.0 with Service Pack 3 or later, or any system running Windows NT Server, Enterprise Edition can run the Cluster Administrator tool. For remote administration, you can install copies of Cluster Administrator through Windows 2000 Administration Tools, included on the Windows 2000 Server and Windows 2000 Advanced Server CD-ROM sets.

The options in the Cluster Administrator utility that deal with groups and resources have been discussed in a previous chapter and will not be included here, but there are many other features that are useful. Before these options are covered, it is important to understand the different icons that may appear in Cluster Administrator. The icons are context sensitive. What this means is that an icon will be interpreted in a slightly different way depending on the type of object it is marking.

The most common icon is a yellow triangle that looks like a yield traffic sign. This icon is displayed as a signal that a resource or a group has been manually taken off-line. When a resource encounters a failure, the Cluster Service will attempt to restart it. After the configured number of failures, the resource is either moved to another cluster member or marked as "failed," which is denoted with a different icon. One thing to keep in mind is that if a resource or group is marked as off-line, and you did not take it off-line, this means someone else did. You probably should not bring the resource or group back on-line without first checking with others who have the privilege and who possibly performed the operation.

This symbol is also used to mark a cluster member that has been paused.

The next icon is a red circle with an "X" in it. This can represent a variety of situations depending on the type cluster object it is associated with. First, if a resource is marked with this icon, it means the resource is in a "failed" state. This will happen when a resource encounters failures and has been restarted by the cluster the configured number of times. Next, the resource will be moved to another cluster member if possible. If there is not another cluster member available to take the resource, the resource is classified as "failed."

This symbol, when associated with a group object, denotes that one or more of the member resources is not on-line. The resource could either be in an off-line or failed state. The remaining members of the group will still function normally.

When this symbol is associated with a node object, the Cluster Service has determined the cluster member to be down. A cluster member could be classified as down if the computer is shut down or the network between the cluster members is not functioning.

Cluster Administrator Options

There are many other options in Cluster Administrator used to perform various configuration tasks. There are always three methods to modify the properties of a cluster object. First, the object can be highlighted and the right mouse button depressed. The other option is to highlight the object and select the File option in the menu bar. Either method leads to the same options available to configure an object.

The third method is the toolbar. The toolbar is limited in its options. It is object sensitive in the options that it provides. For example, the Bring OnLine toolbar button will only be available when a resource or group that is currently off-line is selected. Since the toolbar is limited in the options it provides, I never use it.

One option in Cluster Administrator not bound to an object type is the Open Connection option from the File menu. This option will establish connections to remote clusters for administrative purposes. It may concern administrators that their cluster can be managed remotely, but the Cluster Administrator utility provides the option to define what users and Windows 2000 groups have permission to connect remotely.

Cluster Object

The very first entry in the left pane of Cluster Administrator is the cluster object. There are only two options for modifying this object. See Figure 5-1. The first is Rename. As its name implies, the name of the cluster can be changed with this option. When changing the name of the cluster, there are a few things to keep in mind. First, make sure to follow the NetBIOS naming rules, such as having a name of no more than 15 characters. Second, if the cluster name has been statically defined in a DNS database, it will need to be changed. This should not be a problem with a WINS database as the registration process is usually dynamic. The new name of the cluster will be regis-

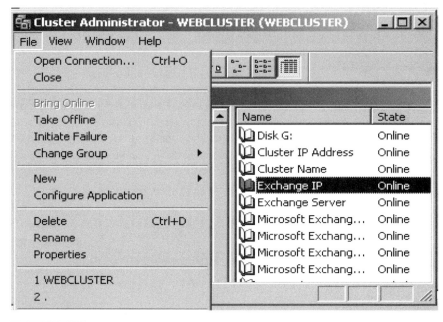

FIGURE 5-1   *Configuring cluster properties.*

tered automatically. Third, the new name assigned to the cluster will not take effect until the Cluster Name resource is taken off-line and put back on-line. Notice the options Open Connection and Close. These are the options an administrator uses to connect to a remote cluster.

Cluster Properties

Selecting the Properties option from the File menu allows the administrator to modify the configuration of the cluster.

Through the General tab in the cluster properties, the cluster name and cluster description can be modified. See Figure 5-2.

SECURITY TAB

This option allows the Cluster Administrator to define what users or groups can manage the cluster, *not* what users can connect to resources. Resource permissions are managed through the Permissions option provided by the type of resource. For example, the only resource at this time that provides a permission option is the file share resource. Since the file share resource parallels the NetBIOS file-sharing mechanism of Windows 2000, the permissions are applied in the same method the operating system uses. Not all resource

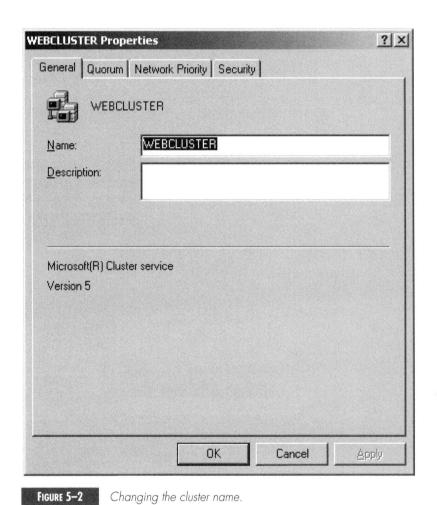

FIGURE 5–2   *Changing the cluster name.*

types will provide this feature, and when they do, there is no guarantee the security interface will be the same.

To assign specific users or groups the ability to manage the cluster, select the Security tab from the WEBCLUSTER Properties window. See Figure 5-3. The only entries after an installation are for the local Administrator and system accounts. To modify this list, use the Add and Remove buttons. Selecting the Remove button will remove the currently highlighted entry from the access list. When the Add button is selected, a list of the groups and users from the Windows 2000 user accounts database is displayed. Select the users or groups to grant access to and select OK. Full control is the only type of access that can be granted. It is also possible to deny a user or group of users by checking the "Deny" box.

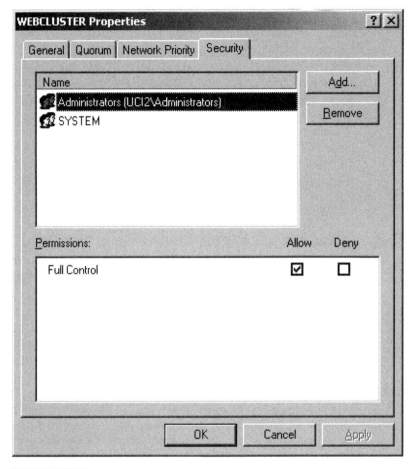

FIGURE 5–3   *Managing administrative access to the cluster.*

QUORUM TAB

The quorum resource location is defined during the cluster installation process. See Figure 5-4. It is possible to change the location of the quorum resource if the disk configuration in the cluster is changed. Select a Partition on the shared I/O bus from the pull-down menu, and if needed change the Root path. If the cluster is started and the quorum files do not exist or are corrupt, the necessary files are created by the Cluster Service at startup time. Do not modify the access permissions on the disk that contain the quorum resource. The Cluster Service must have full access to this device.

The quorum log stores configuration changes made to the cluster. When the quorum log fills, the information is written to the registry. The quorum log

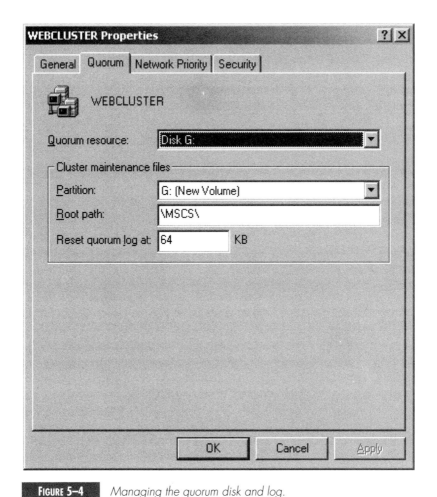

FIGURE 5-4   *Managing the quorum disk and log.*

represents a buffer for storing cluster configuration modifications. This is necessary since changes could occur while one of the cluster members is off-line. In the event a cluster member is planned to be off-line for an extended period of time or if cluster configuration changes appear to be getting lost, the size of the quorum log should be increased from its default size of 64KB.

THE NETWORK PRIORITY TAB

The Cluster Service offers the capability to use multiple network adapters. A typical configuration would have two adapters in each cluster member. If there is more than one physical network connecting the cluster members, one or more of the network interfaces can be designated to handle the internal cluster traffic. This includes cluster heartbeat and failover traffic. Only one adapter is used for cluster communication at any time, but configuring two adapters allows another level of fault tolerance to be designed into the cluster configuration. When more than one network adapter is configured to handle the internal cluster traffic, the adapters can be prioritized to define which should be used. A four-port hub or a short thin-wire Ethernet segment is a perfect configuration for the internal cluster communication network if a hub is not available. Make sure the cluster does not attempt to register with WINS or DNS on both network interfaces. Use the Move Up and Move Down buttons to define the order of precedence of adapters to be used for internal cluster traffic.

A network interface can be used only for internal cluster traffic, client traffic, or both. Client traffic consists of access to all the cluster resources and will introduce the majority of the network traffic. If the network interfaces are of different types, use the faster interface for the client traffic. If there are two network adapters on the cluster members, only configure one for client access, and configure both for all communications. Then prioritize the adapters so that the adapter not used for client access will be used first for cluster communication traffic. See Figure 5-5. The net effect of all this fault tolerant paths for the cluster communication, but only one path for client traffic. But if the network adapter on the client network fails, the cluster resources can be manually failed over to the other node, and users can regain access to their resources. So we do not need to configure multiple adapters for client communications.

To configure the type of traffic that will be allowed on the network interface, highlight the interface and select the Properties button. The network properties screen appears. See Figure 5-6.

Managing Cluster Nodes

Individual cluster members can be managed by right mouse clicking on the target member in the Cluster Administrator tool. See Figure 5-7.

Pause Node

The Pause Node option allows existing groups and resources to stay on-line but does not allow any additional resources or groups to be brought on-line. This option can be used to gradually move resources and groups to other cluster members. Also, if a node has reached its processing capacity, using this option will stop the node from taking over any additional cluster resources.

One recommended sequence for performing maintenance on a cluster member is as follows:

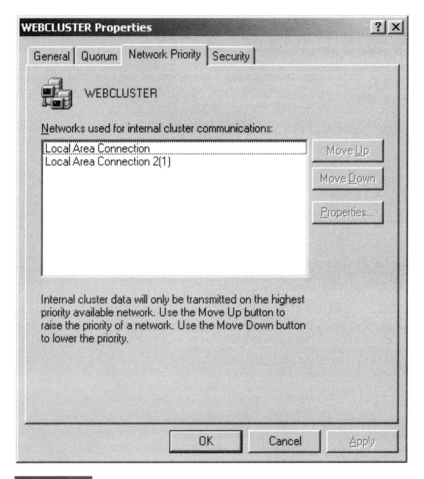

FIGURE 5–5   *Configuring network adapters for cluster use.*

- Pause the node requiring the maintenance.
- Move any remaining groups and resources to other cluster members.
- Perform the maintenance on the paused node.
- When the maintenance is complete, select the Resume Node option.

Make sure that the SCSI bus termination is not interrupted during the maintenance process. This is the reason it is recommended that Y cables be used so that the cluster member can be disconnected from the SCSI bus, and proper termination is preserved.

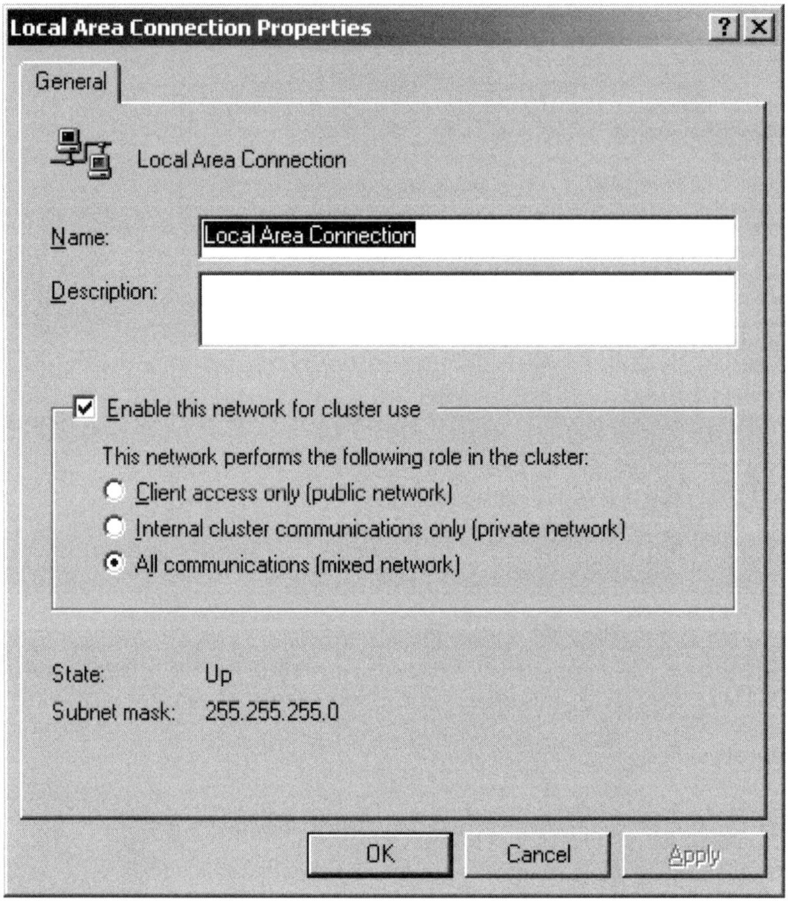

FIGURE 5-6   *Configuring network adapters (continued).*

Evict Node

The Evict Node option is used to permanently remove a node from the cluster. It does not deinstall the Cluster Service; it just removes the node information from the cluster database. The Cluster Service needs to be removed manually by using the Add/Remove Programs option in Control Panel.

Start/Stop Cluster Service

When the Cluster Service is stopped on a node, all groups will be moved to the other node, as long as failover is allowed by the group policies. All client access to resources on the cluster member is immediately terminated. Basi-

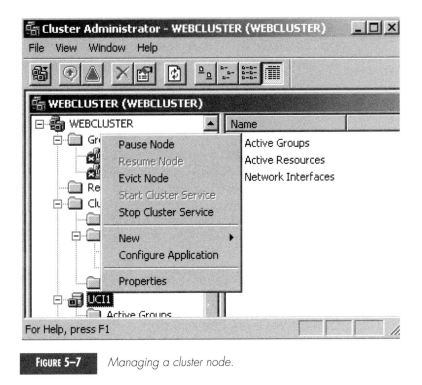

FIGURE 5–7   *Managing a cluster node.*

cally, this is an easy way to fail all resources at once to the other cluster member. This can be used when a cluster member is going to be shut down for maintenance. Even if the computer is not going to be shut down, there are other reasons to disconnect all users. Perhaps a software upgrade is going to be applied that will only affect the local disks, but the upgrade will not succeed with connected users. In this case, when the upgrade is complete, and the node is ready to become a cluster member again, simply select the Start Cluster Service option.

Managing Cluster Security

The Cluster Service depends on Windows 2000 security at all levels of communication, from communication between nodes to client access of cluster resources.

Earlier in the chapter, it was discussed how to specify which Windows 2000 users and groups can manage the cluster. Other tasks relating to security that may need to be carried out by the administrator include:

- change the account under which the Cluster Service runs
- change the password to the account under which the Cluster Service runs
- limit access to shared data (file share resources)
- audit access to shared data
- take ownership of files or folders

CHANGING THE CLUSTER SERVICE ACCOUNT

The Cluster Service must run under a user account, as opposed to the system account, which is the default account that Windows 2000 services are configured to run with. There are certain restrictions and a number of privileges that must be applied to the account to be used:

- The account must be a domain account. It cannot be a local account. This means that a member server must use an account from a domain account database.
- The Cluster Service must run with the same account on both nodes. This guarantees that the Cluster Service on both nodes will have the same security context and be capable of accessing files created by the other node's Cluster Service. If the two nodes do not have the same account, they will not be able to form a cluster.
- The account must be in the Administrators group on both nodes. Violation of this restriction is more likely to happen when the nodes are member servers and have their own account database and therefore their own Administrators group. However, it is possible to encounter this between domain controllers if the account being used is newly created or modified and the two domain controllers have not yet performed an account database synchronization with the new account information.
- The account must have a variety of privileges. Some, but not all, of these privileges will be inherited when the account is placed in the Administrators group. The Cluster Server installation process performed the initial privilege allocation. If the account is being changed, the privileges will need to be granted manually. The privileges required by the Cluster Service account are:
  - back up files and directories
  - increase quotas
  - increase scheduling priority
  - load and unload device drivers
  - lock pages in memory
  - log on as a service
  - restore files and directories

Rather than create a brand new account and assign all the privileges, it may be an acceptable option to rename the account in the Computer Management tool. This will modify the username but preserve the security context and privileges that were originally assigned. Once the account has been granted these privileges, the following procedure can be used to change the account:

1. Verify with the Computer Management tool that, at most, the following restrictions are set:
   - User cannot change password.
   - Password never expires.
2. Stop the Cluster Service on both nodes by navigating to Programs – Administrative Tools – Services.
3. Bring up the properties for the Cluster Service, and select the Logon tab. Make sure the radial button This Account is selected. This will allow the domain and account database to be browsed and the username selected. Enter and reconfirm the password.
4. Perform step 3 on the other cluster member.
5. Restart the Cluster Service on both nodes.
6. Verify that the cluster is functional by using Cluster Administrator to check that both cluster members are on-line.

CHANGING THE PASSWORD TO THE CLUSTER SERVICE ACCOUNT

The security policy of some companies requires that passwords be changed periodically. This task is less complex than changing the username and password. To change the password for the Cluster Service account, perform the following tasks:

1. Use the Services tool in Administrative Tools to stop the Cluster Service on both cluster members.
2. Change the password to the Cluster Service account. Make sure the "User must change password at next logon" option is not selected.
3. Bring up the properties for the Cluster Service, and select the Logon tab. Make sure the radial button This Account is selected. Enter and reconfirm the new password.
4. Perform step 3 on the other cluster member.
5. Restart the Cluster Service on both nodes.
6. Verify the cluster is functional by using Cluster Administrator to check if both cluster members are on-line.

SETTING SECURITY ON FILE SHARE RESOURCES

Security is set on file share resources through the exact same interface that is used from Windows 2000 to assign permissions to shared directories. Make sure that permissions are assigned through the Cluster Administrator interface and not through the standard Windows 2000 permissions interface. Permissions assigned to file share resources from Windows 2000 will be lost when the resource is taken off-line and put back on-line, since the assigned permissions were not stored in the cluster database.

It is a requirement of the Cluster Service that the shared SCSI disks be formatted with the NT File System (NTFS). NTFS supports its own level of security, also known as access control lists. When the permissions assigned at the NTFS level conflict with the permissions assigned to the share directory, a network connection to the resource will provide the most restrictive permissions from the two access control lists. For example, if the NTFS security is set to allow the group Domain Users Read access to a directory, but the file share resource allows Change access, users will end up with the most restrictive permission, which in this case would be Read. It would be a security issue if the granted access were not handled in this manner.

One interesting discovery was that if the NTFS permissions allow "No Access," the Cluster Service software fails when attempting to bring the resource on-line. However, it does not fail when the NTFS permissions allows "Read" and the file share resource wants to allow a higher level permission such as "Change."

AUDITING ACCESS TO DATA

Windows 2000 offers an audit function that can record various successful or failed events generated by the operating system. With regard to data protection, auditing can record access to files. Windows 2000 only supports file-level auditing for NTFS partitions, which means that any disk on the shared I/O bus is a candidate for auditing. Auditing of file access can be enabled at the drive, directory, or file level. Also, it is not necessary to audit every user's access to a file; the users to be monitored can be specified by the administrator. Audit information can be viewed with the Event Viewer utility.

To enable auditing on a file, directory, or drive, simply right mouse click on the object and select Properties. A Security tab will be one of the options to choose. If it is not, the object is most likely not stored on an NTFS partition. Select the Security tab, then select the Advanced box. Select the Audit tab and a configuration screen will appear. See Figure 5-8.

Use the Add button to select the users and groups that are to be audited. Select the events to be audited by selecting the appropriate success or failure boxes. Be aware that auditing consumes system resources. The saying "There ain't no such thing as a free lunch" applies here. The more security features that are enabled on a system, the more of an impact the security logging will have on the overall performance of the system. The new load will be mainly in the areas of processor and disk I/O. The load introduced by enabling auditing can be minimized, however, by carefully choosing the events to be audited. For example, do not choose to audit successful file accesses by everyone. This can slow your system down to the point where it could hang. By limiting the users and the event to audit, the audit utility can be a useful tool for security monitoring.

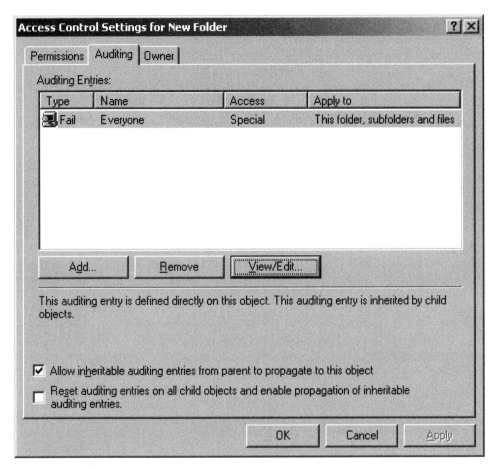

Access Control Settings for New Folder

Permissions | Auditing | Owner

Auditing Entries:

Type	Name	Access	Apply to
Fail	Everyone	Special	This folder, subfolders and files

Add...   Remove   View/Edit...

This auditing entry is defined directly on this object. This auditing entry is inherited by child objects.

☑ Allow inheritable auditing entries from parent to propagate to this object

☐ Reset auditing entries on all child objects and enable propagation of inheritable auditing entries.

OK   Cancel   Apply

FIGURE 5–8   *Auditing the shared disk.*

After auditing is enabled, it should be reviewed periodically by the administrator. The audited events are written to a log file that can be viewed with the Event Viewer utility. The Event Viewer works with three different log files. To examine the collected data, in Event Viewer, select the Security Log. This will display any audited events. See Figure 5-9. To view more detail for any event, simply double-click on it. Information such as the file accessed and the username that requested the access will be among the details displayed.

Cluster.exe

The Cluster Service contains a utility that allows for many of the same tasks that can be done through the Cluster Administrator utility to be performed via

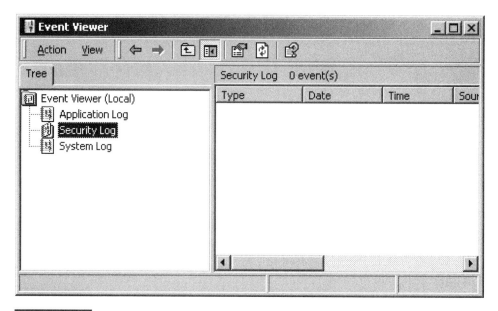

Examining the Audit log.

the command linc. The command is "CLUSTER" and it has a variety of
options. One advantage to the command line version is that batch files can be
written and scheduled to execute on a repeating basis to automate many of
the cluster administration tasks.

Some objects have common settings. For example, all resources can
define dependencies. Other settings are object specific. An IP address
resource requires a TCP/IP address, whereas a network name resource
requires a NetBIOS name.

CLUSTER

The "CLUSTER" command can be used to modify the cluster object. The syntax is:

CLUSTER [cluster name] /option

The cluster name is optional. Supply a cluster name to execute a configuration command on a remote cluster. Any arguments in square brackets are
optional parameters.

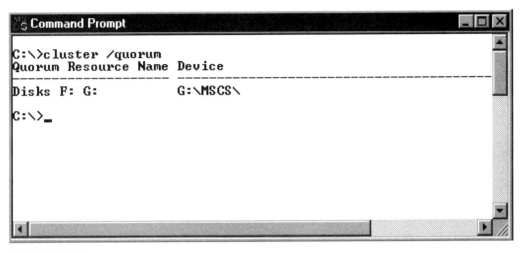

Checking the quorum resource.

TABLE 5.1   *Options for the "CLUSTER" command.*

/RENAME : cluster name	Renames the cluster
/VERSION	Displays the Cluster Service software version number
/QUORUM_RESOURCE ::resource name [/PATH:path][/MAXLOGSIZE :size]	Changes the name or location of the quorum resource or the size of the quorum log
/LIST : [domain name]	

CLUSTER NODE

The "CLUSTER NODE" command is used to configure cluster member nodes. The syntax is:

CLUSTER [cluster name] NODE [node name] /option

The node name is only optional for the "/STATUS" command.

TABLE 5.2   *Options for the "CLUSTER NODE" command.*

/STATUS	Displays the cluster node status, such as up, down, or paused; default option
/PAUSE	Pauses a node
/RESUME	Resumes a node
/EVICT	Evicts a node from the cluster
/PROPERTIES	

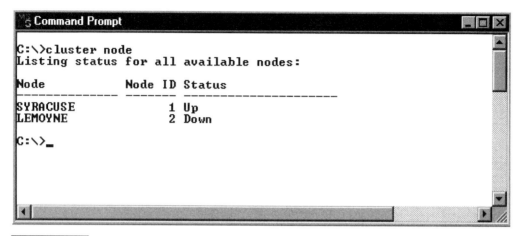

FIGURE 5-11   *Checking the cluster members' current state.*

CLUSTER GROUP

The "CLUSTER GROUP" command is used to display and configure group settings. The syntax is:

CLUSTER [cluster name] GROUP [group name] /option

TABLE 5.3   *Options for the "CLUSTER GROUP" command.*

/STATUS	Displays the status of a group such as Online, Offline, or Partially Online
/NODE : nodename	Displays all the groups on a specific cluster member
/CREATE	Creates a new group
/DELETE	Deletes a group
/RENAME : new group name	Renames a group
/MOVETO : nodename /WAIT : timeout	Moves a group to another node and the amount of time to wait for the move to complete
/ONLINE : nodename /WAIT	Brings a group on-line
/OFFLINE::nodename /WAIT	Takes a group off-line
/PROPERTIES [propname = propvalue]	Displays a group's properties, uses the property names returned to set new values
/PRIVPROPERTIES [propname = propvalue]	Displays the private properties for a group; sets private group properties
/LISTOWNERS	Displays the list of preferred owners
/SETOWNERS : node list	Specifies a preferred owner list

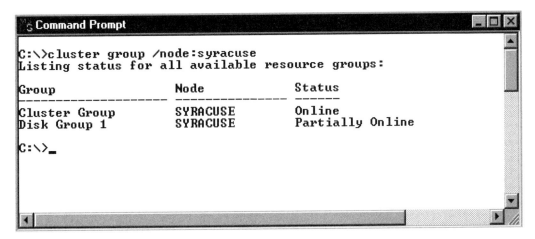

FIGURE 5-12   *Displaying the groups owned by a node.*

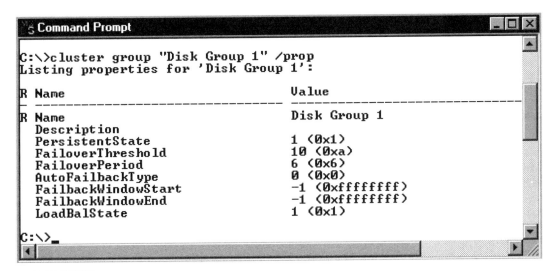

FIGURE 5-13   *Displaying the properties for a group.*

Groups created through Cluster Administrator do not contain private properties, but software developers can take advantage of this feature to store data pertinent to a group's functionality.

CLUSTER RESOURCE

The "CLUSTER RESOURCE" command is used to display and configure cluster resource settings. The basic syntax of the command is:

CLUSTER [cluster name] RESOURCE [resource name] /option

TABLE 5.4	Available options for the "CLUSTER RESOURCE" command.
/STATUS	Displays the status of a resource such as Online, Offline, or Failed

/CREATE
  /GROUP
  /TYPE : resource-type
  [/SEPARATE]
	Creates a new resource
	Group that the new resource should be a member of
	The resource type for the resource such as "File Share"
	Specifies that the resource should run in a separate resource monitor

/DELETE	Deletes a resource
/RENAME : new resource name	Renames a resource
/ADDOWNER : node name	Adds a node name to the list of possible owners
/REMOVEOWNER : node name	Removes a node name from the list of possible owners
/LISTOWNERS	Displays the possible owners of the resource
/MOVETO : group	Moves the resource to the specified group
/PROPERTIES [propname = value]	Displays the common properties of a resource; use propname = value to modify a common property such as the RestartPeriod for a resource

Some properties are common to all types of resources. For example, all resources have a restart threshold, which is how many times to restart the resource on the same cluster member before moving the resource to another node. These properties are displayed and modified with the "/PROPERTIES" option. The properties that can be modified with this option follow.

TABLE 5.5	Properties that can be modified with the "/PROPERTIES" option.
Common Property Name	**Description**
Description	Changes the text that describes the resource.
DebugPrefix	Defines which debugger should be used for the resource.
SeparateMonitor	Indicates whether the resource should run in a separate resource monitor. Valid entries are true or false.
PersistentState	The last known state of a resource. For example, if a resource is taken off-line, and the system is rebooted, the resource will still be off-line because of its persistent state.

TABLE 5.5	*Properties that can be modified with the "/PROPERTIES" option. (Continued)*
Common Property Name	**Description**
LooksAlivePollInterval	The interval in milliseconds that the Cluster Service should perform a quick check to see if the resource "looks" operational. If there is no value for this property, a default value is taken from the same property for the resource type.
IsAlivePollInterval	The interval in milliseconds that the Cluster Service should perform a more thorough check to determine whether a resource is on-line. If there is no setting for this property, a default is taken from the property for the resource type.
/RestartAction	Defines what action should be performed if the resource fails. • 0 – Do not restart the resource • 1 – Allow resource restarts, but not failover • 2 – Perform restarts and failovers
RestartThreshhold	Defines how many times Cluster Server will attempt to restart the resource before failing the group to another node.
RestartPeriod	Specifies the monitoring interval for resource restart attempts to reach the RestartThreshhold before Cluster Server fails over the group to another cluster member.
Pending Timeout	The period of time that a resource can stay in a Pending Online or Pending Offline state without correcting itself. When this timer expires, the resource is placed in an Offline or Failed state.
LoadBalStartupInterval	Reserved for future use.
LoadBalSampleInterval	Reserved for future use.
LoadBalAnalysisInterval	Reserved for future use.
LoadBalMinProcessorUnits	Reserved for future use.
LoadBalMinMemoryUnits	Reserved for future use.
/PRIVPROPERTIES [propname = value]	Displays the private or resource-specific properties for a resource, such as the address for an IP address resource. Use propname = value to modify a private property.

Properties displayed with the /PRIVPROPERTIES switch are known as private properties. These are properties that are unique to the resource type. These properties correspond to the Parameters tab displayed in Cluster Administrator when the properties for a resource are requested.

TABLE 5.6	*Properties displayed with the /PRIVPROPERTIES switch.*
/FAIL	Initiates a resource failure
/ONLINE	Brings a resource on-line

TABLE 5.6	Properties displayed with the /PRIVPROPERTIES switch. (Continued)
/OFFLINE	Takes a resource off-line
/LISTDEPENDENCIES	Lists all the dependencies for a resource
/ADDDEPENDENCY : resource	Adds a new dependency for a resource
/REMOVEDEPENDENCY : resource	Removes a dependency for a resource

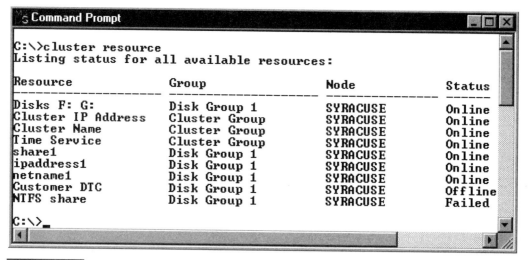

FIGURE 5–14 Displaying all cluster resources.

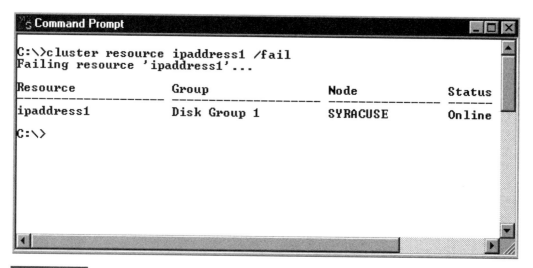

FIGURE 5–15 Forcing a resource to fail.

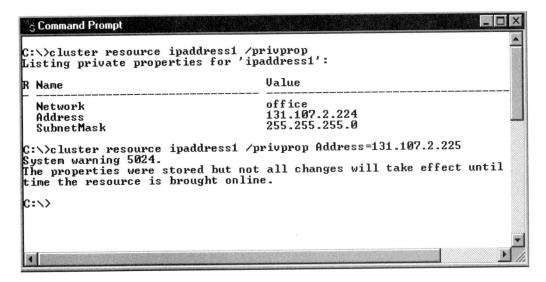

Command Prompt

```
C:\>cluster resource ipaddress1 /privprop
Listing private properties for 'ipaddress1':

R Name                              Value
_ _____      _____
   Network                         office
   Address                         131.107.2.224
   SubnetMask                      255.255.255.0

C:\>cluster resource ipaddress1 /privprop Address=131.107.2.225
System warning 5024.
The properties were stored but not all changes will take effect until
time the resource is brought online.

C:\>
```

FIGURE 5-16 *Examining the private properties of a resource.*

CLUSTER RESOURCETYPE

The "CLUSTER RESOURCETYPE" command allows the administrator to display or modify properties for a resource category such as an IP address. The properties for a resource type are sometimes used as default settings for an instance of the resource. For example, if a resource is created without specifying a LooksAlivePollInterval, the value from the resource type is used. The basic syntax of the command is:

CLUSTER [cluster name] RESOURCETYPE [resource type name] /option

TABLE 5.7 *Available options for the "CLUSTER RESOURCE" command.*

/LIST	Lists the installed resource types
/CREATE	Creates a resource type
/DLLNAME : dllname	Specifies the filename of the resource DLL
/TYPE : type name	Assigns a type name
/ISALIVE : interval	Defines a default IsAlive timer
/LOOKSALIVE : interval	Defines a default LooksAlive timer
/DELETE	Deletes a resource type
/PROPERTIES [propname=value]	Displays or modifies the common properties for a resource type

TABLE 5.8	Common properties available for use in the "CLUSTER RESOURCETYPE" command.
Name	Changes the resource type display name
Description	Changes the text that describes a resource type
DllName	Specifies the name of the Dynamic Link Library (DLL) for the resource type
DebugPrefix	Specifies the debugger to use for the resource type
AdminExtensions	One or more class identifiers for Cluster Administrator extensions
LooksAlivePollInterval	Specifies the interval that the Cluster Service checks the resource of this resource type to determine if the resources "look" operational; this is a very superficial check
IsAlivePollInterval	Specifies the interval that the Cluster Service should use to perform a thorough check to determine if the resource of this resource type is functional
/PRIVPROPERTIES [propname=value]	Displays or modifies the private properties for a resource type

There are currently no private properties for the standard resource types, but programmers may use this feature to store appropriate information when implementing new resource types.

CLUSTER NETWORK

The "CLUSTER NETWORK" command allows the administrator to display or configure any networks used by the Cluster Server software. The basic syntax of the command is:

CLUSTER [cluster name] NETWORK [network name] /option

TABLE 5.9	Options available for the "CLUSTER NETWORK" command.
/STATUS	Displays the status of the network(s), such as Up or Down
/RENAME	Allows the text name of a network to be modified
/LISTINTERFACES	Displays the cluster nodes for a given network and the status of each node; the network name is not optional for this command
/PROPERTIES [propname = value]	Displays or modifies the common properties of a network resource

TABLE 5.10	*Common properties that can be modified.*
Name	The text name assigned to the network
Address	The network portion of the IP address assigned to the network
AddressMask	The subnet mask assigned to the network
Description	The text description of the network
Role	The communication role the network provides to the cluster, represented by a numeric code: • 1 – Use only for internal cluster communications • 2 – Use only for client access • 3 – Use for both cluster and client communications
/PRIVPROPERTIES [propname = value]	Used to modify the private properties of a network. There are no private properties for a network in the standard release of the Cluster Server; the. capability exists to store private properties and may be used in future releases or by software vendors

Administrative Tasks

System administrators are responsible for providing a processing platform to clients that meets their always-changing needs. Hardware and software become antiquated at a faster and faster rate. The impact of this on the administrator is in the area of hardware and software upgrades. One of the benefits of a clustered environment is the ability of the administrator to perform tasks during normal business hours that in the past had to be postponed until after business had completed for the day. Attempting to perform upgrades during non-workday hours can sometimes become an adventure because many times the technical support for the upgrade being done is unavailable after hours, or at best the wait times for technical support can double or triple. In a clustered environment where all applications are implemented as cluster resources, a cluster node could be shut down and removed from the cluster for maintenance without adversely affecting the client base. This statement will hold true as long as every cluster member has sufficient resources, specifically memory, and CPU speed to support all resources with acceptable response time.

Cluster Backup and Restore

You can use the Windows 2000 Backup to perform backup and restore of cluster nodes as long as all nodes are running Windows 2000 Advanced

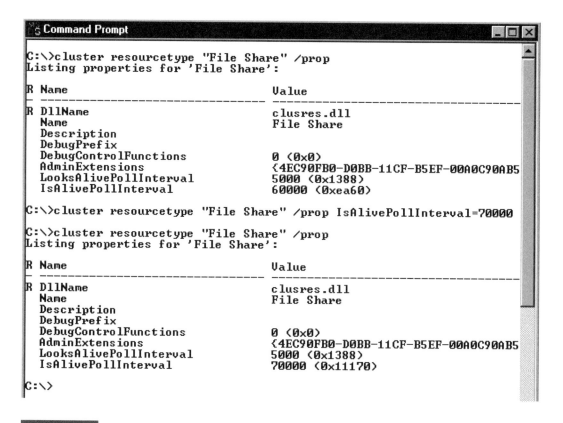

```
Command Prompt                                                    _ □ X

C:\>cluster resourcetype "File Share" /prop
Listing properties for 'File Share':

R Name                                Value
  ------------------------------      --------------------------------
R DllName                             clusres.dll
  Name                                File Share
  Description
  DebugPrefix
  DebugControlFunctions               0 (0x0)
  AdminExtensions                     {4EC90FB0-D0BB-11CF-B5EF-00A0C90AB5
  LooksAlivePollInterval              5000 (0x1388)
  IsAlivePollInterval                 60000 (0xea60)

C:\>cluster resourcetype "File Share" /prop IsAlivePollInterval=70000

C:\>cluster resourcetype "File Share" /prop
Listing properties for 'File Share':

R Name                                Value
  ------------------------------      --------------------------------
R DllName                             clusres.dll
  Name                                File Share
  Description
  DebugPrefix
  DebugControlFunctions               0 (0x0)
  AdminExtensions                     {4EC90FB0-D0BB-11CF-B5EF-00A0C90AB5
  LooksAlivePollInterval              5000 (0x1388)
  IsAlivePollInterval                 70000 (0x11170)

C:\>
```

FIGURE 5–17   *Modifying the properties for a resource type.*

Server. A new feature of Backup is the ability to back up to another disk device. A new feature is also being used in the backup terminology, *system state*. System state is the collection of information that defines the state of a computer and is so interrelated that it must be backed up as a unit to be of any use. This information includes the registry, COM class registration information, and the system's boot files.

Backing Up Data on the First Cluster Node

Use the Backup wizard to perform a backup of a cluster node where the Cluster Service is operational. Use either of the following backup options:

- "Back up everything on my computer." This option will back up everything on a cluster node. The backup will include the clustering software, cluster administrative software, the quorum resource's recovery log, which contains the most recent cluster database information, any resource registry checkpoints, and system state data.

- "Only back up the system state data." This option will back up only the quorum resource's recovery log, which contains the most recent cluster database information.

These options use the BackupClusterDatabase API, which guarantees that a consistent snapshot of the cluster database is saved. Performing a backup of a cluster node using these options will back up the quorum resource's recovery log regardless of which cluster node controls the quorum resource. Do not use the option to back up selected files. It does not use the cluster API and cannot guarantee the integrity of the cluster database.

Backing Up Data on Remaining Cluster Nodes

Once the quorum resource's recovery log has been backed up once, it is not necessary to back up the quorum log on the remaining cluster nodes. You should back up the *%windir%\cluster\CLUSDB* file on the remaining nodes. You can also back up the clustering software, cluster administrative software, system state data, and other cluster disks on the remaining cluster nodes.

First stop the Cluster Service on a cluster node. You should then select "Back up everything on my computer" in the Backup wizard.

Restoring Data on a Server Cluster Node

You can run the Restore wizard to restore the quorum resource recovery log, the cluster database, and any clustering software on a node. The Restore wizard uses the cluster API RestoreClusterDatabase to restore the cluster database to the quorum drive. The RestoreClusterDatabase API automatically:

1. stops the Cluster Service on all cluster nodes if the Cluster Service is running
2. restores the signature of the quorum disk if the signature of the quorum disk has changed since backup time
3. restores the cluster database and any resource registry checkpoints onto the quorum disk
4. restarts the Cluster Service on the restoring node

Then restore another cluster node using the Restore wizard and restart the Cluster Service on that node. Once the cluster database has been restored on the first node and all clustering software restored by the Restore wizard, the restoring node can join the cluster.

NOTES

- The Windows 2000 Backup and Recovery Tools wizard is available only to server clusters where all nodes are running Windows 2000 Advanced Server.
- The Restore wizard does not restore disk signatures or the partition layout of nonquorum cluster disks. If a nonquorum cluster disk changes after the backup time, the corresponding disk resources may fail to come on-line after a restore when the Cluster Service attempts to bring them on-line.
- The Restore wizard will attempt to restore the disk signature of the quorum disk but will not restore the partition layout of the quorum disk. This is necessary for the Cluster Service to be capable of recognizing a replaced quorum disk after a restore.

Performing a Hardware Upgrade

For the first example, assume a hardware upgrade, such as a CPU upgrade, needs to be performed. The node can simply be shut down. At this point, all resources will fail over to the remaining cluster node and still be available to clients. The computer that has been shut down can be taken apart and any new hardware installed.

A couple precautions need to be followed. If the shared I/O bus is SCSI, termination must be maintained when disconnecting the computer that is being taken off-line.

SUPPORTING MORE THAN ONE SCSI ADAPTER

Multiple SCSI adapters are supported, including multiple shared SCSI adapters. There is a lightly documented problem that can occur. Most SCSI controllers have BIOS that can be enabled, which is usually the default. If the controller contains the boot disk, the BIOS should be enabled. On all other SCSI controllers, the BIOS should be disabled. If it is enabled, seemingly unrelated error messages can happen.

Performing a Software Upgrade

Clusters offer the concept of what is sometimes called a rolling upgrade. What this basically means is that it is not necessary to upgrade all operating systems or applications on a cluster at the same time; they can be done independently. The benefit of a rolling upgrade is that many software upgrades require system reboots, and it is advantageous not to be required to reboot all cluster members at the same time. The idea is to perform the installation on one cluster member and then perform any required reboot. When the upgraded cluster member has rejoined the cluster, the upgrade process is now performed on the next cluster member, always making sure there is one running cluster member. If upgrades can be performed successfully on one cluster member at a time, the impact to clients can be minimized. Clients will experience cluster transitions and possibly some degraded performance as one cluster member is forced to own all cluster resources while the other cluster member is rebooted to complete a software installation or upgrade, but all cluster resources will still be available.

Clustering SQL Server

There is a statement from a movie that goes something like this: "It's not money that leads to ultimate power these days; it is control of the data." This is not an exact quote, and in case you find the statement interesting, it's from the movie "Sneakers." It is almost scary to think how accurate the statement is. Unavailability of data can be directly translated to loss of revenue.

The next step in the growth of clusters will be as applications that are written specifically to take advantage of features that a cluster can provide, such as fault tolerance. Some applications can be implemented simply as generic applications or generic services and will not require rewrites, but as new versions of software become available, look for them to include some level of cluster support. There are a few applications that have support built-in to the Cluster Service. For example, two resource types that will be discussed in later chapters are the Distributed Transaction Coordinator and the Message Queue Server. These products are bundled with Windows 2000 Advanced Server along with the Cluster Service. Other products have a separate release that includes cluster support. The Microsoft products that include cluster support are the "enterprise" editions. Two such products with an enterprise edition release are SQL Server and Exchange Server. The SQL Server Enterprise Edition will be discussed here and Exchange Server Enterprise Edition in the next chapter.

SQL Server—Overview

Before discussing the implementation of SQL Server in a clustered environment, a brief overview of SQL Server in a standard environment is necessary for comparison purposes. In a typical standalone SQL Server installation, three services are installed: SQL Executive, SQL Server, and Microsoft Distributed Transaction Coordinator (MSDTC) service. Each service performs specific tasks within the SQL Server umbrella. For example, SQL Executive is responsible for executing scheduled SQL tasks, such as backups. Standard client access to data is provided by the SQL Server service.

Devices and Databases

A device is a preallocated area of a disk that SQL Server will use as a storage device. From Windows NT's perspective, an SQL device is nothing more than a file. From SQL Server's perspective, the device is like a logical drive. SQL Server can create and store multiple databases on a device. A 100MB device might only be 5–10% utilized, but Windows NT only sees the 100MB file and must back up the entire device. This is why it is not practical to perform a Windows 2000 backup of an SQL Server device.

A database consists of tables, which are the basic unit of data storage for SQL Server. Databases are created on an SQL device. Outside of SQL Server, databases are hidden, residing in the file that represents the SQL Server device.

There are a number of devices and databases created during the installation process. The most common device is the master device, which holds the master, model, pubs, and tempdb databases.

Microsoft Cluster Support for SQL Server

The Microsoft Cluster Service supports two types of SQL Server configurations. The configuration used depends on the desired result of the cluster/database administrator. The type of SQL Server implementation desired also influences the hardware required (specifically the shared SCSI disks) by the cluster. The two configurations possible are known as active/active and active/passive configurations. Both configurations use symmetric virtual servers.

Symmetric Virtual Server

A *symmetric virtual server* is an instance of an SQL Server. Each symmetric virtual server can be linked to a standard SQL Server installation. To the client,

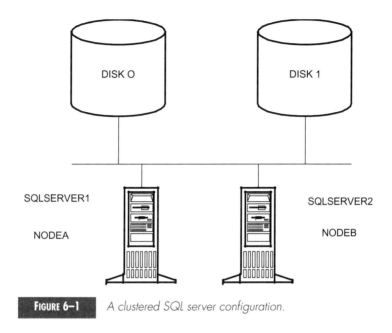

FIGURE 6-1   *A clustered SQL server configuration.*

the virtual server is referenced by a server name just like any other SQL Server. The difference is that the SQL virtual server is a group of resources on the cluster that can be owned by any cluster member. This equates to a fault-tolerant SQL Server, at least from a hardware perspective, because the resources that implement the virtual server can fail over between cluster members. Since SQL virtual servers have their own installation, they also have their own master, model, tempdb, and user databases. One cluster node has the ability to simultaneously run one or more virtual servers.

Examine Figure 6-1. Assume two SQL Server installations have been performed along with cluster support for SQL Server, and the virtual server names are SQLSERVER1 and SQLSERVER2. The two SQL virtual servers are serving access to totally independent databases. If NODE A were to fail, the cluster software would move the virtual server SQLSERVER1 to NODE B along with all the supporting resources such as the physical disk. To a client application, it is equivalent to turning NODE A off and then immediately back on. The client would lose all connections to SQL Server and all uncommitted transactions are rolled back. The client application must reconnect to the sever SQLSERVER1. The virtual server now running on NODE B will be transparent to the client. The server environment is preserved as the virtual server is moved from NODE A to NODE B. Information in all open databases and logs will be consistent after the failover. In reality, the new server is working with the same data, as the physical disk that stores the devices is now owned by NODE B. Any SQL registry information is kept consistent between nodes with registry replication.

Client applications may require slight modification to take full advantage of SQL Server cluster functionality. They should be written to reestablish lost connections when the server fails. Connections to SQL Server can be state oriented or stateless. Any state or data associated with a connection will be lost when the connection is broken. This would include any uncommitted transactions and temporary tables. If the connection to SQL Server is stateless, such as with Microsoft Access or Internet Information Server, the client will be able to reconnect and continue processing with no loss of data. Stateless clients provide a more seamless failover and recovery of the SQL virtual server.

Active/Passive Configuration

In an active/passive configuration, only one cluster member is running SQL Server (the active server), and the other cluster member is available as a backup in the event that the active SQL Server fails. The second server is the passive server. Referring to Figure 6-1, to implement an active/passive configuration, SQL Server could be installed on NODE A only. On NODE B, install the SQL Server utilities. Now, one virtual server can be created, associated with the SQL Server installation on NODE A. This implementation offers fault tolerance and will require no additional hardware. The SQL Server installation, along with the master device, must be located on one of the shared SCSI devices. This allows the SQL virtual server to successfully fail over between cluster members.

Active/Active Configuration

In an active/active configuration, there will be multiple instances of SQL Server running as symmetric virtual servers. Cluster support for SQL Server allows more than one instance of SQL Server to be running on a node in the cluster. In a typical two-node cluster, there could be two SQL virtual servers. Normally, they can be load balanced by defining appropriate preferred owners. In the event that one of the cluster nodes goes off-line, the SQL virtual server resource will fail over to the remaining cluster member and still be reachable by clients.

An active/active configuration requires some additional hardware. There must be multiple installations of SQL Server, one per virtual server. The SQL Server installations must be on separate SCSI devices on the shared bus. To distribute the SQL processing load among the cluster nodes, the SQL Server installations will need to be on separate disk resources that can be owned independent of one another.

Installing SQL Server, Enterprise Edition 6.5

UPGRADING FROM SQL SERVER 6.5 TO SQL SERVER, ENTERPRISE EDITION 6.5

It is possible to upgrade an SQL Server 6.5 installation to SQL Server, Enterprise Edition 6.5. The one major consideration is replication. If replication is in use, all replicated transactions in the distribution database must be distributed before upgrading to SQL Server, Enterprise Edition 6.5. If it is not clear whether all replicated transactions have been processed, users should be unsubscribed before installation and resubscribed after the upgrade has completed.

It is recommended that all servers that function as replication Publishers and Distributors be upgraded to either SQL Server 6.5, Service Pack 3 or to the Enterprise Edition version. A Distribution server running Service Pack 3 or Enterprise Edition can communicate properly with Publisher running versions of SQL Server earlier than Service Pack 3. The reverse is not true, however. A Publisher running Service Pack 3 should not run against a Distributor running an earlier service pack.

Replication depends extensively on server names for each node in the replication configuration. Renaming of a server involved in replication is not supported. When clustering support for SQL Server is installed, a new server name is created. For replication to function properly, it will need to be deinstalled prior to configuring SQL Server cluster support and reinstalled after the configuration is complete.

INSTALLING SQL SERVER, ENTERPRISE EDITION 6.5

Installing SQL Server is a straightforward process. There are some special installation requirements when installing SQL Server to run it in a clustered environment.

For every virtual server desired, there must be a corresponding SQL Server installation. An active/passive configuration will require one installation, an active/active configuration will require two installations, one on each cluster node. In an active/passive configuration, install the utilities such as Enterprise Manager by selecting the option Install Utilities Only (Figure 6-2).

For a symmetric virtual server to be successfully implemented, SQL Server must be installed on one of the shared SCSI disks. See Figure 6-3. If an active/active configuration is being implemented, the two SQL Server installations will need to be on separate shared SCSI devices to allow independent failover of the virtual servers. The virtual server resource will be automatically placed in a group with the disk resource that contains the SQL Server installation. Since only one cluster node can own a disk resource, having two installations of SQL Server on the same disk would not allow SQL Server to be running simultaneously on both cluster nodes.

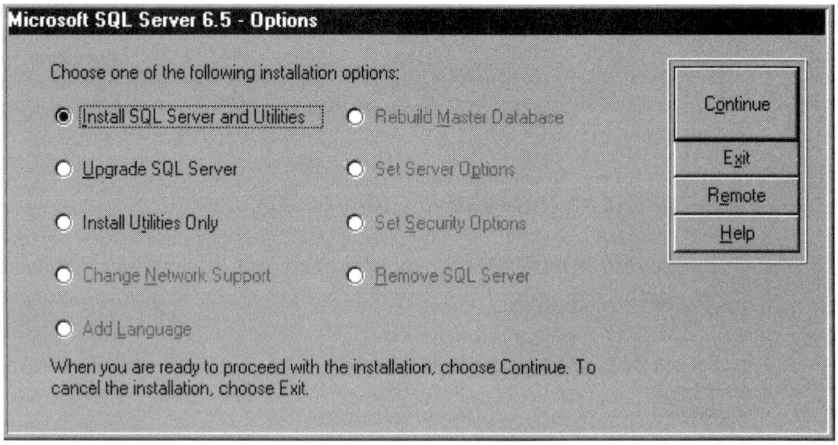

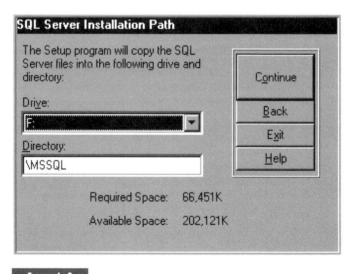

FIGURE 6–2

FIGURE 6–3

The master device must be located on a shared SCSI disk for the virtual server to be able to fail over properly (Figure 6-4). The default location for the master device will be a subdirectory under the device and directory specified as the main SQL Server installation directory entered in Figure 6-3.

From a performance perspective, separating the SQL Server executables and databases can be useful. This is because disk I/O traffic can be spread among

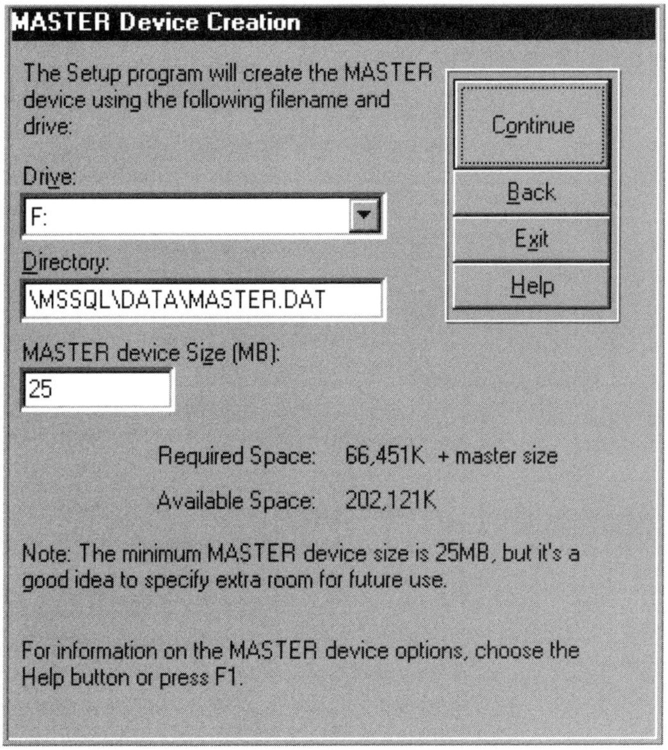

MASTER Device Creation

The Setup program will create the MASTER
device using the following filename and
drive:

Drive:

F:

Directory:

\MSSQL\DATA\MASTER.DAT

MASTER device Size (MB):

25

Continue

Back

Exit

Help

Required Space: 66,451K + master size

Available Space: 202,121K

Note: The minimum MASTER device size is 25MB, but it's a
good idea to specify extra room for future use.

For information on the MASTER device options, choose the
Help button or press F1.

FIGURE 6–4

multiple physical disks. However, when configuring SQL Server to run in a
clustered environment, all files and devices should be located on one physical
disk to minimize the number of shared SCSI disks that need to be moved
between cluster members in the event of a failover.

It is best not to configure the SQL Server and SQL Executive services to
start automatically, as they will need to be stopped anyway when SQL cluster
support is installed. See Figure 6-5. Standard SQL Server offers many options
for network support. SQL Server running in a cluster only supports TCP/IP,
Multi-Protocol, and Named Pipes. In addition, the SQL Cluster installation program only uses Named Pipes for connectivity. Therefore, the Named Pipes
protocol needs to be installed at least until the SQL cluster support software is
installed. It could then potentially be removed. Selecting the Networks button
in Figure 6-5 presents the network protocols screen in Figure 6-6.

If an active/active configuration is being implemented, it is necessary
that the username and password be the same for the SQL Executive service
for both SQL Server installations (Figure 6-7). The username specified for the

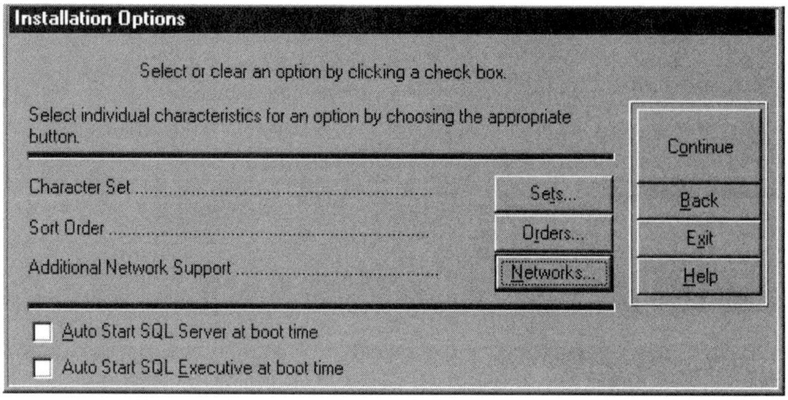

FIGURE 6–5

FIGURE 6–6

SQL Executive service can be verified with the Services option in Control Panel. The password for the account can also be reentered. Realize that if the password for the account is changed in the User Manager utility, it must be manually updated in the Services program in order to work.

SERVICE PACKS AND HOT FIXES

SQL Server, Enterprise Edition supercedes Service Pack 4 and earlier. As a result, applying any service pack other than Service Pack 5 or later, or any hot fixes to these service packs, can corrupt the SQL Server installation.

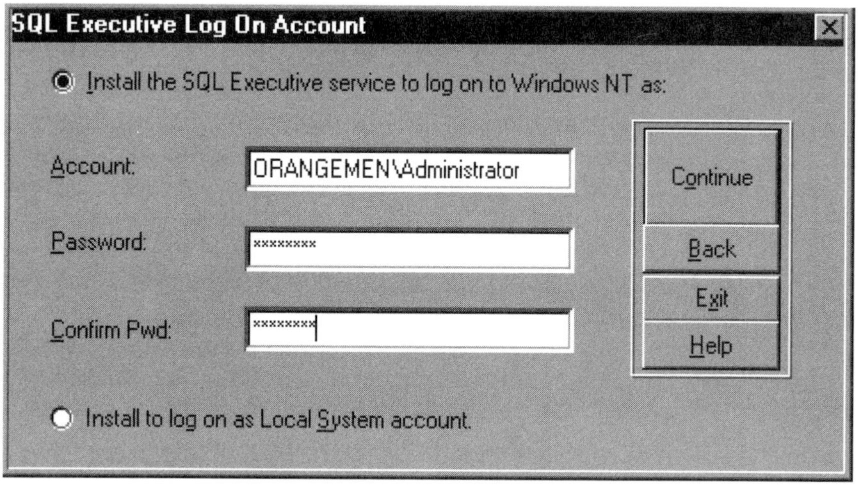

FIGURE 6-7

Installing Cluster Support for SQL Server

Pre-Setup Requirements

Before the SQL Server Cluster software can be loaded, there are some prerequisite tasks that need to be performed. Some tasks are recommendations, but others will block a successful installation if not carried out. These tasks are as follows.

- There must be a two-node functioning cluster. Cluster support for SQL Server will not install if it does not detect a two-node cluster, and both must be up and running.

- SQL Server, Enterprise Edition must be installed on at least one node in the cluster. If SQL Server is not going to be installed on both nodes, the SQL Server utilities must be installed on the second node.

- Stop the SQL Server and Internet Information Server services on both nodes. Use the SQL Service Manager utility in the SQL Server program group to stop the SQL Server services. Stop the MSDTC, MSSQL Server, and SQL Executive services. Use the Internet Service Manager to stop the WWW, FTP, and Gopher services.

- Proper licensing, at this time, requires SQL Server licenses on both cluster nodes, even if only one SQL Server process will be running on the cluster. There have been rumors of cluster licenses for software, but at the time of this writing, they are not yet available.

FIGURE 6–8

- If there are going to be multiple virtual servers, designate which shared disks will belong to each virtual server. Remember, in order to have multiple instances of SQL Server running, they will each need their own disk on the shared SCSI bus.

Cluster Support for SQL Server — Setup

On the SQL Server, Enterprise Edition CD-ROM, switch to the appropriate platform directory, either Alpha or I386. In the Cluster subdirectory, start the installation program named SQL Cluster Setup. The screen in Figure 6-8 appears.

If a message appears at this time that the computer is not a member of a cluster, make sure the other cluster member is up, and shows in the Cluster Administrator utility as being on-line.

Select the option Install virtual server (Figure 6-9). If this is an initial installation, it will be the only option available. If cluster support for SQL Server has already been installed, the Remove virtual server option can be

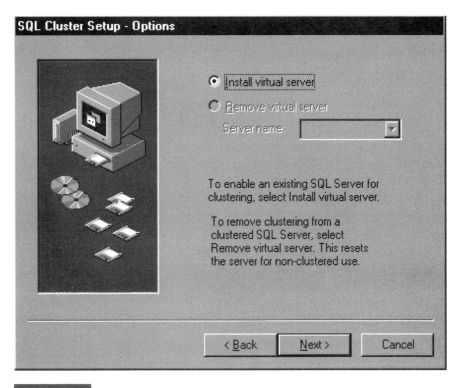

SQL Cluster Setup - Options

⊙ Install virtual server

○ Remove virtual server

Server name:

To enable an existing SQL Server for clustering, select Install virtual server.

To remove clustering from a clustered SQL Server, select Remove virtual server. This resets the server for non-clustered use.

< Back   Next >   Cancel

FIGURE 6—9

used to deinstall the software. Any resources are also removed with this option, so do not remove the SQL Server resources manually through Cluster Administrator.

Multiple virtual servers cannot be installed unless there are separate disks available on the shared SCSI bus. The software allows a maximum of one virtual server per shared SCSI disk. You cannot use separate logical drives on the same SCSI disk and expect to install multiple virtual servers. Remember that the physical disk is a single resource and can only be accessed by one member of the cluster. There must be an SQL Server installation associated with each virtual server specified in this screen.

Enter the password to the "sa" account (Figure 6-10). The "sa" account is the default system administration account for SQL Server. After an SQL Server installation this password will be blank.

I have personally had many problems at this point of the installation. I am not sure, but I think my problems began when I aborted an installation at about two thirds complete. The installation was not going to complete due to another problem I had. Every time I attempted to continue past this screen I

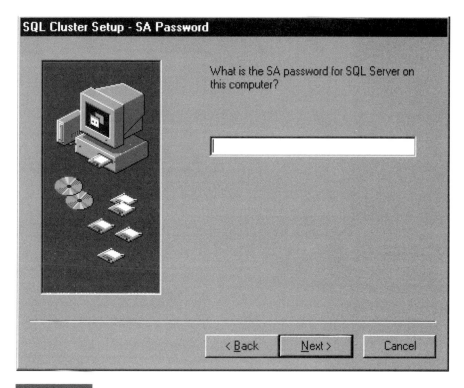

SQL Cluster Setup - SA Password

What is the SA password for SQL Server on this computer?

< Back   Next >   Cancel

FIGURE 6–10

got an error message that said, "Unable to log on to SQL Server. Make sure the SQL Server Service can be started and that the "sa" password supplied is correct." I would check the SQL Server service, and it would be running. It was started by the installation. I could log on to SQL Server through all the tools such as ISQL/W. The only way I was able to fix the problem was to do a complete reload of Windows NT and SQL Server.

Enter the password for the account that SQL Server is configured to run under (Figure 6-11). If the service is configured to run with the System account, this screen will not appear. For the cluster support for the SQL Server installation to proceed beyond this point, the username and password the SQL Server service is running under must be the same on both cluster nodes. If they are different, user the Services program from Control Panel to configure the username and password for the service by double-clicking on the MSSQL Server service. The password is not supplied from the account database when a username is selected. It must be entered for security purposes. To determine whether the username and password are correct, select the service and then the "Start" button. This will attempt to start the service. If no

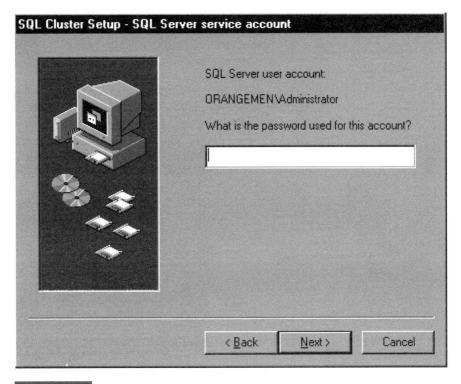

FIGURE 6–11

error messages appear, the service has started successfully. One common configuration problem is the account configured to run the service does not have the privilege to run as a service. This privilege can be granted through the Policies menu in User Manager.

Enter the password the SQL Executive account is configured to run under (Figure 6-12). When doing an SQL Server installation, it is not an option to specify an account for this service. It will be configured to run under the System account. It is necessary that the SQL Executive service run with the same username and password on both nodes in the cluster. To guarantee this, use a domain account rather than a local account if the computers are not configured to be domain controllers. Remember that if the password is changed in the account database, it must also be changed through the Services program in Control Panel. This screen will also not appear if the SQL Executive is running under the System account.

Each symmetric virtual server will have a unique name and address. If this looks familiar, it should. The information in this screen will be used to create an IP address resource in the cluster (Figure 6-13). The TCP/IP address

FIGURE 6-12

entered here is the address that will be exposed on the network for the virtual server. For example, it is not commonly used, but it is possible to connect to an SQL Server in ISQL by using a TCP/IP address. Programmers could use the address when developing applications. This is not good practice, but the point is that the SQL Server name and TCP/IP address are interchangeable. Names are there for our benefit. As far as the computer is concerned, it is just extra work to resolve the name to a TCP/IP address.

Since the virtual server is associated with a TCP/IP address, and this resource can move between cluster members, it is now possible to see the foundation of how cluster support for SQL Server works.

Enter the name by which the SQL Server will be known (Figure 6-14). This is the name that users will enter in ISQL or administrators will register in Enterprise Manager. This name is used to define a network name resource in the cluster. The network name will be the SQL Server that clients and applications connect to. This network name resource has a dependency of the IP address entered in Figure 6-13.

Verify the server name, IP address, and subnet mask, and select Finish (Figure 6-15). The installation completes unattended at this point. When the

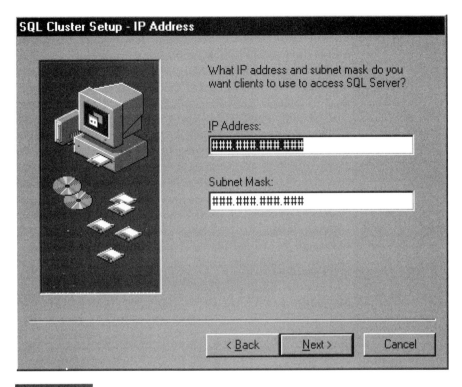

FIGURE 6-13

installation is complete, the virtual server will not be accessible because the resources created to support the cluster will be off-line. To test the virtual server, run Cluster Administrator and bring on-line any resources in the group that have the same name as the server name supplied in Figure 6-15. Once the resources are brought on-line, it will not be necessary to bring them on-line again, even after a system reboot unless there is a resource failure or they are manually taken off-line. This step is only necessary once.

Cluster Support for SQL Server Modifications

When cluster support for SQL Server is installed, various changes are made both to Windows NT and to the cluster configuration. The most significant change to the operating system is the addition of three services. These new services can be viewed with the Services program in Control Panel. Two of the services replace the normal SQL Server and SQL Executive services. The

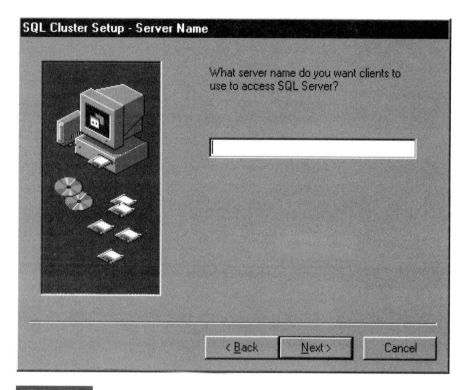

FIGURE 6–14

names will be MSSQLServer$*name*, where *name* is replaced by the virtual server name created during the SQL cluster support software installation. The third service is named VSrvSvc$*name*, again replacing *name* with the name of the symmetric virtual server created. It is interesting that only this service is defined as a generic service in the cluster. The SQL Server and SQL Executive services are not cluster resources, in the sense that they are not generic service resources. There are, however, two new resource types in the cluster configuration. See Figure 6-16.

The software installation creates a new cluster group based on the name supplied for the virtual server. There are six resources in this group. The first is the physical disk resource. The installation will move the necessary disk resource into the group, which could lead to many other resources being automatically moved to this group if the same disk is used to store other resources such as file shares. This forces all the resources to be running on the same node as the virtual server. To distribute the processing load, it will be necessary to have a separate disk on the shared SCSI bus for SQL Server processing. This allows the SQL virtual server resource to be located on a

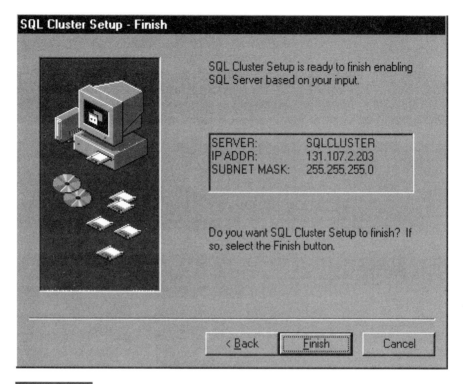

SQL Cluster Setup - Finish

SQL Cluster Setup is ready to finish enabling SQL Server based on your input.

SERVER: SQLCLUSTER
IP ADDR: 131.107.2.203
SUBNET MASK: 255.255.255.0

Do you want SQL Cluster Setup to finish? If so, select the Finish button.

< Back   Finish   Cancel

FIGURE 6–15

cluster node independent of other cluster resources. To balance the load, make one node the preferred owner for the SQL virtual server group and the other node the preferred owner for the other resource groups. To review how to define preferred owners for cluster groups, refer to Chapter 4. The next two resources are standard IP address and network name resources. These together create a unique endpoint on the network that can move between cluster nodes. The next two resources are types that have not been introduced before.

The resource titled SQLCLUSTER SQL Executive 6.5 is a resource of type SQL Executive 6.5. It is directly linked to the new service created during the installation process. When the SQL Executive resource is taken off-line, the service is automatically stopped. When the resource is brought on-line, the service is started. The proper administrative interface to the SQL Server services is through the Cluster Administrator utility, not the Services program. One issue with managing the SQL Server and SQL Executive services is that there are too many methods that appear to manage the services, but the only method that actually brings the resource on-line is Cluster Administrator. For

FIGURE 6–16

example, the services can still be controlled through the SQL Service Manager. The problem with this is that if the SQL Executive resource is off-line, the SQL Service Manager does not bring the resource on-line when it starts the service. The resource must still be brought on-line via the Cluster Administrator utility. It becomes a two-step process to actually start the SQL virtual server. If the resources are brought on-line first via Cluster Administrator, the services are started at the same time without administrator intervention.

The next resource in the group is SQLCLUSTER SQL Server 6.5. This resource has a type of SQL Server 6.5. The resource takes the place of the standard SQL Server service and is associated with the service named MSSQLServer$*name*, where *name* is replaced by the virtual server name created during the SQL cluster support software installation. The administration of this resource is performed identically as the SQL Executive resource. Manage it through the Cluster Administrator utility.

The last resource is the SQLCLUSTER Vserver resource. This resource has a type of generic service.

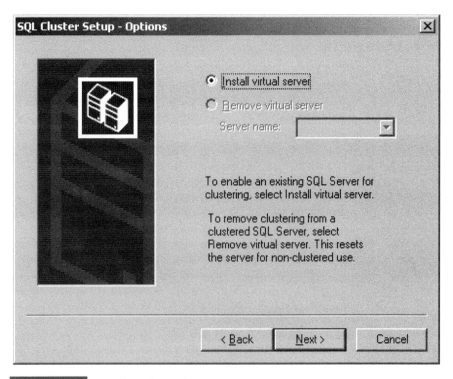

FIGURE 6–17   *Installing clustered SQL Server.*

Clustering SQL Server 7.0

Implementing a cluster running SQL Server 7.0 is very similar to previous versions. After installing SQL Server on a cluster shared disks, run the Cluster Failover Wizard located in the SQL Server Program Group.

Select the option to Install Virtual Server. See Figure 6-17. Notice the option Remove Virtual Server is not available since a server of this type does not already exist.

Enter an IP Address that does not already exist on your network. See Figure 6-18. This information is used by the Wizard to create a new IP Address resource in the cluster. Contact your network administrator if you are unsure of an available address.

Supply a unique name by which to reference the clustered SQL Server. See Figure 6-19. This name is used to create a network name resource that depends on the IP Address resource created in Figure 6-18.

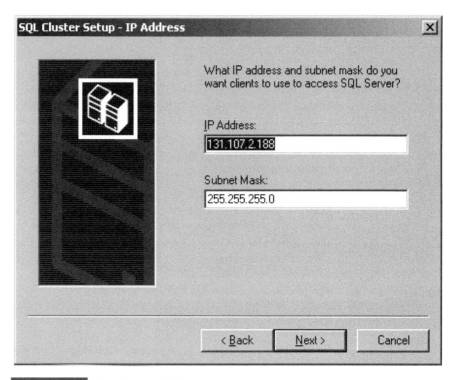

FIGURE 6–18   *Supplying IP Address resource parameters.*

All necessary information has now been supplied to the Cluster Failover Wizard. At this point, the target group and resources will be created. Also, the wizard installs the files necessary for run SQL Server onto any secondary cluster members. If you encounter an error stating that the SQL Manager program is opened, check the processes tab in Task Manager. There seems to be a problem with the SQL Service Manager unloading itself from memory if you use it to start/stop any of the SQL services. You can simply highlight the process and select the "End Task" button. At this point, the installation of SQL Server 7.0 in a cluster is complete. Figure 6-20 shows the resources created by the Cluster Failover Wizard.

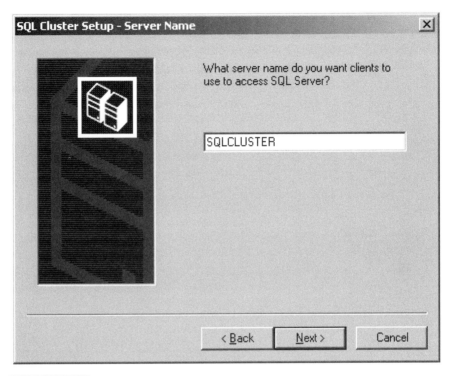

FIGURE 6–19   *Supplying Network name resource parameters.*

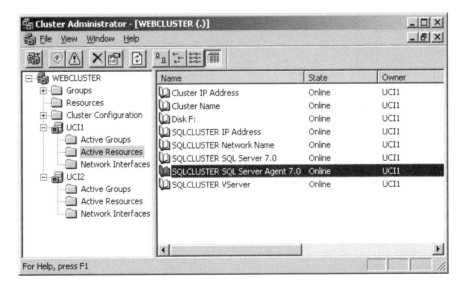

FIGURE 6–20   *The completed clustered SQL Server installation.*

Clustering Exchange Server

Exchange Server is one of two major applications, the other being SQL Server, released by Microsoft in an Enterprise Edition, which provides cluster-aware support for installation into a Microsoft Cluster environment. It also shares with SQL Server an increasing role as a line of business applications whose functionality is essential to corporate workflow. Designed to enhance user access to a wide variety of resources by removing the technical obstacles between the user and the resource, Exchange is itself enhanced by Cluster Server's promise of "high availability." Achieving the cluster "high availability" promise for Exchange Server is the topic of this chapter.

Exchange Server—Overview

Microsoft Exchange Server, as the name implies, facilitates the flow of information within and between organizations. More than simple messaging, it combines a secure and reliable information store with a robust directory database and the necessary services, connectors, and agents to provide authorized users with convenient, enterprise-wide access to corporate information resources. It provides server-side services to a broad range of clients communicating over native MAPI, SMTP, POP3, IMAP4, NNTP, and HTTP messaging protocols. The focus (no surprise here) is on comprehensive and powerful convenience.

Hierarchically, Exchange establishes an inverted tree structure defining a solitary Exchange Organization at the top composed of one or more Exchange Sites, each consisting of one or more Exchange Servers. Logically, the site is the unit of administration. The practical reality is that resources exist on individual servers—sometimes on more than one—that ensure availability and fault tolerance. Scalability is ensured by the distributed granularity of the Exchange topology: Additional sites or servers can be deployed at any point to redress load or performance issues.

Each server maintains its own information stores and a dynamic copy of a shared directory services database, which weaves the server's NetBIOS name into the internal name for all local exchange database objects. This creates a coupling so strong that changing the server's NetBIOS name will incapacitate Exchange Server. The core functionality of Exchange Server is established at installation by the creation and registry of five Windows 2000 services (System Attendant, Directory, Information Store, Message Transfer Agent, and Event Services). Additional functionality, such as connectors or Advanced Security, can be supported with the deployment of the appropriate Windows 2000 services. All Exchange components are stored in an extensive set of file system folders established during installation, some of which are shared to facilitate intercomponent communication. An optional module, Admin.exe, which provides a powerful graphical interface for configuring the properties of individual Exchange objects, provides single-seat organization-wide administrative capability.

As Microsoft Exchange has increasingly become an essential component of mainstream corporate workflow, the issue of service availability has grown. With the failure of an Exchange Server, the user mailboxes and nonreplicated public folders on that server will be unavailable until that server is returned on-line. Any connectors uniquely homed on the failed server will also be down. Users homed on other Exchange Servers will not be affected by the remote server failure unless they need to access a resource uniquely homed on the failed server. Users whose mailboxes are homed on the failed server will not be able to access Exchange Server, but if they are configured for off-line client operation, they will be able to continue working with the resources that were off-line enabled at the time they last synchronized the off-line store with the server store. No updating of these off-line resources will be possible until the server is brought back on-line.

Microsoft Exchange Server has been available in both a Standard Edition and an Enterprise Edition from its first release. Prior to version 5.5, the significant difference between the two editions was the ability and product license to install intersite connectors. With version 5.5, the Enterprise Edition adds cluster awareness to Exchange Server, taking a significant step to ensuring high availability. Note that not all Exchange components and services are cluster aware. The design goals for Exchange Cluster Server include hardware failure protection and high availability and are met with the current active/

standby-clustering model. For this version of Exchange and the Cluster Service, the goals specifically did not include user load balancing (which would require active/active clustering) or dynamic backup capability (available on some third-party products).

Installing Exchange Server, Enterprise Edition

Installation of Microsoft Exchange Server, version 5.5, Enterprise Edition into a Microsoft Cluster environment is a two-stage process. In the first stage, Exchange Server, Enterprise Edition is installed onto the primary node of an existing cluster. This is a full installation, with Exchange's executable, database, component, and support files installed to the shared cluster drive(s), Exchange resources created in the cluster resource group, system libraries and extensions installed into the primary node's local Windows 2000 System32 folder, and Windows 2000 services created and registered on the primary node. This results in a viable Exchange Server installation on the primary cluster node, but not one that would survive being failed over, for there is no Exchange awareness or capability on the secondary cluster node. The second stage of the installation process remedies this by installing system libraries and extensions into the secondary node's local Windows 2000 System32 folder and creating and registering Windows 2000 services on the secondary node.

The installation process begins automatically when you place the Exchange Server, Enterprise Edition CD-ROM in the drive. (If it does not start automatically, it can be initiated by running Launch.exe in the root of the CD-ROM). A helpful menu system appears (Figure 7-1) with options to move to a submenu of installation choices, to open and review the Exchange Server Release Notes, to move to a submenu of documentation choices (including an html document specifically about clustering Exchange Server), to move to a submenu of on-line resource choices, or to exit the installation program. Both the Release Notes and the "Clustering with Exchange Server" web document call attention to the required preexisting cluster environment that must be in place before a clustered installation of Exchange Server can be successful. These topics are taken up in the next section, before moving on to Setup itself.

Pre-Setup Considerations

An Exchange Cluster Server is created by installing Exchange Server into an existing Microsoft Server Cluster; clustering services cannot be added to an existing Exchange Server. So the existence of a viable cluster is one preinstallation requirement, and there are additional required conditions to ensure the cluster will properly support Exchange:

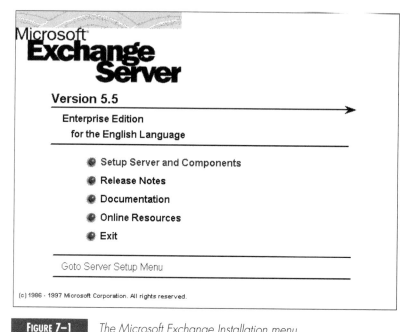

Microsoft®
Exchange Server

Version 5.5

Enterprise Edition
for the English Language

● Setup Server and Components
● Release Notes
● Documentation
● Online Resources
● Exit

Goto Server Setup Menu

(c) 1986 - 1997 Microsoft Corporation. All rights reserved.

FIGURE 7–1   *The Microsoft Exchange Installation menu.*

- The cluster server hardware should be symmetrical. The processor type and capability, installed memory, and local hard drive configuration should be the same on both nodes of the cluster. It must further be adequate to support the cluster OS and all applications, whether cluster aware or not, that might be running on either node at any given time. In addition to the basic requirement that a failed-over application be able to find, configure, and launch the necessary local resources in a compatible environment, Exchange optimizes its use of hardware resources based on a static, point-in-time analysis of the server on which it is running. Performance and, possibly, function may be impaired following fail over, depending on the degree of divergence from hardware symmetry.
- The cluster server hardware should be approved for cluster use in the hardware compatibility list (HCL) found at *http://www.microsoft.com/ hwtest/hcl.* Microsoft will not provide support for noncomplying hardware.
- Exchange Server 5.5, Enterprise Edition is the only version of Exchange that is cluster aware. It must be installed on the shared cluster drive(s) of an active cluster node to take advantage of cluster services. It is possible to install Exchange Server, Enterprise Edition

onto a non-cluster server or to install Exchange Server, Standard Edition onto a non-shared (non-cluster) drive of a cluster node—both will yield viable Exchange Servers—but neither will provide any of the benefits derived from clustering. Should the server fail, the Exchange resources would be unavailable until the problem is resolved. It is also possible to install Exchange Server, Standard Edition onto the shared cluster drive of an active cluster node—the non-cluster-aware Standard Edition setup program does not prevent it—but fail over of the non-cluster-aware Exchange Server installation will result in its destruction and corruption of its files due to Standard Edition's inability to virtualize its network name. Exchange Server, Standard Edition, is not intended for a multisite, multiserver environment and is, by design, utterly unsuited for deployment in a clustered server environment. Unless specifically stated otherwise, further references to Exchange Server will mean version 5.5, Enterprise Edition exclusively.

• Installation of the Enterprise Edition of Exchange Server into a cluster requires two server licenses for Exchange, even though only a single instance of Exchange can be running at any point in time. This requirement is made part of, and detailed in, the on-line license agreement, shown in Figure 7-2, which must be acknowledged to continue the installation process. It would appear that this licensing requirement foreshadows migration to an active/active cluster support mode, where each node is hosting an active Exchange Server installation capable of being failed over to the other node. Microsoft has indicated that the future of Exchange Cluster Server lies in that direction.

A cluster resource group must be created and configured to support the cluster-aware installation of Exchange Server. This resource group will contain the Exchange components and define the administrative and fail over unit for the Exchange Cluster Server. An IP Address resource, a Network Name resource, and a disk resource are all required in the Exchange resource group prior to launching the Exchange setup program. To create a resource group, in Cluster Administrator, choose the FILE menu button, then NEW, and GROUP to open the New Group dialog box (Figure 7-3). Enter the name for the cluster resource group in the Name field—it is good policy to also provide a definitive description. This name is used almost exclusively within the cluster environment—it is exposed in the Exchange environment only early in the setup process, to identify the cluster resource group for installation—so it does not enter into the naming convention consideration for the Exchange topology. If more than one Exchange Cluster Server installation is administered, it is still a good idea to choose uniquely definitive names to help avoid administrative confusion—it is easier to deal with Exch_Cluster_Boston and Exch_Cluster_Dallas than two instances of Exch_Cluster, which will force a

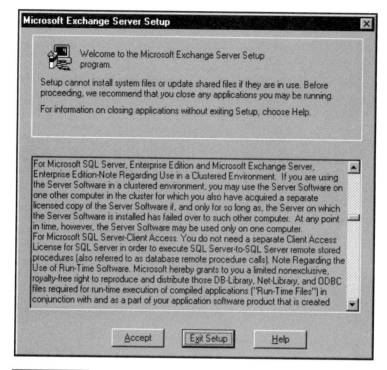

FIGURE 7–2   *License acceptance.*

review of the (hopefully present) description to uniquely identify the cluster resource groups.

To create the IP Address resource, in Cluster Administrator, choose the FILE menu button, then NEW, and RESOURCE to open the New Resource dialog box (Figure 7-4). Enter the name for the IP Address resource in the Name field and add an optional description. This name is used exclusively in the cluster environment and is not exposed in Exchange, so the same general comments made about the cluster resource group name also apply here. Choose IP Address for the Resource type, and be sure the Group field identifies the Exchange cluster resource group created earlier.

The default values are acceptable for the Possible Owners dialog box and Dependencies dialog box (the IP Address resource has no dependencies) that follow. In the TCP/IP Address Parameters dialog box (Figure 7-5), enter the unique IP address and subnet mask assigned to the Exchange virtual server. This IP address is fully exposed in the intranet/internet environment and needs to be handled just as the IP address of a non-clustered Exchange Server would be handled. Also identify the appropriate network for client access (if more than one network is available). Choose Finish to close.

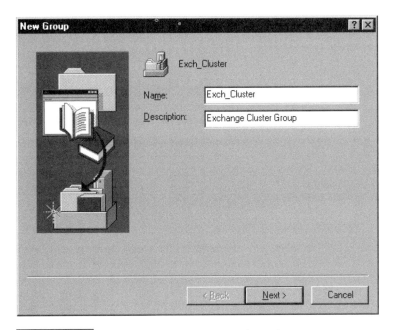

FIGURE 7–3   *Creating the resource group for Exchange.*

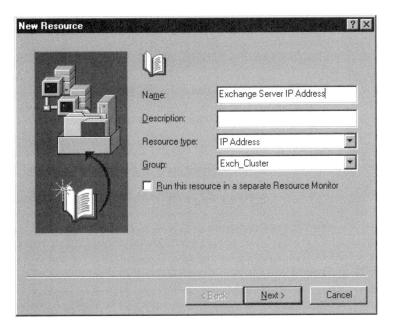

FIGURE 7–4   *Creating the Exchange IP Address resource.*

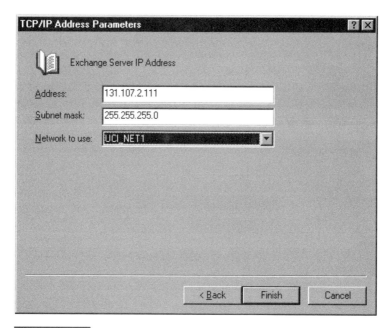

FIGURE 7–5   *Creating the IP Address resource (continued).*

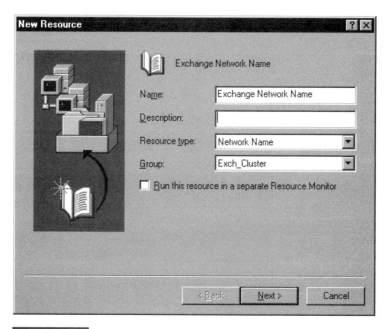

FIGURE 7–6   *Creating the Network Name resource.*

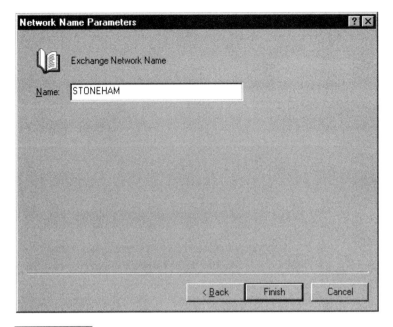

FIGURE 7-7   *Creating the Network Name resource (continued).*

To create the Network Name resource, in Cluster Administrator, choose the FILE menu button, then NEW, and RESOURCE to open the New Resource dialog box (Figure 7-6). Enter the name for the Network Name resource in the Name field and, again, add an optional description. This name is the name of the cluster administrator resource object itself, whose resource type is Network Name; it is not the NetBIOS name of the virtual Exchange Server. This name is used exclusively in the cluster environment and is not exposed in Exchange, so once again the same general comments made about the cluster resource group name also apply here. Choose Network Name for the Resource type, and be sure the Group field identifies the Exchange cluster resource group created earlier.

Once again, the default values are acceptable for the Possible Owners and Dependencies dialog boxes. (This time, however, the Network Name resource is dependent on the IP Address.) In the Network Name Parameters dialog box (Figure 7-7), enter the unique NetBIOS name assigned to the Exchange virtual server. This server name is fully exposed in the Exchange and network environments and needs to be handled just as the server name of a non-clustered Exchange Server would be handled. It is, in fact, a server name, which will be listed in Network Neighborhood or other browser list. It is the Exchange Server name that will be shown in the Exchange Admin.exe program, and it is the name that will form a part of the internal object names

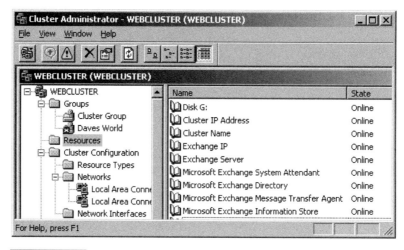

FIGURE 7–8   *Viewing the Exchange resources.*

in the Exchange Directory Services database. This name should be subjected to the same naming convention/suitability consideration accorded any other server name. Choose Finish to close.

The final step in this cluster resource group preparation is to move the shared disk resource into the Exchange resource group. At this point, the view in Cluster Administrator should look like Figure 7-8, with an active, fully configured Exchange cluster resource group containing an IP Address resource, a Network Name resource, and a shared cluster disk resource. The cluster is now ready to support Exchange Server.

The discussion to this point has been largely focused on the cluster aspects of this Exchange Server installation. It may need to be restated, then, that the underlying purpose of this entire process is to create an Exchange Server—one enhanced to cluster-supported high-availability operation—but still, at the core, an Exchange Server. So the standard planning and analysis procedure used to support the deployment of a non-clustered Exchange Server is still fully applicable to the clustered Exchange Server and must be observed. What may be different for the Exchange Cluster Server deployment is the high likelihood that it is a complete replacement for an existing Exchange Server, done to gain the benefits derived from clustering, rather than a topologically new site/server or a load-balancing scalability install, which are the reasons for most non-clustered Exchange Server installations. A complete replacement install has significant server namespace and existing resource preservation/migration implications that simply do not apply to the new site or site extension deployment. This server's role in the Exchange topology needs to be well defined prior to installation.

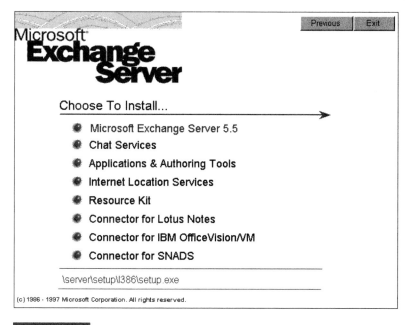

Previous   Exit

Microsoft
Exchange
Server

Choose To Install...

● Microsoft Exchange Server 5.5
● Chat Services
● Applications & Authoring Tools
● Internet Location Services
● Resource Kit
● Connector for Lotus Notes
● Connector for IBM OfficeVision/VM
● Connector for SNADS

\server\setup\I386\setup.exe

(c) 1986 - 1997 Microsoft Corporation. All rights reserved.

FIGURE 7-9   *The Exchange Server installation menu.*

Setup — Primary Cluster Node

Following the activity and involvement of the pre-Setup section, the actual setup of Exchange Server into a Cluster Server environment is something of an anticlimax. This is largely because the process is well defined and executes reliably. From the top level of the Exchange Server installation menu (Figure 7-9), the Setup Server and Components option opens a submenu of choices, as shown in Figure 7-10. Choosing Microsoft Exchange Server 5.5 launches the server setup program appropriate to the installation platform (Intel or Alpha). As shown in the lower portion of the illustration, this can also be launched by running CD:\server\setup\I386\setup.exe or CD:\server\setup\alpha\setup.exe, as appropriate.

The cluster-aware setup program will detect that it is running on an active cluster node and confirm this by displaying the informational dialog box shown in Figure 7-10. Choosing Help for more information about clustered servers opens the Help dialog box, which provides a hot link to basic information on Server Clusters and a reminder to be sure that Enterprise Edition is being installed on symmetrically configured Server Clusters.

The setup program next requires identification of the cluster resource group into which it will install Exchange resources. A choice from the drop-down box of all cluster resource groups is offered. This is the single point,

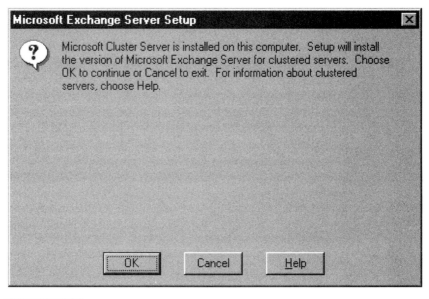

FIGURE 7-10   *Cluster detection notification.*

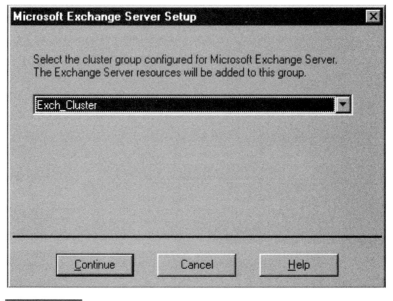

FIGURE 7-11   *Selecting the resource group.*

FIGURE 7-12   *Selecting the type of Exchange installation.*

mentioned earlier, where the name of the cluster resource group is exposed in the Exchange Server Environment. The setup program proceeds, requiring, among other things, a site services account and password. (It will default to the administrator account used for the install, but this should not be accepted—use a dedicated account for this purpose.) This portion of the process is indistinguishable from a non-clustered install until the installation type (Typical, Complete/Custom, Minimum) dialog box is displayed (Figure 7-11).

The difference at this point between a cluster-aware installation and a non-cluster installation is not readily apparent until an unacceptable action is attempted, which causes the cluster-aware setup program to define the operational environmental rules in place. This dialog box (Figure 7-12), in addition to allowing the choice of installation scope, displays the installation directory for the Exchange Server files, in this case, X:\exchsrvr, on the shared SCSI cluster disk. An attempt to specify an alternative installation directory via the Change Directory button, pointing to a non-cluster disk, generated the error message shown in Figure 7-13.

FIGURE 7–13   *Attempting to use a non-shared disk.*

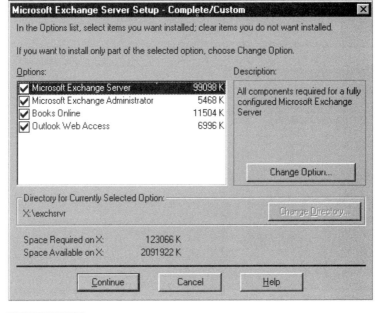

FIGURE 7–14   *Performing a custom install.*

The fourth explanation for the error, that the proposed directory is not a cluster disk resource, is the operative one, and drives home the point that what continuity exists between a failed cluster node and its surviving twin exists solely on the shared cluster drive(s). Installation to a shared cluster drive, specifically one identified as a disk resource in the Exchange resource group, is mandatory, and will be enforced by the system.

Setup proceeds, supporting a complete installation, with all components installing to the shared cluster drive, as shown in Figure 7-14. Setup copies Exchange executable, database, component, and support files to the shared

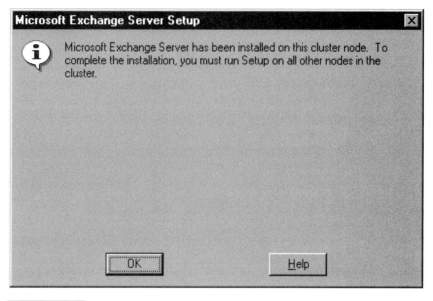

FIGURE 7–15   *Reminder to run setup on secondary node.*

cluster drive, establishes cluster resources in the Exchange cluster resource group, copies system libraries and extensions to the local \System32 directory, and creates and registers Windows 2000 services on the primary node. The setup program then uses two dialog boxes to declare itself finished, to provide reminders to run Setup on the secondary node, and to run Performance Optimizer on the active node (Figures 7-15 and 7-16).

Except for running Performance Optimizer, installation on the primary node is complete, and the Exchange Server is available for use, but only on the primary node. Until Setup is completed on the secondary node, fail over of the Exchange installation will be fatal, so it is recommended to proceed directly to the setup of the secondary node.

Setup—Secondary Cluster Node

Running Setup on the secondary node is a very straightforward process, only requiring knowledge of the Exchange site service account login ID and password and access to the primary (active) Exchange Cluster Server and the Exchange setup program. The Welcome screen (Figure 7-17) provides two choices: Update Node, which duplicates the primary node's local Exchange environment (system libraries and extensions, services) on the secondary

FIGURE 7-16   *Exchange Server setup completion message-Primary node.*

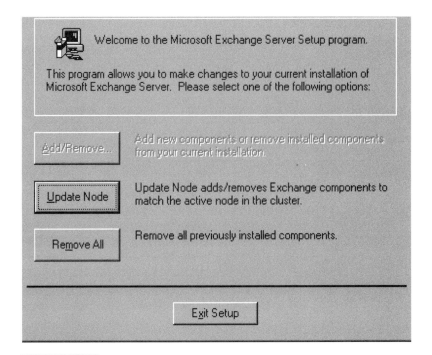

FIGURE 7-17   *Secondary node installation.*

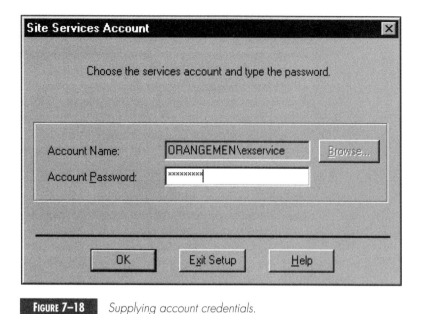

FIGURE 7–18   *Supplying account credentials.*

node, and Remove All, which permits removal of Exchange functionality from the server.

Note that the option to Add/Remove Exchange components is not available on the secondary node. All such initiating configuration decisions are restricted to the active Exchange Cluster Server node, which is the only node that can access the Exchange files on the shared cluster disk; the secondary node is slaved to the primary configuration via Update Node. The administrator will be required to supply the Exchange site service account password to demonstrate his or her right to administer this installation (Figure 7-18).

After copying system libraries and extensions to the local \System32 directory and creating and registering Windows 2000 services on the secondary node, the Exchange setup program declares its successful completion (Figure 7-19). Note that, unlike the analogous dialog box at the end of primary node setup, there is no suggestion to run Performance Optimizer on the secondary node. If Performance Optimizer has been run on the active node, the logical extension of the symmetrical server hardware assumption is that there is no reason to run it again on the secondary node—it's identical. More practically, the secondary node cannot access the shared cluster disk, has no administrative access to the Exchange environment, and therefore has neither resources to optimize nor an executable to run.

The Exchange cluster is now installed, functional, and capable of failing over from one node to the other as required by component failure or administrator intervention. To clients, the clustered Exchange environment is indis-

FIGURE 7-19   *Exchange Server setup completion message-Secondary node.*

tinguishable from a non-clustered environment, but administration of the clustered Exchange environment has some singular differences that must be observed. These differences will be discussed shortly.

Replacing an Existing Exchange Server

Typically, an Exchange cluster is either a new Exchange Server in a new or an existing site, or a complete replacement for an existing, non-clustered Exchange Server. The setup already outlined suffices for the new server scenario-just populate with recipients. The replacement scenario, however, requires some additional effort. It can be accomplished in one of two ways:

- By moving mailboxes from the existing, non-clustered Exchange Server to the new Exchange cluster in the same site
- By using disaster recovery techniques to restore the existing Exchange Server objects and resources into the new Exchange cluster's framework.

The first method is conceptually easier and completes without an interruption in service, but requires, at least temporarily, two servers: both the old and new servers must be online simultaneously. The second method requires no additional hardware beyond the target servers, but must be planned and implemented differently than outlined above, involves an interruption in service, and relies upon disaster recovery techniques with which make many administrators feel less than comfortable.

To move users and implement the first method above, set up the Exchange cluster in the same site as the existing Exchange Server, and ensure that directory replication on both the old and new servers is up to date. In the Exchange Administrator program, highlight all the mailboxes on the existing Exchange Server, then in the Tools menu, select "Move Mailbox", identify the Exchange cluster as the target server, and the contents of the selected mailboxes will be moved from the old server to the new one. (This process can take some time to complete.) The existing public folders created and owned by the users, originally on the old Exchange Server, do not move with the mailboxes. It is necessary to re-home the public folders separately. One way to do this is to replicate all the public folders on the original Exchange Server to the new Exchange cluster. Once replication has completed (be sure the new replicas show a recent Last Received Time in the Public Information Store\Folder Replication Status tab and match the original values in the Total K and Total number of items columns of the Public Information Store\Public Folder Resources tab) the instances can be removed from the original Exchange Server Public Information Store and re-homed on the new Exchange cluster. If the old Exchange Server was the first server installed into the site, it will also be necessary to re-home the Site Folders Forms folder and reset the Offline Address Book server and Routing Calculation server to the new Exchange cluster. See Knowledge Base article Q152959 for further details. The result is that the resources of the original server are now completely duplicated on the new cluster. Note that it is not possible to maintain the same Exchange Server name for the new server: it must have a distinct (although virtual) network name of its own, which becomes its Exchange Server name. This, of course, impacts each user's messaging profile, which identifies the user's home server. As long as the old server remains online and in the site, the next time the users log into email, their messaging profile will automatically be updated to identify he new server. So it is important that the old server not be removed from the site until all users have logged into email once, subsequent to the migration. The old server can then be retired.

To replace and existing, non-clustered Exchange Server using disaster recovery techniques, no additional hardware beyond that needed to form a cluster is required: the original server can be reinstalled as one node in the cluster. It does, however, require additional planning and installation steps. The original Exchange Server must be upgraded to Exchange version 5.5, then backed up and taken offline. (If the server is going to be reused in the new environment, the upgrade to Windows 2000 can be done at the same time.) The cluster resources must be prepared, as described previously, except that the Network Name resource must match the NetBIOS name of the original Exchange Server. Using the command prompt, change directory to the platform-appropriate subdirectory of the Exchanger Server 5.5 Enterprise Edition CD and run Setup.exe in Recovery Mode by supplying the switch "/r". Recovery Mode tells the setup program to install a new exchange environment, but that the Directory and Information Store databases will be restored from a previous backup. Complete the setup of the primary node as before, and run Performance Optimizer without restarting services. Using the Cluster Administrator program, bring the Exchange Server System Attendant resource online. Next, restore the Directory and Information Store databases to the shared cluster disk, again without starting services after completion of the process. Using the Cluster Administrator program, bring the Exchange Server Directory resource online. Now right click the Exchange Server Information Store resource, choose Properties/Registry Replication tab, and force a new registry checkpoint by removing the existing Root Registry Key entry and adding the following new entry:

SYSTEM\CurrentControlSet\Services\MSExchangeIS.

Choose OK twice to return to the Cluster Administrator program main window, and bring the Exchange Server Information Store resource online. This process can take some time to complete, particularly with large information stores, since the system must first recover the databases prior to bringing the resource online. It is possible the default startup timeout interval—600 seconds—will expire and Cluster Administrator will post a resource failure message. Ignore this message and let the process complete recovery, and bring the IS resource online. Finally, select the Exchange Server resource group name and bring the entire resource group online. Installation of the primary node is complete. Run Setup.exe in the secondary node and choose Update Node, as before. Installation and replacement is complete.

Supporting Exchange Server, Enterprise Edition

Supporting an Exchange Server Cluster, for the most part, is very similar to supporting a non-clustered Exchange Server. The majority of the daily administrative workload is still accomplished as before, through the Exchange Administrator program, Admin.exe. The two most significant differences are the need for a two-step setup process (primary node and then secondary node update) whenever Exchange services are installed or removed, and the general use of Cluster Administrator instead of Control Panel/Services to start and stop Exchange services. These issues, and a few other one-time changes, are discussed in the following sections.

Administration — Operational Differences

WHERE TO RUN ADMIN.EXE

Generally, run Exchange's Administrator program, Admin.exe, on any conventional Windows 2000 computer except and Exchange Server Cluster. By default, Admin.exe is installed for each node in the cluster, but like most other Exchange components, the executable is physically installed on the shared Exchange disk resource (in \Exchsrvr\bin). Thus, each node has a valid shortcut for the Exchange Administrator program, but only the active node, which controls the shared disk resource, can successfully access and run the program. The inactive node, without access to the shared disk resource, simply cannot find the executable referenced by the shortcut.

The problem with running the Administrator program on the active node of a clustered Exchange Server is that the node may not remain the active node. Fail over of the Exchange resource group, and consequent loss of access to the shared disk resource, will cause an Administrator program running locally on the clustered Exchange Server to crash, even if the node itself remains up. In contrast, an Administrator program connected to the Exchange Server Cluster, but physically running on a computer outside of the cluster, will experience only a server-specific interruption in activity (and may display component or server access or timeout errors). It is otherwise unaffected and resumes activity once the Exchange environment is restarted on the other (now active) node.

STARTING, STOPPING AND PAUSING EXCHANGE SERVICES

In a typical non-clustered environment, Exchange components implemented as Windows 2000 services are configured to start automatically with server startup. Individual Exchange services can be stopped, restarted, or paused manually using Control Panel/Services, Server Monitor/Services or "net stop" and "net start" commands. In the clustered environment, these Exchange services are configured for manual startup on both nodes, and the cluster software methodically starts the services (in dependency order) on the active node only. Generally, Exchange services in a clustered environment should only be stopped and restarted using the Cluster Administrator program, by changing the state of the resource between offline and online. The cluster resource manager recognizes five resource states: online, online pending, offline, offline pending, and failed. Note that, using Control Panel/Services, a clustered service, when started, is specifically not online and a clustered service that is stopped is not specifically offline. From the perspective of cluster services, a stopped service that is not offline must have failed, and this triggers an appropriate corrective response from the cluster, which may involve a service restart or a resource group move to another cluster member. The administrator of a mixed clustered and non-clustered Exchange environment must be particularly careful with regard to stopping and restarting Exchange services.

One exception to the above rule is the Key Management Server service. The KM Server creates and manages the public and private keys to enable Advanced Security digital signing and encryption of messages. For security, the KM service requires entry of a specific password at each and every service initialization, or it will not load. The password can be read from a floppy disk or entered manually, but in either case, it will not typically be so readily available that automatic restart of the KM service is possible or desirable. When installed in a clustered environment, the KM Server resource is configured not to restart in the event of service failure or fail over. This also means that failure of the KM Server service cannot trigger a fail over of the cluster group, since Affect the Group is disabled. So in this case, the KM service can be stopped and restarted using any method, without adversely affecting the clustered Exchange environment. Microsoft recommends starting the clustered KM Server service via Control Panel/Services, and then using Cluster Administrator to bring the resource online. Moreover, Microsoft does not recommend installing KM Server into a cluster environment in the first place, since the security requirements defeat the fail over capability of the resource.

A second exception to the above rule result from the lack of a Paused service state within the Cluster Administrator program. There are times when a service needs to be paused in order to support a specific process (for example, in order to cycle a manual Dirsync process, with Exchange server as the Dirsync server, the Directory Synchronization service must be paused at specific points in the process). In order to achieve this, it is necessary to take the resource offline in Cluster Administrator (service is stopped and offline), restart the service outside of Cluster Administrator (service is started but still offline), and then pause the running service (service is paused and still offline). When the process requiring the service pause is complete, just continue the service and then bring it online.

Server monitors defined in the Exchange Admin.exe program are prevented from taking actions to restart services or servers when an Exchange Cluster installation is involved. The role of server monitors is to monitor specifically defined services on one or more Exchange Servers in an organization. An Exchange administrator defines a series of responses, triggered by the server monitor when an abnormal condition is detected on one of the monitored Exchange Servers. The responses range from, minimally, a pop-up message on one or more operators' consoles, and escalate, with the passage of time, through sending email alerts, launching specified processes, and taking the actions of attempting to restart the affected service or restarting the Exchange Server on which the service runs.

This activity of server monitors duplicates the capabilities and responsibilities of the Cluster Service itself and might, if permitted, block the Cluster Service's ability to ensure resource availability. Imagine Cluster Services trying

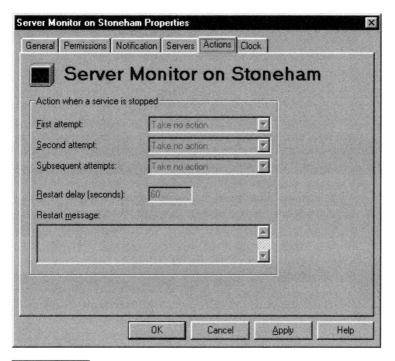

FIGURE 7-20   *Server Monitor actions disabled for clustered Exchange Server.*

to take resources off-line preparatory to fail over while server monitors dart in to restart those same resources! To avoid this possibility, the server monitor properties pages have been made cluster aware, so that if an Exchange Cluster Server is added to the list of monitored servers, the Actions tab options are disabled and appear grayed out, as shown in Figure 7-20. It is recommended that the Exchange administrator run dual sets of server monitors—one for non-clustered servers for which restart actions are supported and one for clustered servers for which restart actions are disabled. It is also up to the Exchange administrator to ensure that any process launched by a server monitor does not independently attempt to stop and restart services, conflicting with Cluster Service actions.

ADDING AND REMOVING EXCHANGE COMPONENTS

Once Exchange Server has been installed on both nodes and Performance Optimizer has been run, the Exchange installation is fully and optimally functional, but it may not be complete. It is a common administrative task to add or remove messaging connectors or other components as workflow, needs, and capabilities change. Some components (Internet Mail Service [IMS], Internet News Service [INS], Microsoft Mail [PC] Connector, Lotus cc:Mail Connector, Exchange Scripting Service, Key Management [KM] Server) are implemented as distinct Windows 2000 Services, while others (Site Connector, X.400 Connector) are not. Whenever one of the Exchange services is installed or removed on the primary node, Setup.exe/Update Node must be run on the secondary node, as during the initial Exchange cluster install.

Microsoft's Exchange Server 5.5 Resource Guide contains a list of Exchange components that are not supported in a cluster environment:

- Dial-up connection services including: Dynamic RAS Connector, dial-up Internet Mail Service, dial-up Internet News Service
- Microsoft Exchange Connector for IBM OfficeVision OV/VM (PROFS)
- Microsoft Exchange Connector for Lotus Notes
- Microsoft Exchange Connector for SNADS
- Microsoft Mail for AppleTalk Networks (now Quarterdeck Mail)
- Microsoft Outlook Web Access (OWA)
- X.400 Connector using X.25
- X.400 Connector using TCP/IP

Fortunately, unsupported does not necessarily mean unstable, and some of the components can be fixed (OWA and X.400 using TCP/IP), although others cannot, such as Microsoft Mail for AppleTalk. See the Knowledge Base article Q175563. The inability of the component process to properly resolve the virtual Exchange Server resources distinctly from the physical cluster node resources appears to be the common problem.

The issue with using the X.400 connector over TCP/IP in a cluster environment lies in how the remote Exchange Server is identified. If identified by IP address, an MTA communication failure results because the physical IP address of the cluster node gets substituted for the Exchange Server IP address. The solution is to identify the remote server by Exchange Server name, not IP address, on the X.400 Stack tabs of both Exchange servers. The MTAs will then connect properly.

A workable solution for Outlook Web Access is to install Internet Information Server (IIS) on both cluster nodes. Outlook Web Access will then by default establish a virtual IIS root (IIS 3.0) or instance (IIS 4.0) on the shared disk resource. After updating the secondary cluster node, each node will have an Exchange IIS virtual directory pointing identically to the shared disk. A client's browser access against the Exchange Server's virtual network name resolves properly to the IIS virtual directory via the active node.

For the remaining unsupported components, reliability testing in a non-production setting, which emulates your production environment, will illuminate the field support issues. Following the logic of the problems outlined above, the failure of the component process to properly resolve virtual from physical resources, may suggest fruitful avenues of investigation.

E   I   G   H   T

Network Load Balancing Clusters

*S*erver clusters perform their task well. They are designed to eliminate the processor as a single point of failure for your applications.
Server clusters are not designed to spread the load generated by a
single application across multiple servers. For example, assume you
have a cluster as a dedicated web server. If you have implemented
this as a server cluster, one of your cluster members is doing all the
work, while the other one is either idle or running a different application. If the web application is generating too much of a load for
the cluster member's processor, the only solution is to upgrade to a
faster processor. This is a shame, since you have another processor
doing little or nothing at all!

Enter network load balancing clusters, which are pretty much new with Windows 2000. There was an add-on product for Windows NT, but this version is
much better. Network load balancing clusters offer the capability to run the
same application on multiple machines and have user connections load-balanced among the systems. A user will be directed to one machine in the cluster, and remain there for the duration of their connection. The advantage is
being able to make use of all processors in the cluster. The disadvantage is
that multiple installations of application software must be maintained.

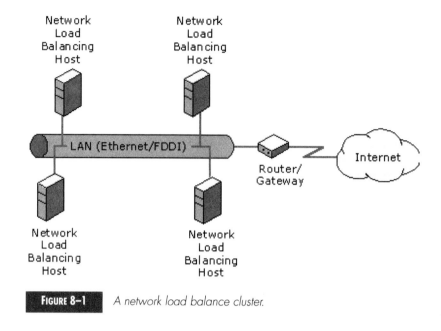

FIGURE 8-1   *A network load balance cluster.*

Introduction

Windows 2000 Network Load Balancing service enhances the availability of Internet server programs such as those used on web servers and FTP servers. A single computer running Windows 2000 provides a limited level of server reliability and performance scalability. However, by combining the resources of two or more computers running Windows 2000 Advanced Server into a single Network Load Balancing cluster, the reliability and performance that web servers and other critical servers require can be achieved. Figure 8-1 depicts a cluster having four hosts within the cluster:

Each host must run a separate copy of the desired server application, such as that for a web, FTP, Telnet, and email server. Network Load Balancing load balances the workload among them. For other services, such as email, only one copy of the service handles the workload within the cluster. Instead of load balancing these services, Network Load Balancing allows the network traffic to flow to one host, moving the traffic to another host only in cases of failure.

Network Load Balancing clusters together several computers running server programs that use the TCP/IP networking protocol. Network Load Balancing allows all of the computers in the cluster to be addressed by the same set of cluster IP addresses (while maintaining their existing addressability using unique, dedicated IP addresses). Network Load Balancing distributes incoming client requests in the form of TCP/IP traffic across the hosts.

To scale server performance, Network Load Balancing can load balance the incoming TCP/IP traffic across all the hosts in the cluster. In this case, a copy of the server program runs on all of the load-balanced hosts, and the load is partitioned among the hosts. The load weight to be handled by each host can be configured as necessary. You can also add hosts dynamically to the cluster to handle increased load. In addition, Network Load Balancing can direct all traffic to a designated single host, called the default host.

Network Load Balancing manages the TCP/IP traffic to maintain high availability for server programs. When a host fails or goes off-line, Network Load Balancing automatically reconfigures the cluster to direct client requests to the remaining computers. For load-balanced programs, the load is automatically redistributed among the computers still operating. Programs with a single server have their traffic redirected to a specific host. Connections to the failed or off-line server are lost. Once the necessary maintenance is completed, the off-line computer can transparently rejoin the cluster and regain its share of the workload.

Overview of Network Load Balancing Configuration

Network Load Balancing runs as a Windows 2000 networking driver. Its operations are transparent to the TCP/IP networking stack. To ensure maximum network performance, Network Load Balancing normally uses one network adapter to handle client-to-cluster traffic, whereas other network traffic to the server goes through a separate network adapter. However, a second network adapter is not required.

Database Access from Load-Balanced Server Applications

Some server programs access a database that is updated by client requests. When these programs are load balanced in the cluster, these updates need to be properly synchronized. Each host can use local, independent copies of databases, which are merged off-line as necessary. Alternatively, the clustered hosts can share access to a separate, networked database server. A combination of these approaches can also be used. For example, static web pages can be replicated among all clustered servers to ensure fast access and complete fault tolerance. However, database requests would be forwarded to a common database server that handles updates for multiple web servers.

Some mission-critical programs may require the use of highly available database engines to ensure complete fault tolerance for the service. Increasingly, cluster-aware database software will be deployed to deliver highly

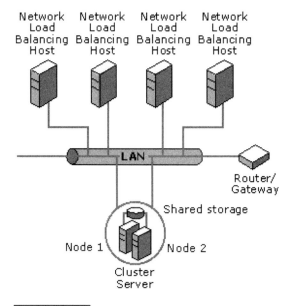

Network   Network   Network   Network
Load   Load   Load   Load
Balancing Balancing   Balancing   Balancing
Host   Host   Host   Host

LAN

Router/
Gateway

Shared storage

Node 1   Node 2

Cluster
Server

FIGURE 8–2   *A combined cluster solution.*

available and scalable database access within an overall clustering scheme. One such example of this is Microsoft SQL Server, which can be deployed in a two-node configuration with the Cluster Service in a server cluster. The Cluster Service ensures that if one node fails, the remaining node will assume the responsibilities of the failed computer, thus providing almost continuous service to Microsoft SQL Server clients. It is able to do this because both computers share a common disk subsystem.

It is important to distinguish between the two cluster solutions under discussion. The first, Network Load Balancing, is intended primarily to load balance incoming TCP/IP traffic. The computers participating in this solution form one type of cluster. The second, the Cluster Service, is intended primarily to provide failover service from one computer to another. The computers participating in this solution form a different type of cluster. Moreover, the Network Load Balancing cluster would most commonly be running web server programs. In contrast, the Cluster Service would most commonly be running database programs (when used in conjunction with Network Load Balancing). By joining the two clusters to function in a complementary fashion, the user creates an overall clustering scheme that achieves high availability and load balancing (Figure 8-2).

How Network Load Balancing Works

Network Load Balancing provides high availability and scalability of web servers using a cluster of two or more host computers working together. Internet clients access the cluster using a single IP address (or a set of addresses for a multihomed host). The clients are unable to distinguish the cluster from a single server. Server programs do not identify that they are running in a cluster. However, a Network Load Balancing cluster differs significantly from a single host running a single server program because it provides uninterrupted service even if a cluster host fails. The cluster also can respond more quickly to client requests than can a single host (for load-balanced ports).

Network Load Balancing delivers high availability by redirecting incoming network traffic to working cluster hosts if a host fails or is off-line. Existing connections to an off-line host are lost, but the Internet services remain available. In most cases (e.g., with web servers), client software automatically retries the failed connections, and the clients experience only a few seconds' delay in receiving a response.

Network Load Balancing delivers better performance by distributing the incoming network traffic among one or more virtual IP addresses assigned to the Network Load Balancing cluster. The hosts in the cluster then concurrently respond to different client requests, even to multiple requests from the same client. For example, a web browser may obtain each of the multiple images in a single web page from different hosts within a Network Load Balancing cluster. This speeds up processing and shortens the response time to clients.

Network Load Balancing enables all cluster hosts on a single subnet to concurrently detect incoming network traffic for the cluster's primary IP address (and for additional IP addresses on multihomed hosts). On each cluster host, the Network Load Balancing driver acts as a filter between the cluster adapter driver and the TCP/IP stack to allow a portion of the incoming network traffic to be received by the host.

Network Load Balancing employs a fully distributed algorithm to statistically map incoming clients to the cluster hosts based on their IP address, port, and other information. When inspecting an arriving packet, all hosts simultaneously perform this mapping to quickly determine which host should handle the packet. The mapping remains invariant unless the number of cluster hosts changes. The Network Load Balancing filtering algorithm is much more efficient in its packet handling than are centralized load-balancing programs, which must modify and retransmit packets. This enables Network Load Balancing to provide much higher aggregate bandwidth. By running directly on the cluster hosts, Network Load Balancing performance is not limited by a specific generation of processor or network technology.

Distribution of Cluster Traffic

Network Load Balancing controls the distribution of TCP and UDP traffic from the Internet clients to selected hosts within a cluster as follows: After Network Load Balancing has been configured, incoming client requests to the cluster IP addresses are received by all hosts within the cluster. Network Load Balancing filters incoming datagrams to specified TCP and UDP ports before these datagrams reach the TCP/IP protocol software. Network Load Balancing manages only the TCP and UDP protocols within TCP/IP, controlling their actions on a per-port basis.

Network Load Balancing does not control any incoming IP traffic other than TCP and UDP traffic for specified ports. It does not filter ICMP, IGMP, ARP (except as described below), or other IP protocols. All such traffic is passed unchanged to the TCP/IP protocol software on all of the hosts within the cluster. Because of the robustness of TCP/IP and its ability to deal with replicated datagrams, other protocols behave correctly in the clustered environment. However, you will see duplicate responses from certain programs such as Ping when the cluster IP address is used. These programs can use the dedicated IP address for each host to avoid this behavior.

Convergence

To coordinate their actions, Network Load Balancing hosts periodically exchange multicast or broadcast messages within the cluster. This allows them to monitor the status of the cluster. When the state of the cluster changes (such as when hosts fail, leave, or join the cluster), Network Load Balancing invokes a process known as convergence, in which the hosts exchange messages to determine a new, consistent state of the cluster and to elect the host with the highest host priority as the new default host. When all cluster hosts have reached consensus on the correct new state of the cluster, they record the completion of convergence in the Windows 2000 event log.

During convergence, the hosts continue to handle incoming network traffic as usual, except that traffic for a failed host does not receive service. Client requests to working hosts are unaffected. At the completion of convergence, the traffic for a failed host is redistributed to the remaining hosts. Load-balanced traffic is repartitioned among the remaining hosts to achieve the best possible new load balance for specific TCP or UDP ports. If a host is added to the cluster, convergence allows this host to take over handling ports for which it has the highest priority and to receive its share of the load-balanced traffic. Expansion of the cluster does not affect ongoing cluster operations and is achieved transparently to both Internet clients and server programs. However, it may affect client sessions that span multiple TCP connections when client affinity is selected because clients may be remapped to different cluster hosts between connections.

Network Load Balancing assumes that a host is functioning properly within the cluster as long as it participates in the normal message exchange among the cluster hosts. If other hosts do not receive a response from any member for several periods of message exchange, they initiate convergence to redistribute the load previously handled by the failed host. You can control both the message exchange period and the number of missed messages required to initiate convergence by setting default values of 1000 milliseconds (1 second) and five missed message exchange periods, respectively. Because these parameters are not usually modified, they are not configurable through the Network Load Balancing Properties dialog box. They can be adjusted manually in the registry as necessary.

Cluster Troubleshooting

Troubleshooting can be one of the most aggravating tasks an administrator has to perform, but at the same time, it is one of the most gratifying. All of the time invested and mistakes made are forgotten with the adrenaline rush of solving a new problem. As we gloat in our success, we ponder whether we should document our victory or let the same problem challenge the troubleshooting skills of someone else.

In my opinion, troubleshooting should be a methodical process. I have seen many individuals troubleshoot by randomly trying various combinations until the problem goes away. This generally works, but being methodical can usually narrow down the possible cause of the problem faster. I use what I once heard referred to as "the divide and conquer" method. This method involves making one change that eliminates one possible cause of the problem. For example, if a client cannot access a server, you may want to use the Ping utility to verify potential connectivity between the client and the server. If the Ping utility is successful, the network is functional, and you move on to another test. If the test fails, the network may be having a problem. Next, ping devices between the client and the server, such as routers, isolate the network segment or router that may be malfunctioning.

Successful troubleshooting requires knowledge in many areas, such as NetBIOS, network protocols and hardware, computer hardware, Windows 2000 security, and Window 2000 performance. To test and eliminate various components as potential problems, it is necessary to know what tool to use. For example, the Ping utility tests the ability for two computers to communicate via TCP/IP. The "NET VIEW *computername*" command, however, tests

NetBIOS connectivity. If TCP/IP is the only protocol loaded, a successful "NET VIEW" command proves that both TCP/IP and NetBIOS are functional.

Portions of this chapter may repeat material in previous chapters, and some new information will be provided. The goal of this chapter is to give a cluster administrator consolidated information on how to troubleshoot various cluster problems that could arise.

Troubleshooting Tools

Successful troubleshooting begins with using the correct tool for the problem. Windows 2000 provides many such tools. Each is useful for testing one or more components of the operating system.

Disk Administration

A successful installation of the Cluster Service requires that both cluster members assign the same drive letters for the partitions on the shared I/O bus. This is accomplished with the Disk Management tool. The same feature of Disk Management that allows the administrator to properly configure drive letters also allows drive letter problems to be introduced. If an administrator changes drive letter assignments to a device on the shared I/O bus but fails to perform the same configuration on the other cluster member, problems will result. The Disk Management tool provides the capability to view drive letter assignments. If a mismatch in drive letters occurs, use the Assign drive letter option under Tools to again make the drive letters consistent between cluster members. Disk Administrator can also be used to determine which cluster member has control of a disk. See Figure 9-1. This is useful when there are problems bringing resources (such as the quorum resource) on-line. The cluster member that has control of the disk will properly display the partition information of the disk. The cluster member that does not have control of the device will display an entry for the device with the wording "Configuration information not available."

Task Manager

The Task Manager program provides a method for the administrator to perform a quick view of the operating system and its current load. Task Manager

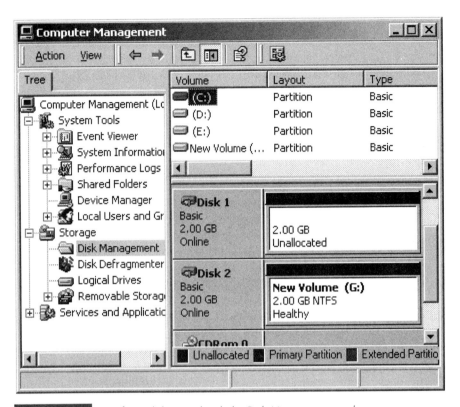

FIGURE 9—1   *Verifying disk control with the Disk Management tool.*

is invoked by right mouse clicking on the taskbar and selecting the Task Manager option. Task Manager allows three different views of the operating system. The first one is the Applications view. This shows what Windows applications are running. This view can be used to terminate a malfunctioning application by highlighting the application and selecting the End Task button. This view is the equivalent of the Windows task list.

The second view offered by Task Manager is the Processes view. See Figure 9-2. The Processes view displays all processes currently running on the system. The amount of activity that is displayed for a process is the amount of activity of the process since it was created. If the Task Manager utility is closed, it has no effect on the counters. For example, the CPU time displayed for a process will be the total amount of CPU time the process has consumed since it was created. Processes created by the Cluster Service can be monitored for activity. The processes pertinent to the Cluster Service are:

- Clussvc.exe—This is the main cluster service
- Resrcmon.exe

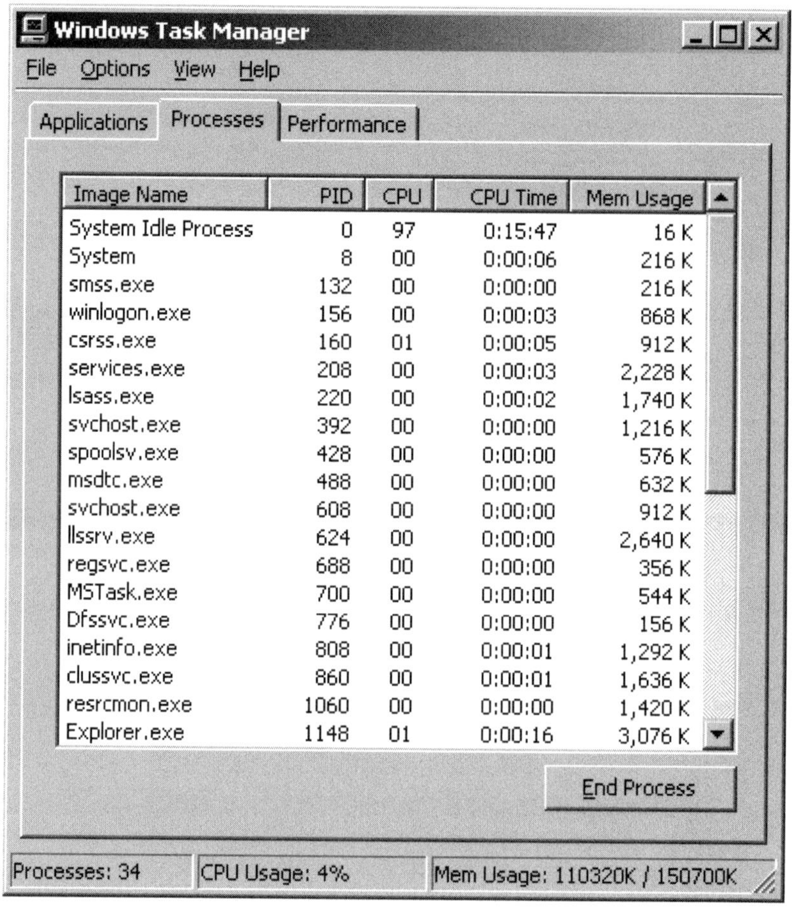
Windows Task Manager
File Options View Help
Applications Processes Performance
Image Name PID CPU CPU Time Mem Usage
System Idle Process 0 97 0:15:47 16 K
System 8 00 0:00:06 216 K
smss.exe 132 00 0:00:00 216 K
winlogon.exe 156 00 0:00:03 868 K
csrss.exe 160 01 0:00:05 912 K
services.exe 208 00 0:00:03 2,228 K
lsass.exe 220 00 0:00:02 1,740 K
svchost.exe 392 00 0:00:00 1,216 K
spoolsv.exe 428 00 0:00:00 576 K
msdtc.exe 488 00 0:00:00 632 K
svchost.exe 608 00 0:00:00 912 K
llssrv.exe 624 00 0:00:00 2,640 K
regsvc.exe 688 00 0:00:00 356 K
MSTask.exe 700 00 0:00:00 544 K
Dfssvc.exe 776 00 0:00:00 156 K
inetinfo.exe 808 00 0:00:01 1,292 K
clussvc.exe 860 00 0:00:01 1,636 K
resrcmon.exe 1060 00 0:00:00 1,420 K
Explorer.exe 1148 01 0:00:16 3,076 K
End Process
Processes: 34
CPU Usage: 4%
Mem Usage: 110320K / 150700K

FIGURE 9–2 *Examining current processes with Task Manager.*

Use the Processes display to determine whether any of the cluster-related processes are logging CPU activity. The cluster processes will not log any activity unless there is a request sent to the process. For example, the "clussvc" process will log CPU activity when the Cluster Administrator utility is executed and makes a connection to the Cluster Service. A resource monitor will log CPU time when one of the resources it manages has activity. There is other process-related data that can be displayed, such as the number of page faults. To add or remove columns from the window, use the View menu option and then the Select Columns option. Make changes to the fields displayed by selecting and deselecting the appropriate fields.

The Performance display gives a quick overview of the load on various system resources such as processor and memory consumption. See Figure 9-3.

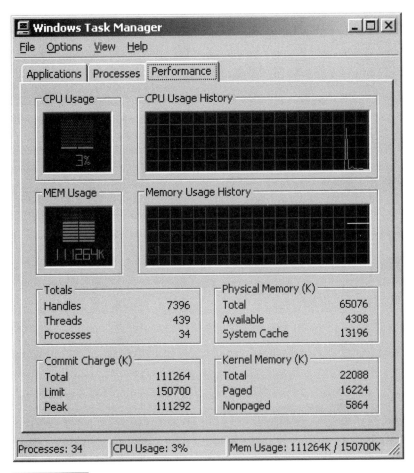

FIGURE 9–3   *Examining system load with Task Manager.*

Use this display to determine if the system is being overloaded. If it is, further analysis with Performance Monitor may be necessary.

A couple of useful items in the Performance display include the size of the file cache and the number of handles. The file cache is used to keep certain data read from the disk in memory. If this data is needed again, a disk I/O is saved. When free memory is limited, the size of the file cache will be reduced. The impact will be increased physical disk activity, which is slow compared with retrieving the same data from memory.

The amount of available memory is important. There should always be at least between 4 and 6MB of free memory on a system.

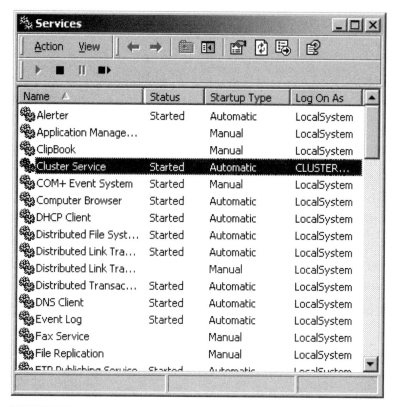

FIGURE 9–4   *Examining installed service with the Services tool.*

Services Tool

The Services tool in the Administrative Tools group can be used to verify that the Cluster-related services are running. See Figure 9-4. These services include the Cluster Service and the Remote Procedure Call (RPC) service. The Cluster Service and RPC Service should have a status of Started. Services have configuration information that is accessed by double-clicking on the specific service. See Figure 9-5. The Services tool provides the capability to perform tasks such as changing the password for the account the Cluster Service is running under. Remember to also change the password in the operating system's account database.

Services also have the option of accepting one or more startup parameters. The Cluster Service has parameters to fix certain problems that may arise. To pass a startup parameter to a service:

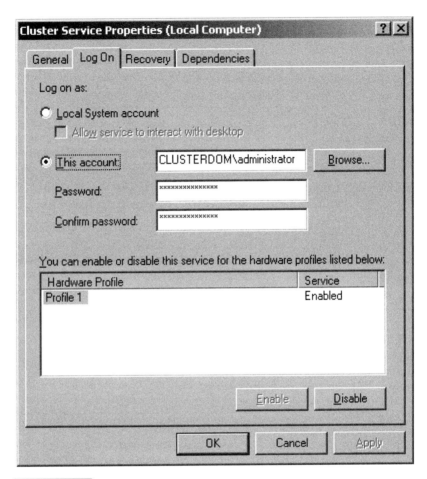

FIGURE 9–5   *Configuring the Cluster Service.*

1. Stop the service by highlighting the service and selecting the Stopoption.
2. Enter the data to be supplied to the service in the Startup Parameters box on the Services screen. See Figure 9-4.
3. Restart the service by selecting the Start option.

   Startup parameters are not saved. If the service is stopped and started, it will be running without the startup parameter. If you wish to restart the service with the startup value, the data will need to be reentered into the Startup Parameters box.

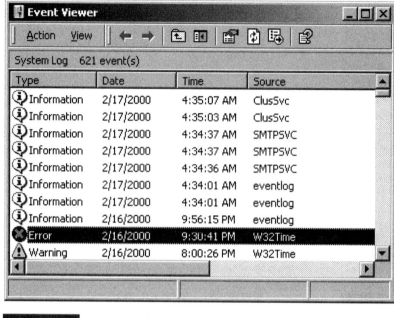

FIGURE 9-6   *Examining the event log.*

Event Viewer

The Event Viewer utility displays the Windows NT logging files. It is located in the Administrative Tools group. There are actually three logs that can be viewed through Event Viewer. The Cluster Service writes messages into the system log. See Figure 9-6.

  The cluster administrator should review the logs in Event Viewer regularly, even when there are no noticeable problems. If there is an entry in the event log, the detail can be displayed by simply double-clicking on the entry. See Figure 9-7.

Net Helpmsg

The command "net helpmsg *error-number*," when issued from a command prompt, displays the text message of the error number supplied. This is very useful because program error handling often only displays an error number. See Figure 9-8.

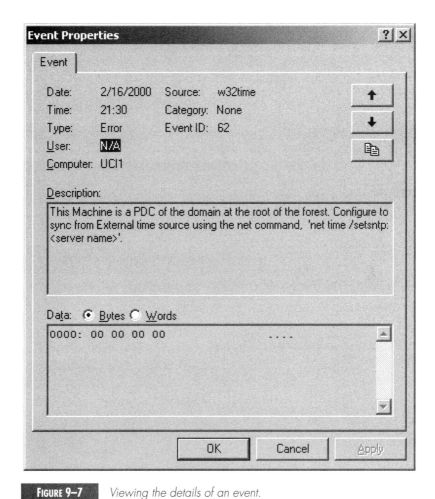

FIGURE 9–7   *Viewing the details of an event.*

In this example, the error number to be translated is 5. The error text for error number 5 is "Access is denied." This utility works for a majority of error numbers encountered.

Net View

The command "NET VIEW *computername*" or "NET VIEW *network_name*" tests the ability to connect to a server with NetBIOS. See Figure 9-9. This is useful in testing whether file share resources are available

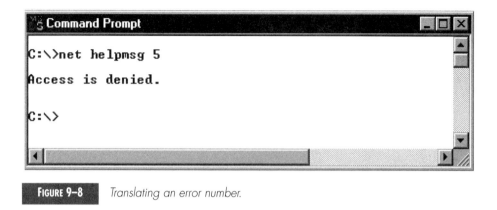

FIGURE 9–8   *Translating an error number.*

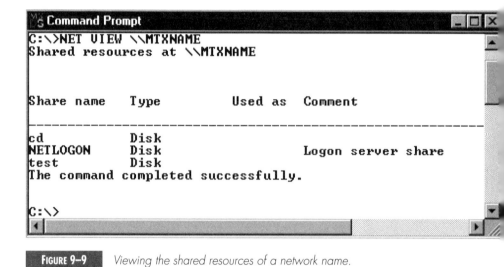

FIGURE 9–9   *Viewing the shared resources of a network name.*

or testing the validity of any cluster Network Name resource. If the command fails, it does not prove that NetBIOS is not functioning. The problem could be with NetBIOS name resolution. To test whether NetBIOS name resolution is the problem, issue the command "NET VIEW *ip_address*." This command is new with Window NT 4.0. If this command works and the first one does not, NetBIOS is functional, but NetBIOS name resolution is not working properly.

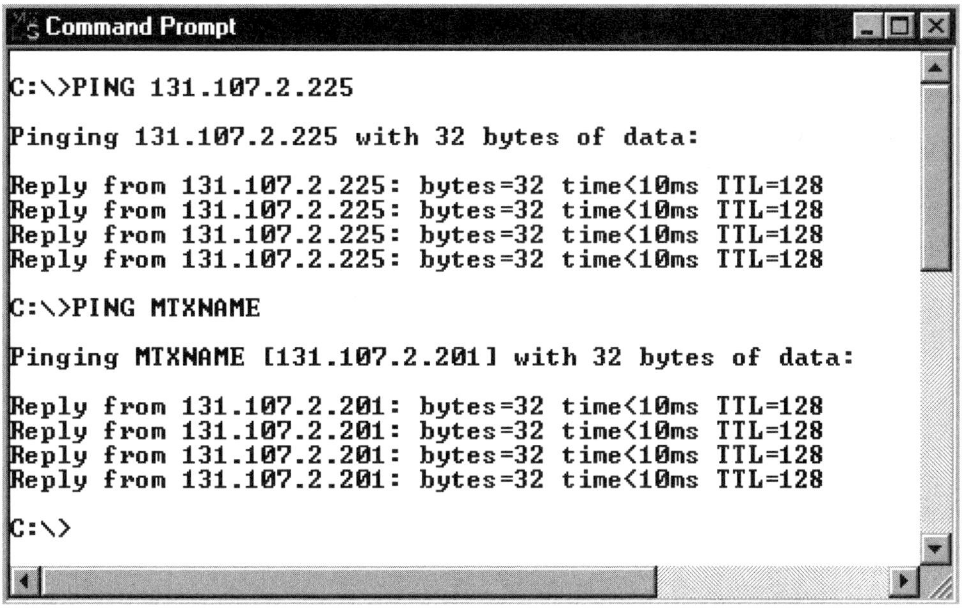

```
Command Prompt                                          _ □ ✕

C:\>PING 131.107.2.225

Pinging 131.107.2.225 with 32 bytes of data:

Reply from 131.107.2.225: bytes=32 time<10ms TTL=128
Reply from 131.107.2.225: bytes=32 time<10ms TTL=128
Reply from 131.107.2.225: bytes=32 time<10ms TTL=128
Reply from 131.107.2.225: bytes=32 time<10ms TTL=128

C:\>PING MTXNAME

Pinging MTXNAME [131.107.2.201] with 32 bytes of data:

Reply from 131.107.2.201: bytes=32 time<10ms TTL=128
Reply from 131.107.2.201: bytes=32 time<10ms TTL=128
Reply from 131.107.2.201: bytes=32 time<10ms TTL=128
Reply from 131.107.2.201: bytes=32 time<10ms TTL=128

C:\>
```

FIGURE 9–10   *Testing IP Address and Network Name resources.*

Ping Utility

The Ping utility is a TCP/IP connection test. Since the Cluster Service only works with TCP/IP protocol, it is the only protocol that needs to be tested to troubleshoot cluster problems. To test whether TCP/IP is functional between a client and the cluster or between cluster members, issue the command "PING *hostname,*" where *hostname* is the name of the system that is encountering connection problems. If the command is successful, TCP/IP is functional. If the command is not successful, some of the possible problems could be:

- an invalid TCP/IP address, subnet mask, or router entry on the server or client
- a network failure between the client and the server
- host name resolution is not working properly

To determine if host name resolution is the problem, issue the command "PING *address,*" where *address* is the TCP/IP address of the system being tested. If pinging by TCP/IP address is successful, but pinging by name fails, the problem is with host name resolution.

A slight anomaly occurs when testing Network Name and IP Address resources with the Ping utility. In Figure 9-10, the IP Address resource of

131.107.2..225 is tested. Also, the network name of MTXNAME, which has a dependency on the same IP address resource, is tested. The test is successful, but notice the TCP/IP address that replies to the test. It is not the TCP/IP address of the resource, but the actual TCP/IP address of the cluster member that currently owns the tested resources.

Network Monitor

Network Monitor is a graphical utility that functions like a network "sniffer." It can provide information such as the overall load on a network segment and the source and destination addresses of each packet. This can be useful for determining whether data is moving between the client and the server. The network monitor utility is covered more thoroughly in the chapter on performance. From a troubleshooting perspective, we could use the Network Monitor tool to verify that cluster members are *heartbeating* and capable of communicating with each other.

System Information

The System Information tool has numerous screens to view various operating system-related data. See Figure 9-11.

TIP   To use the System Information tool, select Programs, Accessories, System Tools, and System Information.

One display I find useful is the Resources display. This tab displays the settings of the devices for which Windows 2000 has assigned an IRQ and loaded a device driver. If there are problems getting Windows 2000 to recognize a device, check here to determine whether another device is using the same hardware settings and is stopping the device in question from being loaded.

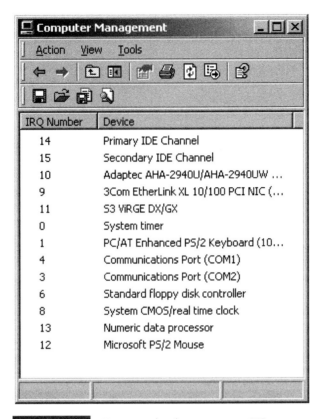

FIGURE 9–11 *Examining hardware resource IRQs.*

Cluster Logging

The Cluster Service can write detailed information to a file regarding significant events or problems. This is known as cluster logging. Cluster logging is enabled by default. To enable cluster logging or to verify that is already running, an environment variable must be defined.

TIP

To examine environment variables, select Settings, Control Panel, System, the Advanced tab, and the Environment Variables option. You can also type "set" at the command prompt. This will list all environment variables and their definitions.

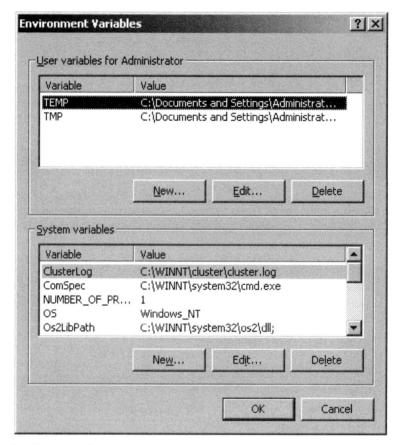

FIGURE 9–12 *Setting the cluster log environment variable.*

There are two sets of environment variables displayed. See Figure 9-12. The system variables are environment variables that are available systemwide. The user environment variables are available only to the current logged-on user. To enable cluster logging:

- Select the System Environment area by mouse-clicking anywhere in the System Variables display.
- Erase the data in the Variable and Data boxes and add the system environment variable CLUSTERLOG with a value that represents the path and filename that the Cluster Server software should use to record events and error messages, and select the Set button. Verify that the entry appears in the System Variables window.
- Restart the system for cluster logging to take effect.

The environment variable does need to be a system environment variable. A user variable will not work because the Cluster Service is generally running under a different username. Make sure to enable cluster logging on all nodes in the cluster. The cluster log file has a maximum size of 8MB. If the log file reaches this limit, Cluster Server will start overwriting the data in the file. The 8MB limit on the log file can be overridden by adding the value ClusterLogSize in the registry path:

HKEY_LOCAL_MACHINE\System\CurrentControlSet\ClusSvc\Parameters.

The ClusterLogSize parameter has a type of DWORD, and it should specify the maximum size for the log file.

Sample Cluster Log

A great deal can be learned about the underlying cluster functionality by examining a cluster log in detail. The following entries were logged during a cluster startup when the quorum disk was unavailable.

000004e0.00000414::2000/02/12-14:16:40.946 [CS] Service Starting...
000004e0.00000414::2000/02/12-14:16:40.956 [EP] Initialization...
000004e0.00000414::2000/02/12-14:16:40.956 [DM]: Initialization
000004e0.00000414::2000/02/12-14:16:40.956 [DM] DmpRestartFlusher: Entry
000004e0.00000414::2000/02/12-14:16:40.966 [DM] DmpStartFlusher: Entry
000004e0.00000414::2000/02/12-14:16:40.966 [DM] DmpStartFlusher: thread created
000004e0.00000414::2000/02/12-14:16:40.966 [NM] Initializing...
000004e0.00000414::2000/02/12-14:16:40.976 [NM] Local node name = UCI2.
000004e0.00000414::2000/02/12-14:16:40.976 [NM] Local node ID = 2.
000004e0.00000414::2000/02/12-14:16:40.976 [NM] Creating object for node 2 (UCI2)
000004e0.00000414::2000/02/12-14:16:40.976 [NM] Initializing networks.
000004e0.00000414::2000/02/12-14:16:40.976 [NM] Initializing network interfaces.
000004e0.00000414::2000/02/12-14:16:41.126 [NM] Initialization complete.
000004e0.00000414::2000/02/12-14:16:41.126 [FM] Starting worker thread...
000004e0.00000414::2000/02/12-14:16:41.126 [API] Initializing
000004e0.00000414::2000/02/12-14:16:41.126 [LM] :LmInitialize Entry.
000004e0.00000414::2000/02/12-14:16:41.126 [LM] :TimerActInitialize Entry.
000004e0.00000498::2000/02/12-14:16:41.126 [FM] Worker thread running
000004e0.00000414::2000/02/12-14:16:41.136 [CS] Service Domain Account = CLUSTERDOM\administrator
000004e0.00000414::2000/02/12-14:16:41.136 [CS] Initializing RPC server.
000004e0.00000414::2000/02/12-14:16:41.236 [INIT] Attempting to join cluster WEBCLUSTER

000004e0.00000414::2000/02/12-14:16:41.236 [JOIN] Spawning thread to connect to sponsor 169.254.186.236
000004e0.00000414::2000/02/12-14:16:41.236 [JOIN] Spawning thread to connect to sponsor 131.107.2.61
000004e0.00000414::2000/02/12-14:16:41.236 [JOIN] Spawning thread to connect to sponsor UCI1
000004e0.00000128::2000/02/12-14:16:41.236 [JOIN] Asking 169.254.186.236 to sponsor us.
000004e0.000004e8::2000/02/12-14:16:41.236 [JOIN] Asking 131.107.2.61 to sponsor us.
000004e0.00000464::2000/02/12-14:16:41.246 [JOIN] Asking UCI1 to sponsor us.
000004e0.00000464::2000/02/12-14:16:41.286 [JOIN] Sponsor UCI1 is not available (JoinVersion), status=1722.
000004e0.00000464::2000/02/12-14:16:41.286 [JOIN] JoinVersion data for sponsor UCI1 is invalid, status 1722.
000004e0.00000414::2000/02/12-14:16:42.238 [JOIN] Spawning thread to connect to sponsor 131.107.2.63
000004e0.00000414::2000/02/12-14:16:42.238 [JOIN] Waiting for all connect threads to terminate.
000004e0.00000464::2000/02/12-14:16:42.238 [JOIN] Asking 131.107.2.63 to sponsor us.
000004e0.000004e8::2000/02/12-14:17:13.282 [JOIN] Sponsor 131.107.2.61 is not available (JoinVersion), status=1722.
000004e0.000004e8::2000/02/12-14:17:13.282 [JOIN] JoinVersion data for sponsor 131.107.2.61 is invalid, status 1722.
000004e0.00000128::2000/02/12-14:17:13.282 [JOIN] Sponsor 169.254.186.236 is not available (JoinVersion), status=1722.
000004e0.00000128::2000/02/12-14:17:13.282 [JOIN] JoinVersion data for sponsor 169.254.186.236 is invalid, status 1722.
000004e0.00000464::2000/02/12-14:17:14.244 [JOIN] Sponsor 131.107.2.63 is not available (JoinVersion), status=1722.
000004e0.00000464::2000/02/12-14:17:14.244 [JOIN] JoinVersion data for sponsor 131.107.2.63 is invalid, status 1722.
000004e0.00000414::2000/02/12-14:17:14.244 [JOIN] All connect threads have terminated.
000004e0.00000414::2000/02/12-14:17:14.244 [JOIN] Unable to connect to any sponsor node.
000004e0.00000414::2000/02/12-14:17:14.244 [INIT] Failed to join cluster, status 53
000004e0.00000414::2000/02/12-14:17:14.244 [INIT] Attempting to form cluster WEBCLUSTER
000004e0.00000414::2000/02/12-14:17:14.244 [API] On-line read only
000004e8.00000128::2000/02/12-14:17:14.554 [RM] Main: Initializing.

000004e0.00000414::2000/02/12-14:17:14.604 [FM] Creating group 30db106e-3a1f-41c1-94a4-60e819e3b0f2

000004e0.00000414::2000/02/12-14:17:14.634 [FM] Initializing group 30db106e-3a1f-41c1-94a4-60e819e3b0f2 from the registry.

000004e0.00000414::2000/02/12-14:17:14.644 [FM] Name for Group 30db106e-3a1f-41c1-94a4-60e819e3b0f2 is 'Cluster Group'.

000004e0.00000414::2000/02/12-14:17:14.644 [FM] Group 30db106e-3a1f-41c1-94a4-60e819e3b0f2 contains Resource 2b06bed3-5e43-4ea3-bbfe-51a3f1f92b4b.

000004e0.00000414::2000/02/12-14:17:14.644 [FM] Creating resource 2b06bed3-5e43-4ea3-bbfe-51a3f1f92b4b

000004e0.00000414::2000/02/12-14:17:14.644 [FM] Initializing resource 2b06bed3-5e43-4ea3-bbfe-51a3f1f92b4b from the registry.

000004e0.00000414::2000/02/12-14:17:14.644 [FM] Name for Resource 2b06bed3-5e43-4ea3-bbfe-51a3f1f92b4b is 'Cluster IP Address'.

000004e0.00000414::2000/02/12-14:17:14.644 [FM] Warning, failed to find node 1 for Resource 2b06bed3-5e43-4ea3-bbfe-51a3f1f92b4b

000004e0.00000414::2000/02/12-14:17:14.644 [FM] FmpAddPossibleEntry: adding node 2 as possible host for resource 2b06bed3-5e43-4ea3-bbfe-51a3f1f92b4b.

000004e0.00000414::2000/02/12-14:17:14.644 [FM] FmpAddPossibleNode: Warning, node 1 not found

000004e0.00000414::2000/02/12-14:17:14.654 [FM] FmpAddPossibleNode: adding node 2 to resource type's possible node list

000004e0.00000414::2000/02/12-14:17:14.654 [FM] All dependencies for resource 2b06bed3-5e43-4ea3-bbfe-51a3f1f92b4b created.

000004e0.00000414::2000/02/12-14:17:14.654 [FM] Group 30db106e-3a1f-41c1-94a4-60e819e3b0f2 contains Resource 09c032c4-4012-4229-9644-bfe8383a1438.

000004e0.00000414::2000/02/12-14:17:14.654 [FM] Creating resource 09c032c4-4012-4229-9644-bfe8383a1438

000004e0.00000414::2000/02/12-14:17:14.654 [FM] Initializing resource 09c032c4-4012-4229-9644-bfe8383a1438 from the registry.

000004e0.00000414::2000/02/12-14:17:14.654 [FM] Name for Resource 09c032c4-4012-4229-9644-bfe8383a1438 is "Cluster Name."

000004e0.00000414::2000/02/12-14:17:14.654 [FM] Warning, failed to find node 1 for Resource 09c032c4-4012-4229-9644-bfe8383a1438

000004e0.00000414::2000/02/12-14:17:14.654 [FM] FmpAddPossibleEntry: adding node 2 as possible host for resource 09c032c4-4012-4229-9644-bfe8383a1438.

000004e0.00000414::2000/02/12-14:17:14.654 [FM] FmpAddPossibleNode: Warning, node 1 not found

000004e0.00000414::2000/02/12-14:17:14.654 [FM] FmpAddPossibleNode: adding node 2 to resource type's possible node list

000004e0.00000414::2000/02/12-14:17:14.654 [FM] Resource 09c032c4-4012-4229-9644-bfe8383a1438 depends on 2b06bed3-5e43-4ea3-bbfe-51a3f1f92b4b. Creating...

000004e0.00000414::2000/02/12-14:17:14.654 [FM] CreateResource, Opened existing resource 2b06bed3-5e43-4ea3-bbfe-51a3f1f92b4b

000004e0.00000414::2000/02/12-14:17:14.654 [FM] All dependencies for resource 09c032c4-4012-4229-9644-bfe8383a1438 created.

000004e0.00000414::2000/02/12-14:17:14.654 [FM] Group 30db106e-3a1f-41c1-94a4-60e819e3b0f2 contains Resource a4c3dc2d-79c5-4988-8dac-799010afa020.

000004e0.00000414::2000/02/12-14:17:14.654 [FM] Creating resource a4c3dc2d-79c5-4988-8dac-799010afa020

000004e0.00000414::2000/02/12-14:17:14.654 [FM] Initializing resource a4c3dc2d-79c5-4988-8dac-799010afa020 from the registry.

000004e0.00000414::2000/02/12-14:17:14.654 [FM] Name for Resource a4c3dc2d-79c5-4988-8dac-799010afa020 is "Disk G:."

000004e0.00000414::2000/02/12-14:17:14.654 [FM] FmpAddPossibleEntry: adding node 2 as possible host for resource a4c3dc2d-79c5-4988-8dac-799010afa020.

000004e0.00000414::2000/02/12-14:17:14.654 [FM] FmpAddPossibleNode: Warning, node 1 not found

000004e0.00000414::2000/02/12-14:17:14.654 [FM] FmpAddPossibleNode: adding node 2 to resource type's possible node list

000004e0.00000414::2000/02/12-14:17:14.654 [FMX] Found the quorum resource a4c3dc2d-79c5-4988-8dac-799010afa020.

000004e0.00000414::2000/02/12-14:17:14.654 [FM] All dependencies for resource a4c3dc2d-79c5-4988-8dac-799010afa020 created.

000004e0.00000414::2000/02/12-14:17:14.674 [FM] arbitrate for quorum resource id a4c3dc2d-79c5-4988-8dac-799010afa020.

000004e0.00000414::2000/02/12-14:17:14.674 [FM] Initializing resource a4c3dc2d-79c5-4988-8dac-799010afa020 from the registry.

000004e0.00000414::2000/02/12-14:17:14.674 [FM] Name for Resource a4c3dc2d-79c5-4988-8dac-799010afa020 is "Disk G:."

000004e0.00000414::2000/02/12-14:17:14.674 [FM] FmpRmCreateResource: creating resource a4c3dc2d-79c5-4988-8dac-799010afa020 in shared resource monitor

000004e8.00000494::2000/02/12-14:17:15.425 Physical Disk: PnP window created successfully.

000004e0.00000414::2000/02/12-14:17:15.476 [FM] FmpRmCreateResource: created resource a4c3dc2d-79c5-4988-8dac-799010afa020, resid 665608

000004e0.00000414::2000/02/12-14:17:15.526 [MM] MmSetQuorumOwner(2,1), old owner 0.

000004e8.00000334::2000/02/12-14:17:15.566 Physical Disk <Disk G:>: [DiskArb]------- DisksArbitrate -------.

000004e8.00000494::2000/02/12-14:17:16.767 Physical Disk: AddVolume : \\?\Volume{90d2b832-de2f-11d3-89fd-806d6172696f}\ "C", 6 (561376)
000004e8.00000494::2000/02/12-14:17:17.318 Physical Disk: AddVolume : \\?\Volume{90d2b833-de2f-11d3-89fd-806d6172696f}\ "D", 1 (562184)
000004e8.00000494::2000/02/12-14:17:17.809 Physical Disk: AddVolume : \\?\Volume{90d2b834-de2f-11d3-89fd-806d6172696f}\ "E", 1 (562592)
000004e8.00000494::2000/02/12-14:17:17.819 Physical Disk: AddVolume: Get-PartitionInfo(\??\Volume{90d2b831-de2f-11d3-89fd-806d6172696f}), error 1
000004e8.00000494::2000/02/12-14:17:18.900 Physical Disk: AddVolume: Get-PartitionInfo(\??\Volume{90d2b830-de2f-11d3-89fd-806d6172696f}), error 1
000004e8.00000494::2000/02/12-14:17:18.900 Physical Disk: NotifierThread is waiting for messages.
000004e8.00000334::2000/02/12-14:17:19.922 Physical Disk <Disk G:>: SCSI, error attaching to signature 68da304b, error 2.
000004e8.00000334::2000/02/12-14:17:19.922 Physical Disk <Disk G:>: Arbitrate: Unable to attach to signature 68da304b. Error: 2.
000004e0.00000414::2000/02/12-14:17:19.922 [MM] MmSetQuorumOwner(0,0), old owner 2.
000004e0.00000414::2000/02/12-14:17:19.922 [FM] FmGetQuorumResource failed, error 2.
000004e0.00000414::2000/02/12-14:17:19.922 [INIT] ClusterForm: Could not get quorum resource. No fixup attempted. Status = 5086
000004e0.00000414::2000/02/12-14:17:19.922 [INIT] Cleaning up failed form attempt.
000004e0.00000414::2000/02/12-14:17:19.922 [INIT] Failed to form cluster, status 5086.
000004e0.00000414::2000/02/12-14:17:19.922 [CS] ClusterInitialize failed 5086
000004e0.00000414::2000/02/12-14:17:19.932 [INIT] The cluster service is shutting down.
000004e0.00000414::2000/02/12-14:17:19.932 [EVT] EvShutdown
000004e0.00000414::2000/02/12-14:17:19.992 [FM] Shutdown: Failover Manager requested to shutdown groups.
000004e0.00000414::2000/02/12-14:17:19.992 [FM] FmpCleanupGroups: Entry
000004e0.00000414::2000/02/12-14:17:19.992 [FM] FmpCleanupGroups: Exit
000004e0.00000414::2000/02/12-14:17:20.002 [Dm] DmShutdown
000004e0.00000414::2000/02/12-14:17:20.002 [DM] DmpShutdownFlusher: Entry
000004e0.00000414::2000/02/12-14:17:20.002 [DM] DmpShutdownFlusher: Setting event
000004e0.000003f4::2000/02/12-14:17:20.002 [DM] DmpRegistryFlusher: got 0
000004e0.000003f4::2000/02/12-14:17:20.002 [DM] DmpRegistryFlusher: exiting
000004e0.00000414::2000/02/12-14:17:20.082 [MM] MMLeave is called when rgp=NULL.

000004e0.00000414::2000/02/12-14:17:20.082 [CS] Service Stopped. exit code = 5086

000004e8.00000128::2000/02/12-14:17:20.353 [RM] Going away, Status = 1, Shutdown = 0.
000004e8.00000494::2000/02/12-14:17:20.353 Physical Disk <Disk G:>: Stop watching disk 68da304b
000004e8.00000494::2000/02/12-14:17:20.353 Physical Disk <Disk G:>: RemoveDisk: disk 68da304b not found
000004e8.00000128::2000/02/12-14:17:20.353 Physical Disk <Disk G:>: [DiskArb] StopPersistentReservations is called.
000004e8.00000128::2000/02/12-14:17:20.353 Physical Disk <Disk G:>: [DiskArb] StopPersistentReservations is complete.
000004e8.00000128::2000/02/12-14:17:20.383 Physical Disk <Disk G:>: [DiskArb] ArbitrationInfoCleanup.
000004e8.00000458::2000/02/12-14:17:20.383 [RM] PollerThread stopping. Shutdown = 1, Status = 0, WaitFailed = 0, NotifyEvent address = 104.
000004e8.00000128::2000/02/12-14:17:20.383 [RM] RundownResources posting shutdown notification.
000004e8.000004d8::2000/02/12-14:17:20.383 [RM] NotifyChanges shutting down.

Cluster Troubleshooting

Performing troubleshooting on a cluster requires familiarity with both the Windows 2000 and cluster configurations. Also, knowledge of any applications, such as SQL Server, that are integrated into the cluster is an absolute necessity. There is no way to list every possible problem you will encounter and its resolution because every implementation will be slightly different. Also, as clusters become more widely implemented, you may encounter problems that have never occurred before. What follow are some checklists of possible ways to resolve various problems. Also, some of the standard issues and problems that have been prevalent with the Cluster Service to date are included.

Windows 2000 Configuration Checklist

The following is a basic checklist of configuration rules to determine whether the target Windows 2000 computers can install and form a cluster.

- Windows NT Server, Enterprise Edition and Service Pack 3, or Windows 2000 Advanced Server, must be installed on both nodes.

- Both computers must be members of the same domain. Valid configurations include:
  - Both computers are member servers of a domain.
  - Both computers are domain controllers in a domain.
  - One computer is a domain controller, the other is not.
- Both computers must be in the same domain.
- A computer can only be a member of one cluster.
- Each member must have a common SCSI bus or be connected to a common fiber channel hub.
- The shared disks must be formatted NTFS.

Windows 2000 Procedure Checklist

Various tasks that can be performed on a standalone server without severely impacting the operating system can have very negative affects on the cluster. Some of these tasks include:

- *Repartitioning*—Make sure any disk resources are removed before repartitioning the target disk.
- *Computer names*—The name of a cluster member cannot be changed after installing the Cluster Server software. To change the computer name, the Cluster Server software must first be removed; then the name can be changed. Last, reinstall Cluster Server, joining the already existing cluster.
- *TCP/IP addresses*—The TCP/IP address of an IP Address resource should not be changed if a Network Name resource has the IP address as a dependency. The network name and IP address are automatically registered with WINS, and unexpected results could occur if the address were changed.
- *Do not* modify logical drive letters after Cluster Server has been installed.

Installation Problems

CLUSTER SERVICE INSTALLATION FAILS ON FIRST NODE

If the Cluster Service installation fails on the first node of the cluster, check the following:

- Does the cluster name used already exist? A removed or aborted installation may have already registered the cluster name and IP address with a WINS server. Check the WINS database, and if there is an entry for the cluster name, remove it.
- If the installation fails when the username and password for the Cluster Service are supplied, verify that:

- the username and password are accurate
- the account does not have the User must change password at next logon box checked
- the account has the privilege to log on as a service
- the account has administrative privilege
- If the installation fails to display any shared I/O devices, either the I/O bus and devices are not configured properly or the Windows 2000 system drive is on the same bus. The Cluster Service does not allow the I/O bus containing the operating system to be used as part of the cluster configuration.

CLUSTER SERVICE INSTALLATION FAILS ON SECOND NODE

If the Cluster Service installation fails on the second node, check the following:

- Is the first node of the cluster running? Verify a successful installation of the first node by running Cluster Administrator.
- Is the cluster name resource reachable? Open a command prompt on the second node and ping the cluster name and cluster IP address. If this fails, there is a network problem, either with the TCP/IP address or subnet on one of the cluster members or with the cluster IP Address resource and subnet mask.
- Is there an outdated entry for the cluster name in the WINS database or a DNS from a previous installation? If so, delete it.

SCSI Device Problems

Because the Cluster Service uses SCSI configurations in a very atypical manner, many problems seem to arise in this area. Most problems appear at hardware configuration time with a few exceptions.

SCSI BUS OR SCSI DEVICE NOT RECOGNIZED

If problems occur while attempting to get the SCSI bus or a SCSI device to be recognized by the hardware, check the following:

- If the entire bus is not functional, verify:
  - Is the SCSI bus properly terminated?
  - Have SCSI cabling specifications, such as distance limitations, been violated?
  - Are both SCSI controllers on the shared bus the exact same type? It is not guaranteed that two different SCSI controllers will support the shared bus. In fact, not once have I been successful with that type of configuration.
  - No two devices, including controllers, can share the same SCSI id.

- It is recommended to configure the SCSI controllers of the cluster members to SCSI ids 6 and 7.
- Does Windows 2000 recognize the SCSI controller? Use the System Information tool to verify that the SCSI controller is known by the operating system. If it is not, two possible problems could be an IRQ conflict or a plug-and-play problem.
- If there are multiple SCSI controllers in a cluster member, make sure that only the SCSI controller that contains the cluster member's boot disk has its BIOS enabled. If BIOS is enabled on multiple controllers, very obscure errors can occur. For example, someone might receive the message "Not enough disk space" when attempting to load Internet Information Server, even though there is over 1GB free on the installation drive.
- If a specific SCSI device is not functional, check:
  - Does the SCSI device have power? External SCSI devices must be powered on before the operating system boots in order to detect their existence.
  - Verify that the SCSI id does not conflict with another device on the bus. The SCSI ids assigned to the various devices can usually be viewed with the software used to configure the SCSI controller.
  - If the messages "Device not Ready" or "Device timeout" appear after a long delay when the second cluster member is booting, disable the option on the SCSI controller to scan for SCSI devices. What is happening is the first cluster member has taken control of the SCSI bus. The second computer is attempting to detect the devices on the bus but is getting blocked by the first system. Disabling the SCSI device scan has no negative impacts on Windows 2000 or the Cluster Service.

Cluster Member Connectivity Problems

DISKS DO NOT FAIL OVER SUCCESSFULLY

- Verify that the I/O bus is connected to both cluster members.
- Run Disk Administrator on the cluster member the disk will not fail over to and check the configuration. The physical disk should appear in Disk Administrator with the message that configuration information is not available. This at least proves that Windows 2000 is aware of the disk's existence.

When the Cluster Service is installed, it displays disks on all buses other than the system I/O bus. There can only be one shared SCSI bus, so all other devices are considered to be local. The problem is that the Cluster Service does not know which bus will be the shared bus, so it displays all options. The installation by default displays all SCSI devices found on any nonsystem

SCSI bus as shared disks. It is the responsibility of the administrator to remove devices from the Cluster Service configuration for all but one bus. If this is not done, resources could be defined on disks, and the disks will not fail over between cluster members because they are not resident on the shared bus.

Be aware that resources can sometimes be intentionally configured to reference local disks. In this case, the application needs to be installed on local disks on both cluster members. For example, if both cluster members have a local drive D:, a resource could be created with its file location as that drive. In this case, the application should be installed on the local disk of each cluster member. The cluster concept is used to fail over the availability of the application, not the data, since data will be on a local disk and unavailable to be moved between cluster members.

QUORUM RESOURCE FAILS

If the device that holds the quorum resource fails and cannot be brought online, the Cluster Service will not be able to start. To fix the problem, the Cluster Service can be started with a special parameter that bypasses the quorum resource. After the Cluster Service is started, the administrator can use the Cluster Administrator utility to select a new quorum resource. To correct a quorum resource failure:

1. Shut down one cluster member. Only one node should be running.
2. Use the Services option from Control Panel to stop the Cluster Service if it is running.
3. In the Startup Parameters box, enter "-fixquorum," then start the Cluster Service.
4. Use the Cluster Administrator utility to modify the properties of the cluster and select a new quorum resource.
5. Use the Services option in Administrative Tools to stop and restart the Cluster Service. This clears the fixquorum parameter that was passed. It is not necessary to clear anything from the Startup Parameters box, since parameters entered are not saved between service restarts.
6. Reboot the second cluster member.

QUORUM DISK OR QUORUM LOG IS CORRUPTED

If the quorum disk or quorum log becomes corrupted, the Cluster Service will attempt to correct the problem by resetting the log file. This can be determined by examining the Windows 2000 event log and looking for the message, "The log file quolog.log was found to be corrupt." The source of the message will be the Cluster Service. If the quorum log cannot be reset, the Cluster Service will fail to start. If the Cluster Service fails to determine that the quorum log is corrupt and starts, the message ERROR_CLUSTERLOG_CORRUPT will be entered in the cluster log. To correct this problem:

1. Use the Services option in Administrative Tools to stop the Cluster Service if it is started. Do this on both cluster members.
2. On one node, enter "-noquorumlogging" in the Startup Parameters box for the Cluster Service and start the service. This starts the Cluster Service without quorum logging, which means that the cluster files on the quorum disk will not be open.
3. Run a disk repair utility, such as CHKDSK, against the quorum disk. If the disk shows errors, allow CHKDSK to correct them. If CHKDSK reports no errors, the next most likely problem is that the quorum log itself is corrupted. Delete the file quolog.log and any temporary files from the MSCS directory on the quorum disk.
4. Use the Services program to stop and restart the Cluster Service.

The only potential problem with the above procedure is that the quorum log stores cluster configuration changes until they can be communicated to all nodes. When the Cluster Service is configured to start without a quorum log, it is possible that recent configuration changes to the cluster could be lost. But, since the quorum log is corrupted anyway, this is the best solution.

SECOND NODE CANNOT CONNECT TO SHARED DEVICES

When the second cluster member is started, it establishes a connection to the shared devices. The shared disks will not display in Disk Management, but they will appear in My Computer. If the shared disks fail to appear:

- Verify that the drive letters assigned to the drives are the same on both cluster members.
- Perform all the SCSI device and bus checks discussed previously

Client—Cluster Connectivity Problems

All communications between clients and the cluster members will occur via TCP/IP. Most connection issues can usually be attributed to TCP addressing or name resolution problems.

CLIENT CANNOT CONNECT TO VIRTUAL SERVERS

A virtual server consists of a TCP/IP address and a network name. If a client is having problems connecting to a virtual server:

1. Attempt to ping the TCP/IP addresses of both cluster members and the cluster IP address. If the test fails, there is a network problem, possibly TCP/IP addressing.
2. Attempt to ping the TCP/IP address associated with the IP Address resource the virtual server uses. If this test fails, but step 1 is successful, there is a problem with the IP Address resource. Check to see if it is online and that the address has not been changed.

3. Attempt to ping the network name of the virtual server. If the client is on a different subnet than the cluster members, this will test name resolution mechanisms such as WINS and DNS. If the client on a remote subnet fails this test, verify that a name resolution mechanism is available and that an entry for the virtual server network name exists.

4. If the client is having problems accessing file shares, verify that the user has been granted access to the share and is not receiving "Access denied" messages.

CLIENTS CANNOT ACCESS A GROUP THAT HAS FAILED OVER

If a client is using a resource, and the resource fails over to the other cluster member, communications will be temporarily interrupted by the cluster transition. Also, depending on the application, the client may need to manually reconnect. The exact result of an application failover depends entirely on how the application deals with interruptions on the network and loss of any application *state* resident in memory. If the client cannot reconnect to the resource, verify that it is on-line. The cluster software has the capability of using two network adapters, one for client access and the other for cluster communications. It is possible that the network adapter used for client access on the second cluster member is misconfigured or not functional. The cluster will be able to fail over the resources on its private network segment, but the resources will be unavailable to clients.

CLIENTS CANNOT ACCESS A FILE SHARE RESOURCE

If a client cannot access a file share resource:

- File share resources use a virtual server. Perform the troubleshooting for virtual servers discussed earlier.
- Verify that the user has access permissions to the share.

Group and Resource Failure Problems

A RESOURCE FAILS BUT IS NOT BROUGHT BACK ON-LINE

When a resource fails, the Cluster Service will attempt to restart it unless:

- the option Don't Restart is selected in the Advanced page of the resource properties.
- a dependent resource is off-line.
- the resource has reached its failure threshold. A resource has a threshold defining how many failures to accept for a given resource. If the threshold is reached, and the resource cannot be moved to another cluster member, the resource will go into a Failed state and must be brought on-line manually.

A GROUP CANNOT BE BROUGHT ON-LINE

When a group is brought on-line, the Cluster Service attempts to bring all the resources in the group on-line. If one or more resources cannot be brought on-line, the group will have a warning symbol next to it denoting this fact. Resource failures need to be examined individually. If none of the resources in a group can be brought on-line, verify that the disk is accessible.

A GROUP WILL NOT MOVE OR FAIL OVER TO ANOTHER NODE

If a group will not automatically or manually move to another cluster member, check:

- Can the other node accept all the resources in the group? The cluster member needs to be configured as a possible owner of every resource in the group.
- Do the properties of the resources have the Affect the group option selected? This option notifies the group to fail over to the other cluster member. Also check the threshold setting for the resources. The resource threshold defines how many times the resource should be restarted on the same node before it is failed over to another cluster member. There is also a group threshold value that defines how many total resource failures can occur before the group is failed over to another member. For example, assume a group with six resources. If each resource fails twice, neither resource has reached the default threshold of three. However, the total of 12 failures does exceed the default group threshold of 10, and the group will be failed over to another cluster member on the eleventh failure.
- Is the group failing over to another cluster member, then immediately failing back? The Cluster Service will move groups to their preferred owner in the cluster if one is defined.

A GROUP FAILS OVER BUT WILL NOT FAIL BACK

If a group successfully fails over to another cluster member but does not automatically fail back to the original cluster member:

- Make sure the Prevent Failback option is not selected in the group's properties.
- If failback is enabled, is it configured to only occur during specific hours of the day? If so, has that time occurred?
- Are *preferred owners* defined for the group? The Cluster Service will only failback groups to their preferred owners.

A GROUP FAILS IMMEDIATELY WHEN BROUGHT ON-LINE

If a group fails immediately when it is brought on-line, the cause is that one or more resources are not starting properly, reaching their threshold, and affecting the group. Take all the resources in the group off-line. Bring the resources on-line one at a time to determine which resource(s) is the cause of the problem.

General Cluster Issues

THE CLUSTER SERVICE WILL NOT START

If the Cluster Service fails to start, it could be due to a problem with the account used by the Cluster Service. An easy method to verify the validity if the account and password is simply to log in with them. If the system rejects the login attempt, the password has possibly been changed and not updated in the properties for the service. Reset the password in both the user account database and in the service properties. Make sure that the account has not been locked out by the operating system by checking that the Account locked out option is cleared on the account.

THE MESSAGE "RPC SERVER IS UNAVAILABLE" IS DISPLAYED

This message can occur when Cluster Administrator is attempting to connect to a cluster. Possible causes are:

- The system has just completed rebooting. The Cluster Service probably has not started yet. Wait a minute or two and try the Cluster Administrator utility again.
- Attempt to connect to the cluster by TCP/IP address instead of the cluster name when entering Cluster Administrator. If the connection by TCP/IP address is successful, the problem may be in the WINS or DNS databases. Verify that there are no invalid entries for the cluster in the WINS and DNS servers.

CLUSTER ADMINISTRATOR FAILS TO CONNECT TO A NODE

If the Cluster Administrator utility cannot establish a connection to a node:

- Make sure that the Cluster Service and RPC Service are both started.
- Attempt to connect by TCP/IP address. If this succeeds, name resolution is not working.

A RUNNING APPLICATION CANNOT BE CLOSED

If a Windows application is configured as a generic application resource in the cluster, when the resource is brought on-line, the application will open on the desktop. If the application is closed on the desktop, the Cluster Service automatically restarts it, and the application will reappear on the desktop. To properly close the application, use the Cluster Administrator tool and take the resource off-line.

Troubleshooting by Resource Type

This section provides various tests to perform when troubleshooting a specific resource type, such as a file share resource.

TROUBLESHOOTING A PHYSICAL DISK RESOURCE

If one or more of the cluster members will not recognize a physical disk resource or bring the disk resource on-line, check the following items.

- The disk on the shared SCSI bus should not be repartitioned if the cluster has disk resources referencing the physical disk. To repartition a disk, first remove any disk resources for the disk in Cluster Administrator. This could require the quorum device to be relocated if the disk to be repartitioned currently is the quorum resource.
- If disks have been repartitioned, both cluster members need to be rebooted to recognize the changes.
- Make sure drive letters for the disks on the shared SCSI bus are consistent on all cluster members.
- When the second server in a cluster boots, registry information from the existing cluster member is written to the registry of the joining cluster member. This may include updated disk signature information. The registry information should update successfully within 60–90 seconds. If one or two disk signature error messages have been logged, but the cluster is functioning properly, this is probably the cause of the message.

TROUBLESHOOTING AN IP ADDRESS RESOURCE

Even though TCP/IP networking can be very complex, an IP Address resource is fairly simple because it has no dependencies, and the data, which consists of a TCP/IP address and a subnet mask, are easy to troubleshoot using standard TCP/IP testing procedures.

The most common problem with IP Address resources is misconfigured data for the IP Address resource. This can be either the TCP/IP address or subnet mask. Verify that the subnet mask is proper and that the TCP/IP address is in the proper subnet. If necessary, reconfirm the data with the network administrator or whoever is responsible for handing out TCP/IP addresses. The one test that can be used for an IP Address resource is the Ping utility. Use the Ping utility to test access to the IP Address resource from a computer on the same subnet and also from a computer on a remote subnet. If the local test is successful but the remote test fails, this is most likely an invalid subnet, assuming the physical network is functional. The Cluster Service does not complain if addresses and subnet masks are configured incorrectly for the IP Address resource. In fact, an IP Address resource with an address for an entirely different subnet can be configured and brought on-line successfully. It would be nice if the software compared the IP address settings against the TCP/IP configuration at the operating system level and warned of any discrepancies.

TROUBLESHOOTING A NETWORK NAME RESOURCE

To troubleshoot a Network Name resource, check the following items.

- Network Name resources are used as NetBIOS names and host names. They have a dependency on an IP Address resource, so the first check performed should be to verify that the IP Address resource is on-line.
- If there is no noticeable problem with the IP Address resource, try to ping the network name. If this is successful, TCP/IP is functioning properly. If there is a delay of approximately 60–90 seconds before the ping test is successful, the problem is likely that the system initiating the test is configured to use a DNS server, and there is no entry in the DNS database for the Network Name resource. Even though there may be entries in a WINS server for the network name, DNS is checked before WINS is when a ping test is issued. This can be confusing because if the "NET VIEW *network_name*" command is used to test the network name, it may respond much quicker. This is because the "NET VIEW" command uses NetBIOS name resolution, which does not use a DNS until last in its name resolution sequence.
- If Network Name resources are constantly created and deleted, as in the case of a test cluster, another potential problem exists. The Cluster Service will automatically register Network Name resources with the WINS server or DNS configured for the cluster member. If the WINS server then replicates its database to other WINS servers, and the network name is deleted or modified by Cluster Administrator, some WINS servers will have stale information in their databases regarding the network name. Always check the WINS and DNS servers used by the system experiencing problems with the network name. If necessary, delete the database entries.

TROUBLESHOOTING A FILE SHARE RESOURCE

To research a file share resource problem, check the following items.

- File share resources have dependencies on a network name and physical disk resource, so the first step in troubleshooting should be to check the functionality of these two resources. Make sure both dependent resources are on-line.
- If the problem occurs when bringing the file share resource on-line, verify that the directory exists. Also check the local file security if the directory is on an NTFS-formatted partition. If there is no access to

the directory with NTFS security, the Cluster Service cannot bring the resource on-line.

- If users are encountering problems such as saving or writing to files, the problem may also be at the NTFS permission level. Even if the file share resource is created with the proper user access, the permissions at the NTFS level can possibly restrict access further. The actual access that users will have to file share resources will be the most restrictive permissions granted to the file share resource and to the files and directories via NTFS.

TROUBLESHOOTING A GENERIC SERVICE RESOURCE

Generic services are a pretty simple resource. The complicated work has been performed by making a program run as a service. If a generic service resource is not functioning properly, check the following items.

- If the service logs in with a specific account, manually attempt to log in with the account to make sure the password has not been changed or that the password has not expired.
- If the generic service resource functions properly on one cluster member but fails on the other, does the service require information from the registry that may not be getting replicated properly?

TROUBLESHOOTING A GENERIC APPLICATION RESOURCE

To troubleshoot a generic application resource, check the following items.

- A generic application resource does not require any dependent resources, but there is a good chance it has a dependency on a physical disk resource. Make sure the disk resource is functioning properly.
- If the application works on one cluster member but not on another, check to see if the application stores information in the registry. If it does, check the properties of the resource to verify that registry replication has been configured.
- Since virtually any program can be installed as a generic application resource, this introduces the possibility of configuring a malfunctioning program to run as a cluster resource. Run the program interactively and observe its behavior. Does it open a window? Does it end in error? Does it just run to completion and end? If the answer is "yes" to any of these questions, check the following when troubleshooting the resource.
  - If the program is a Windows application, the checkbox Allow application to interact with desktop must be checked. If the box is not selected, and the application is a Windows application, it does not fail when brought on-line. It will be running in the background, not having been able to open a window.

- If the application resource keeps restarting and eventually goes into a failed state, it could be one of two problems. The Cluster Service will restart any resource that fails. If the application ends with an error, this is considered a failure, and the application is restarted. If the application ends normally, this is also considered a resource failure, and the application is restarted. In either case, the application will eventually reach it failure threshold and either be failed over to another cluster member or placed into a failed state.

TROUBLESHOOTING A PRINT SPOOLER RESOURCE

To troubleshoot a print spooler resource, check the following items.

- A print spooler resource is dependent on a physical disk and Network Name resource. Verify that these dependent resources are functioning properly, are in the same group as the print spooler resource, and are on-line.
- Make sure that access to the disk and directory used by the print spooler has not been restricted through NTFS permissions. Also check that the disk that contains the spool directory is not full. This will cause print jobs to hang.
- Check the LPR port mapping for the print device in question. The LPR port must be created for each cluster member. If the print spooler works from one cluster member but not from the other, this could be the problem.
- The printer driver must be manually loaded on each cluster member. If the print spooler functions properly on only one of the cluster members, this could also be the problem.

TROUBLESHOOTING AN IIS SERVER INSTANCE RESOURCE

To troubleshoot an IIS Server Instance resource, check the following items.

- An IIS Server Instance resource has a dependency on an IP Address resource, verify that it is functioning properly.
- If the resource does not work with a domain name such as *www.uci-corp.com*, does it work by using the TCP/IP address? If so, the problem is with name resolution and DNS.
- If the resource is a WWW or FTP virtual root, the allowed access can be Read or Execute. The granted access must be "Execute" for a client to run a program in the directory.
- If the resource functions properly on only one of the cluster members, verify that the directory used is on a shared disk. If the directory is on a local disk, it must exist on both cluster members.

TROUBLESHOOTING AN SQL SERVER RESOURCE

To troubleshoot an SQL Server resource, check the following items.

- Clustering support for SQL Server uses a network name and disk resource as dependencies. Verify that they are functioning and are on-line.
- When clustering support for SQL Server is installed, it replaces the standard SQL services of MSSQL Server and SQL Executive. Use the Services option from Administrative Tools to determine whether the original SQL services have been started, and stop them if necessary. The proper method to start and stop a clustered SQL Server is by taking the SQL-associated resources off-line or by bringing them on-line.
- If the SQL virtual server resource functions properly on one of the cluster members but not on the other, make sure that the username and password used for the SQL Server service account is identical on both nodes.

TROUBLESHOOTING A DISTRIBUTED TRANSACTION COORDINATOR RESOURCE

To troubleshoot a distributed transaction coordinator resource, check the following items.

- Verify that the problem is not with the Transaction Server software or with the database server, such as SQL Server, that the transaction coordinator is accessing.
- A distributed transaction coordinator resource has dependencies on a disk and a Network Name resource. Verify that both dependent resources are functioning properly.

TROUBLESHOOTING A MESSAGE QUEUE SERVER RESOURCE

To troubleshoot a Message Queue Server resource, check the following items.

- Verify that the problem is not with the Message Queue Server software.
- A Message Queue Server resource has a dependency on a disk and a Network Name resource. Verify that both of these resources are functioning properly.
- The Message Queue Server software has various settings that can stall the message queue. This is specific to the software and is not a cluster issue.

The Cluster API

As clusters continue to increase in popularity, the need will arise for applications to be written that are "cluster aware." While the basic functionality of the application will not change, there are a few additional steps an application must take to participate as a fully functional, clustered application.

The platform SDK shipped with Visual Studio 6.0 provides an interface for applications to communicate with the Cluster Service. The interface is a library of routines known as the Cluster Server API. The Cluster Server API can be subdivided into categories that develop applications to manage the cluster or that develop applications that run within the context of a cluster resource. These categories are:

- network management functions
- cluster management functions
- resource group management functions
- resource management functions

An understanding of the basics of the cluster, groups, and resources is necessary to understand and implement the cluster API routines.

Network Management Functions

The network management functions in the Cluster API provide access to information about physical networks that are known and in use by the Cluster Service. The first step in accessing network information is to open a connection to the cluster. This is accomplished with the **OpenCluster** function, which returns a handle to the cluster. Next, the function **ClusterOpenEnum** is called to create a resource enumerator. For the dwtype parameter, use CLUSTER_ENUM_RESOURCE. Loop through all of the resources in the cluster by calling **ClusterEnum** repeatedly with the contents of the *lpdwType* parameter set to CLUSTER_ENUM_RESOURCE. For each resource:

- Call **OpenClusterResource**, setting the *lpszResourceName* parameter to the contents of the *lpszName* parameter returned from **ClusterEnum**.
- Call **ClusterResourceControl** with the *dwControlCode* parameter set to CLUSCTL_RESOURCE_GET_RESOURCE_TYPE.
- If the resource type is "Network Name," an occurrence of a network has been located. One of the values set by **ClusterResourceControl** is a buffer with the network name.

Next, take the network name that was returned and call **OpenCluster-Network**. This will return a handle to a network name. With a handle to a network, we can next call **ClusterNetworkOpenEnum** to create an enumeration object for the objects on the network. Calls to **ClusterNetworkEnum** will return the name of one object with each call.

As you can see, it is not a trivial task to develop an application to interact with a cluster. What follows in the rest of this chapter is the list of API routines, organized by type. Be aware that, just like in the above example, it will be necessary to use routines from more than one category to perform most tasks.

CloseClusterNetwork

The **CloseClusterNetwork** function closes a connection to a network. The function takes one argument, a network handle.

```
BOOL WINAPI CloseClusterNetwork(
  HNETWORK hNetwork
);
```

ClusterNetworkCloseEnum

The **ClusterNetworkCloseEnum** function closes an enumerator for iterating through objects on a network. The function takes one argument, a handle to a network enumerator. This handle was originally created by the **ClusterNetworkOpenEnum** function.

```
DWORD WINAPI ClusterNetworkCloseEnum(
  HNETWORKENUM hNetworkEnum
);
```

ClusterNetworkEnum

The **ClusterNetworkEnum** function can be used to process a collection of network objects. If, for example, an application wants to enumerate all of the network interface objects on a network, it calls **ClusterNetworkOpenEnum** to open a network enumerator that can process network interface objects. The *dwType* parameter is set to CLUSTER_NETWORK_ENUM_NETINTERFACES to specify network interfaces as the object type to be enumerated. With the handle that **ClusterNetworkOpenEnum** returns, the application calls **Cluster-NetworkEnum** repeatedly to retrieve each of the objects. The *lpdwType* parameter points to the type of object that is retrieved.

```
DWORD WINAPI ClusterNetworkEnum(
   HNETWORKENUM hNetworkEnum,
   DWORD dwIndex,
   LPDWORD lpdwType,
   LPWSTR lpszName,
   LPDWORD lpcbName
);
```

PARAMETERS

hNetworkEnum

> [in] Handle to an existing enumeration object originally returned by the **ClusterNetworkOpenEnum** function.

dwIndex

> [in] Index used to identify the next entry to be enumerated. This parameter should be zero for the first call to **ClusterNetworkEnum** and then incremented for subsequent calls.

lpdwType

> [out] Pointer to the type of object returned. The following object type is returned with each call:
> CLUSTER_NETWORK_ENUM_NETINTERFACES
> The object is a network interface.

lpszName

> [out] Pointer to the name of the returned object, a NULL-terminated string.

lpcbName

> [in, out] On input, pointer to a buffer. On output, pointer to the count of characters in the name pointed to by the *lpszName* parameter minus the terminating NULL character.

ClusterNetworkOpenEnum

The **ClusterNetworkOpenEnum** function opens an enumerator for iterating through objects on a network. Call this function to iterate through all of the objects on a network or only through the network interface objects.

```
HNETWORKENUM WINAPI ClusterNetworkOpenEnum(
  HNETWORK hNetwork,
  DWORD dwType
);
```

PARAMETERS

hNetwork
> [in] Handle to a network.

dwType
> [in] Bitmask describing the type of objects to be enumerated. One or more of the following values are valid:
> CLUSTER_NETWORK_ENUM_NETINTERFACES
> Enumerate the network interface objects on the network.
> CLUSTER_NETWORK_ENUM_ALL
> Enumerate all objects on the network.

ClusterNetworkControl

Use the **ClusterNetworkControl** function to perform an operation on a network. **ClusterNetworkControl** performs a variety of tasks based on the control code passed to the function. The scope of allowable operations is defined by the set of control codes specified for networks.

```
DWORD WINAPI ClusterNetworkControl(
  HNETWORK hNetwork,
  HNODE hHostNode,
  DWORD dwControlCode,
  LPVOID lpInBuffer,
  DWORD cbInBufferSize,
  LPVOID lpOutBuffer,
  DWORD cbOutBufferSize,
  LPDWORD lpcbBytesReturned
);
```

PARAMETERS

hNetwork
> [in] Handle to the network to be affected by the operation.

hHostNode

[in] Optional handle to the node hosting the affected network.

dwControlCode

[in] Control code that defines the operation to perform

Valid Control codes are:
CLUSCTL_NETWORK_ENUM_COMMON_PROPERTIES
CLUSCTL_NETWORK_ENUM_PRIVATE_PROPERTIES
CLUSCTL_NETWORK_GET_CHARACTERISTICS
CLUSCTL_NETWORK_GET_COMMON_PROPERTIES
CLUSCTL_NETWORK_GET_FLAGS
CLUSCTL_NETWORK_GET_NAME
CLUSCTL_NETWORK_GET_PRIVATE_PROPERTIES
CLUSCTL_NETWORK_GET_RO_COMMON_PROPERTIES
CLUSCTL_NETWORK_GET_RO_PRIVATE_PROPERTIES
CLUSCTL_NETWORK_SET_COMMON_PROPERTIES
CLUSCTL_NETWORK_SET_PRIVATE_PROPERTIES
CLUSCTL_NETWORK_UNKNOWN
CLUSCTL_NETWORK_VALIDATE_COMMON_PROPERTIES
CLUSCTL_NETWORK_VALIDATE_PRIVATE_PROPERTIES

lpInBuffer

[in] Pointer to the input buffer with information needed for the operation, or NULL if no information is needed.

InBuffersize

[in] Number of bytes in the buffer pointed to by *lpInBuffer*.

lpOutBuffer

[out] Pointer to the output buffer with information resulting from the operation, or NULL if nothing needs to be returned.

cbOutBufferSize

[in] Number of bytes in the output buffer pointed to by lpOutBuffer, or zero if the caller does not know how much data will be returned.

lpcbBytesReturned

[in, out] Pointer to the number of bytes in the buffer pointed to by *lpOutBuffer* that were actually filled in as a result of the operation. The caller can pass NULL for *lpcbBytesReturned* if **ClusterNetworkControl** need not pass back the number of bytes in the output buffer.

GetClusterNetworkState

The **GetClusterNetworkState** function returns the current state of a network, represented by one of the following values:

State	Description
ClusterNetworkStateDown	The network is not operational; none of the nodes on the network can communicate.
ClusterNetworkStatePartitioned	The network is operational, but two or more nodes on the network cannot communicate. Typically a path-specific problem has occurred.
ClusterNetworkStateUp	The network is operational; all of the nodes in the cluster can communicate.
ClusterNetworkStateUnavailable	State information for the network is unavailable. The network's **Role** property is set to ClusterNetworkRoleNone.

```
CLUSTER_NETWORK_STATE WINAPI GetClusterNetworkState(
  HNETWORK hNetwork
);
```

If the operation was unsuccessful, **GetClusterNetworkState** returns ClusterNetworkStateUnknown.

OpenClusterNetwork

The **OpenClusterNetwork** function opens a connection to a network and returns a handle to it.

```
HNETWORK WINAPI OpenClusterNetwork(
  HCLUSTER hCluster,
  LPCWSTR lpszNetworkName
);
```

SetClusterNetworkName

The **SetClusterNetworkName** function modifies the name for a network.

```
DWORD WINAPI SetClusterNetworkName(
  HNETWORK hNetwork,
  LPCWSTR lpszName
);
```

PARAMETERS

hNetwork
> [in] Handle to a network name.

lpszName
> [in] Pointer to the new network name.

SetClusterNetworkPriorityOrder

The **SetClusterNetworkPriorityOrder** function sets the priority order for the set of networks used for internal communication between cluster nodes.

```
DWORD WINAPI SetClusterNetworkPriorityOrder(
  HCLUSTER hCluster,
  DWORD NetworkCount,
  HNETWORK NetworkList[]
);
```

PARAMETERS

hCluster
> [in] Handle to the cluster to be affected.

NetworkCount
> [in] Number of items in the list specified by the *NetworkList* parameter.

NetworkList
> [in] Prioritized array of handles to network objects. The first handle in the array has the highest priority. The list must contain only those networks that are used for internal communication between nodes in the cluster. All networks that can be used for node-to-node communication must appear in the list, and there can be no duplicates.

Cluster Management Functions

As the name implies, this set of API routines allows for manipulation of cluster-wide information. In most cluster programming scenarios, a single application will need to use functions from more than one category. For example, in order to create a new group or resource, each of which have their own group of API routines, a notification port must first be created. Notification ports are the conduit through which applications communicate with the Cluster Service. This is the thread used by the resource monitor. Notification ports are found iin the Cluster Management function set. For an example of using a notification port, examine the code listing at the end of the chapter or on the enclosed CD.

CloseCluster

The **CloseCluster** function closes a connection to a cluster.

```
BOOL WINAPI CloseCluster(
  HCLUSTER hCluster
);
```

PARAMETERS

hCluster
    [in] Handle to the cluster to close.

CloseClusterNotifyPort

The **CloseClusterNotifyPort** function closes a notification port.

```
BOOL WINAPI CloseClusterNotifyPort(
  HCHANGE hChange
);
```

PARAMETERS

hChange
    [in] Handle to the notification port to close.

ClusterCloseEnum

The **ClusterCloseEnum** function closes a cluster enumerator handle.

```
DWORD WINAPI ClusterCloseEnum(
  HCLUSENUM hEnum
);
```

PARAMETERS

hEnum
    [in] Handle to the cluster enumerator to close. This is a handle originally returned by the **ClusterOpenEnum** function.

ClusterEnum

The **ClusterEnum** function enumerates objects in a cluster, returning the name of one object with each call.

```
DWORD WINAPI ClusterEnum(
  HCLUSENUM hEnum,
  DWORD dwIndex,
  LPDWORD lpdwType,
  LPWSTR lpszName,
  LPDWORD lpcbName
);
```

PARAMETERS

hEnum

> [in] Handle to an existing enumeration object originally returned by the **ClusterOpenEnum** function.

dwIndex

> [in] Index used to identify the next entry to be enumerated. This parameter should be zero for the first call to **ClusterEnum** and then incremented for subsequent calls.

lpdwType

> [out] Pointer to the type of object returned. One of the following object types is returned with each call:
>
> CLUSTER_ENUM_NODE
>
> The object is a node in the cluster.
>
> CLUSTER_ENUM_RESTYPE
>
> The object is a resource type in the cluster.
>
> CLUSTER_ENUM_RESOURCE
>
> The object is a resource in the cluster.
>
> CLUSTER_ENUM_GROUP
>
> The object is a group in the cluster.

lpszName

> [out] Pointer to the name of the returned object, a NULL-terminated string.

lpcbName

> [in, out] On input, pointer to a buffer. On output, pointer to the count of characters in the name pointed to by the *lpszName* parameter minus the terminating NULL character.

ClusterOpenEnum

The **ClusterOpenEnum** function opens an enumerator for iterating through objects in a cluster. Applications call the **ClusterOpenEnum** function to create a particular type of object.

```
HCLUSENUM WINAPI ClusterOpenEnum(
  HCLUSTER hCluster,
  DWORD dwType
);
```

PARAMETERS

hCluster
> [in] Handle to a cluster.

dwType
> [in] Bitmask describing the type of objects to be enumerated. One or more of the following values are valid:
> CLUSTER_ENUM_GROUP
> Enumerate the groups in the cluster.
> CLUSTER_ENUM_NODE
> Enumerate the nodes in the cluster.
> CLUSTER_ENUM_RESTYPE
> Enumerate the resource types in the cluster.
> CLUSTER_ENUM_RESOURCE

ClusterResourceTypeControl

The **ClusterResourceTypeControl** function performs an operation on a resource type. **ClusterResourceTypeControl** is a general-purpose function where the task performed is defined by the control code specified for resource types.

```
DWORD WINAPI ClusterResourceTypeControl(
  HCLUSTER hCluster,
  LPCWSTR ResourceTypeName,
  HNODE hHostNode,
  DWORD dwControlCode,
```

> Valid control codes are:
> CLUSCTL_RESOURCE_TYPE_ENUM_COMMON_PROPERTIES
> CLUSCTL_RESOURCE_TYPE_ENUM_PRIVATE_PROPERTIES
> CLUSCTL_RESOURCE_TYPE_GET_CHARACTERISTICS
> CLUSCTL_RESOURCE_TYPE_GET_CLASS_INFO
> CLUSCTL_RESOURCE_TYPE_GET_COMMON_PROPERTIES
> CLUSCTL_RESOURCE_TYPE_GET_FLAGS
> CLUSCTL_RESOURCE_TYPE_GET_PRIVATE_PROPERTIES
> CLUSCTL_RESOURCE_TYPE_GET_REGISTRY_CHECKPOINTS
> CLUSCTL_RESOURCE_TYPE_GET_REQUIRED_DEPENDENCIES
> CLUSCTL_RESOURCE_TYPE_GET_RO_COMMON_PROPERTIES
> CLUSCTL_RESOURCE_TYPE_GET_RO_PRIVATE_PROPERTIES

CLUSCTL_RESOURCE_TYPE_SET_COMMON_PROPERTIES
CLUSCTL_RESOURCE_TYPE_SET_PRIVATE_PROPERTIES
CLUSCTL_RESOURCE_TYPE_STORAGE_GET_AVAILABLE_DISKS
CLUSCTL_RESOURCE_TYPE_UNKNOWN
CLUSCTL_RESOURCE_TYPE_VALIDATE_COMMON_PROPERTIES
CLUSCTL_RESOURCE_TYPE_VALIDATE_PRIVATE_PROPERTIES

```
  LPVOID lplnBuffer,
  DWORD cblnBufferSize,
  LPVOID lpOutBuffer,
  DWORD cbOutBufferSize,
  LPDWORD lpcbBytesReturned
);
```

PARAMETERS

hCluster

[in] Handle to the cluster containing the resource type identified in *ResourceTypeName*.

ResourceTypeName

[in] Pointer to the name of the resource type to be affected.

hHostNode

[in] Optional handle to the node hosting the affected resource type.

dwControlCode

[in] Control code that defines the operation to perform.

lplnBuffer

[in] Pointer to the input buffer with information needed for the operation, or NULL if no information is needed.

cblnBufferSize

[in] Number of bytes in the buffer pointed to by *lplnBuffer*.

lpOutBuffer

[out] Pointer to the output buffer with information resulting from the operation, or NULL if nothing need be returned.

cbOutBufferSize

[in] Number of bytes in the output buffer pointed to by *lpOutBuffer*, or zero if the caller does not know how much data will be returned.

lpcbBytesReturned

[in, out] Pointer to the number of bytes in the buffer pointed to by *lpOutBuffer* that were actually filled in as a result of the operation. The caller can pass NULL for *lpcbBytesReturned* if **ClusterResourceType-Control** need not pass back the number of bytes in the output buffer.

CreateClusterNotifyPort

The **CreateClusterNotifyPort** function creates a notification port to handle cluster event notification. A notification port stores notifications of events occurring within a cluster for applications.

```
HCHANGE WINAPI CreateClusterNotifyPort(
  HCHANGE hChange,
  HCLUSTER hCluster,
  DWORD dwFilter,
  DWORD dwNotifyKey
);
```

PARAMETERS

hChange

[in] Handle to a notification port or INVALID_HANDLE_VALUE, indicating that a new handle should be created. If *hChange* is an existing handle, the events specified in *dwFilter* are added to the notification port.

hCluster

[in] Handle to the cluster to be associated with the notification port identified by *hChange* or INVALID_HANDLE_VALUE, indicating that the notification port should not be associated with a cluster. If *hChange* is not set to INVALID_HANDLE_VALUE, *hCluster* cannot be set to INVALID_HANDLE_VALUE.

dwFilter

[in] Bitmask of flags that describes the events to cause notifications to be stored in the queue. One or more of the following flags can be used:
CLUSTER_CHANGE_CLUSTER_PROPERTY
CLUSTER_CHANGE_CLUSTER_STATE
CLUSTER_CHANGE_GROUP_ADDED
CLUSTER_CHANGE_GROUP_DELETED
CLUSTER_CHANGE_GROUP_PROPERTY
CLUSTER_CHANGE_GROUP_STATE
CLUSTER_CHANGE_HANDLE_CLOSE
CLUSTER_CHANGE_NETINTERFACE_ADDED
CLUSTER_CHANGE_NETINTERFACE_DELETED
CLUSTER_CHANGE_NETINTERFACE_PROPERTY
CLUSTER_CHANGE_NETINTERFACE_STATE
CLUSTER_CHANGE_NETWORK_ADDED
CLUSTER_CHANGE_NETWORK_DELETED
CLUSTER_CHANGE_NETWORK_PROPERTY
CLUSTER_CHANGE_NETWORK_STATE
CLUSTER_CHANGE_NODE_ADDED
CLUSTER_CHANGE_NODE_DELETED

CLUSTER_CHANGE_NODE_PROPERTY
CLUSTER_CHANGE_NODE_STATE
CLUSTER_CHANGE_QUORUM_STATE
CLUSTER_CHANGE_REGISTRY_ATTRIBUTES
CLUSTER_CHANGE_REGISTRY_NAME
CLUSTER_CHANGE_REGISTRY_SUBTREE
CLUSTER_CHANGE_REGISTRY_VALUE
CLUSTER_CHANGE_RESOURCE_ADDED
CLUSTER_CHANGE_RESOURCE_DELETED
CLUSTER_CHANGE_RESOURCE_PROPERTY
CLUSTER_CHANGE_RESOURCE_STATE
CLUSTER_CHANGE_RESOURCE_TYPE_ADDED
CLUSTER_CHANGE_RESOURCE_TYPE_DELETED

dwNotifyKey

[in] Any value that is to be associated with retrieving notifications from the created notification port. The *dwNotifyKey* is returned from **GetClusterNotify** when an event of one of the types specified in *dwFilter* occurs.

CreateClusterResourceType

The **CreateClusterResourceType** function creates a new resource type in a cluster. Be aware that the **CreateClusterResourceType** function only defines the resource type in the cluster database and registers the resource type with the Cluster Service.

```
DWORD WINAPI CreateClusterResourceType(
  HCLUSTER hCluster,
  LPCWSTR lpszResourceTypeName,
  LPCWSTR lpszDisplayName,
  LPCWSTR lpszResourceTypeDll,
  DWORD dwLooksAlivePollInterval,
  DWORD dwIsAlivePollInterval
);
```

PARAMETERS

hCluster

[in] Handle to the cluster to receive the new resource type.

lpszResourceTypeName

[in] Pointer to the name of the new resource type. The specified name must be unique within the cluster.

lpszDisplayName
> [in] Pointer to the display name for the new resource type. While the contents of *lpszResourceTypeName* should uniquely identify the resource type on all clusters, the contents of *lpszDisplayName* should be a localized friendly name for the resource, suitable for displaying to administrators.

lpszResourceTypeDll
> [in] Pointer to the fully qualified name of the resource DLL for the new resource type.

dwLooksAlivePollInterval
> [in] Default millisecond value to be used as the poll interval needed by the new resource type's *LooksAlive* function. The *dwLooksAlivePollInterval* parameter is used to set the resource type's *LooksAlivePollInterval* property.

dwIsAlivePollInterval
> [in] Default millisecond value to be used as the poll interval needed by the new resource type's *IsAlive* function. The *dwIsAlivePollInterval* parameter is used to set the resource type's *IsAlivePollInterval* property.

DeleteClusterResourceType

The **DeleteClusterResourceType** function removes a resource type from a cluster. The **DeleteClusterResourceType** function only removes the resource type, with the name pointed to by *lpszResourceTypeName* from the cluster database, and unregisters it with the Cluster Service. It will be necessary to delete any resources of this type before deleting the type. This can be accomplished with the function **DeleteClusterResource**.

```
DWORD WINAPI DeleteClusterResourceType(
  HCLUSTER hCluster,
  LPCWSTR lpszResourceTypeName
);
```

PARAMETERS

hCluster
> [in] Handle to the cluster containing the resource type to be removed.

lpszResourceTypeName
> [in] Pointer to the name of the resource type to be removed.

GetClusterInformation

The **GetClusterInformation** function retrieves a cluster's name and version. When **GetClusterInformation** returns, the variable pointed to by *lpcchClusterName* contains the number of characters stored in the buffer.

```
DWORD WINAPI GetClusterInformation(
  HCLUSTER hCluster,
  LPWSTR lpszClusterName,
  LPDWORD lpcchClusterName,
  LPCLUSTERVERSIONINFO lpClusterInfo
);
```

PARAMETERS

hCluster
> [in] Handle to a cluster.

lpszClusterName
> [out] Pointer to the name of the cluster identified by *hCluster*, including the terminating NULL character.

lpcchClusterName
> [in, out] On input, pointer to a buffer. On output, pointer to a count of characters in the cluster name pointed to by *lpszClusterName*, including the terminating NULL character.

lpClusterInfo
> [out] Either NULL or a pointer to a CLUSTERVERSIONINFO structure describing the version of the Cluster API for the cluster.

GetClusterNotify

The **GetClusterNotify** function returns information relating to the next notification event stored for a notification port.

```
DWORD WINAPI GetClusterNotify(
  HCHANGE hChange,
  LPDWORD lpdwNotifyKey,
  LPDWORD lpdwFilterType,
  LPWSTR lpszName,
  LPDWORD lpcchName,
  DWORD dwMilliseconds
);
```

PARAMETERS

hChange
> [in] Handle to a notification port created with the **CreateClusterNotify-Port** function.

lpdwNotifyKey
> [out] Pointer to the notification key for the port identified by *hChange*.

lpdwFilterType
> [out] Pointer to the type of returned event.

lpszName

[out] Pointer to the name of the object that triggered the event. The following table describes the contents of *lpszName* by event type.

Value of *lpdwFilterType*	Value of *lpszName*
CLUSTER_CHANGE_GROUP_ADDED	New group name
CLUSTER_CHANGE_GROUP_DELETED	Deleted group name
CLUSTER_CHANGE_GROUP_PROPERTY	Name of changed group
CLUSTER_CHANGE_GROUP_STATE	Name of changed group
CLUSTER_CHANGE_HANDLE_CLOSE	Name of object being closed
CLUSTER_CHANGE_NODE_ADDED	Name of new node
CLUSTER_CHANGE_NODE_DELETED	Name of deleted node
CLUSTER_CHANGE_NODE_PROPERTY	Name of changed node
CLUSTER_CHANGE_NODE_STATE	Name of changed node
CLUSTER_CHANGE_REGISTRY_ ATTRIBUTES	Relative name of changed cluster database key
CLUSTER_CHANGE_REGISTRY_NAME	Relative name of changed cluster database key
CLUSTER_CHANGE_REGISTRY_VALUE	Relative name of changed cluster database key
CLUSTER_CHANGE_RESOURCE_ADDED	New resource name
CLUSTER_CHANGE_RESOURCE_ DELETED	Deleted resource name
CLUSTER_CHANGE_RESOURCE_ PROPERTY	Name of changed resource
CLUSTER_CHANGE_RESOURCE_STATE	Name of changed resource
CLUSTER_CHANGE_RESOURCE_ TYPE_ADDED	Name of new resource type
CLUSTER_CHANGE_RESOURCE_ TYPE_DELETED	Name of deleted resource type

lpccbName

[in, out] On input, pointer to the count of characters in the buffer pointed to by *lpszName*. On output, pointer to the count of characters stored in the buffer pointed to by *lpszName*, excluding the trailing NULL.

dwMilliseconds

[in] Optional time-out value that specifies how long the caller is willing to wait for the notification.

GetClusterQuorumResource

The **GetClusterQuorumResource** function returns the name of a cluster's quorum resource.

```
DWORD WINAPI GetClusterQuorumResource(
  HCLUSTER hCluster,
  LPWSTR lpszResourceName,
  LPDWORD lpcbResourceName,
  LPWSTR lpszDeviceName,
  LPDWORD lpcbDeviceName,
  LPDWORD lpdwMaxQuorumLogSize
);
```

PARAMETERS

hCluster
> [in] Handle to an existing cluster.

lpszResourceName
> [out] Pointer to a NULL-terminated string containing the name of the cluster's quorum resource.

lpcbResourceName
> [in, out] On input, pointer to the count of characters in the buffer pointed to by the *lpszResourceName* parameter, including the terminating NULL character. On output, pointer to the count of characters stored in the buffer, excluding the terminating NULL character.

lpszDeviceName
> [out] Pointer to a NULL-terminated string containing the name of the device on which the quorum resource resides.

lpcbDeviceName
> [in, out] On input, pointer to the count of characters in the buffer pointed to by the *lpszDeviceName* parameter, including the terminating NULL character. On output, pointer to the count of characters stored in the buffer, excluding the terminating NULL character.

lpdwMaxQuorumLogSize
> [out] Pointer to the maximum size of the log being maintained by the quorum resource.

OpenCluster

The **OpenCluster** function opens a connection to a cluster and returns a handle to it.

```
HCLUSTER WINAPI OpenCluster(
  LPCWSTR lpszClusterName
);
```

PARAMETERS

lpszClusterName
> [in] Pointer to the name of an existing cluster or NULL, indicating that a handle to the cluster to which the local computer belongs should be returned.

RegisterClusterNotify

The **RegisterClusterNotify** function adds an event type to the list of events stored for a notification port. The **RegisterClusterNotify** function enables an application that has already created a notification port with **CreateClusterNotifyPort** to register for an additional event that affects a node, resource, or group.

To receive notifications of cluster database changes, flags must be set in the *dwFilter* parameter. Applicable flags start with the prefix CLUSTER_CHANGE_REGISTRY. Making manual changes to the cluster database through the registry editor, REGEDT32, will not cause notifications to be generated.

```
DWORD WINAPI RegisterClusterNotify(
  HCHANGE hChange,
  DWORD dwFilter,
  HANDLE hObject,
  DWORD dwNotifyKey
);
```

PARAMETERS

hChange
> [in] Handle to a notification port created with the **CreateClusterNotifyPort** function.

dwFilter
> [in] Bitmask of flags that describes the event to be added to the set of events currently being monitored by the notification port. The *dwFilter* parameter can be set to one of the following flags:
> CLUSTER_CHANGE_GROUP_DELETED
> CLUSTER_CHANGE_GROUP_PROPERTY
> CLUSTER_CHANGE_GROUP_STATE
> CLUSTER_CHANGE_NODE_DELETED
> CLUSTER_CHANGE_NODE_PROPERTY
> CLUSTER_CHANGE_NODE_STATE
> CLUSTER_CHANGE_REGISTRY_ATTRIBUTES
> CLUSTER_CHANGE_REGISTRY_NAME
> CLUSTER_CHANGE_REGISTRY_SUBTREE
> CLUSTER_CHANGE_REGISTRY_VALUE

CLUSTER_CHANGE_RESOURCE_DELETED
CLUSTER_CHANGE_RESOURCE_PROPERTY
CLUSTER_CHANGE_RESOURCE_STATE

hObject

[in] Handle to the object affected by the event specified in the *dwFilter* parameter. The type of handle depends on the value of *dwFilter* as described in the following table.

Value of *dwFilter*	Value of *hObject*
CLUSTER_CHANGE_GROUP_DELETED	HGROUP
CLUSTER_CHANGE_GROUP_PROPERTY	HGROUP
CLUSTER_CHANGE_GROUP_STATE	HGROUP
CLUSTER_CHANGE_NODE_DELETED	HNODE
CLUSTER_CHANGE_NODE_PROPERTY	HNODE
CLUSTER_CHANGE_NODE_STATE	HNODE
CLUSTER_CHANGE_REGISTRY_ATTRIBUTES	HKEY
CLUSTER_CHANGE_REGISTRY_NAME	HKEY
CLUSTER_CHANGE_REGISTRY_SUBTREE	HKEY
CLUSTER_CHANGE_REGISTRY_VALUE	HKEY
CLUSTER_CHANGE_RESOURCE_DELETED	HRESOURCE
CLUSTER_CHANGE_RESOURCE_PROPERTY	HRESOURCE
CLUSTER_CHANGE_RESOURCE_STATE	HRESOURCE

The cluster database functions return a valid cluster database key that can be used to set *hObject* when *dwFilter* is set to an event type affecting the cluster database.

dwNotifyKey

[in] Notification key that will be returned from **GetClusterNotify** when the requested event occurs.

SetClusterName

The **SetClusterName** function sets the name for a cluster. The cluster name is the **Name** property of the primary Network Name resource of the cluster. Changing this property does not take effect until the next time the cluster is started.

```
DWORD WINAPI SetClusterName(
  HCLUSTER hCluster,
  LPCWSTR lpszNewClusterName
);
```

PARAMETERS

hCluster
> [in] Handle to a cluster to rename.

lpszNewClusterName
> [in] Pointer to the new cluster name.

SetClusterQuorumResource

The **SetClusterQuorumResource** function sets the quorum resource for a cluster.

```
DWORD WINAPI SetClusterQuorumResource(
  HRESOURCE hResource,
  LPCWSTR lpszDeviceName,
  DWORD dwMaxQuoLogSize
);
```

PARAMETERS

hResource
> [in] Handle to the new quorum resource.

lpszDeviceName
> [in] Pointer to the name of the device where the quorum resource resides.

dwMaxQuoLogSize
> [in] Maximum size for the log file to be maintained by the quorum resource.

Resource Group Management Functions

CloseClusterGroup

The **CloseClusterGroup** function closes a group by invalidating its handle.

```
BOOL WINAPI CloseClusterGroup(
  HGROUP hGroup
);
```

PARAMETERS

hGroup
> [in] Handle to the group to close.

ClusterGroupCloseEnum

The **ClusterGroupCloseEnum** function closes a group enumerator object by invalidating its handle.

```
DWORD WINAPI ClusterGroupCloseEnum(
  HGROUPENUM hGroupEnum
);
```

PARAMETERS

hGroupEnum
> [in] Handle to the enumerator object to close.

ClusterGroupControl

The **ClusterGroupControl** function initiates an operation that affects a group. **ClusterGroupControl** is a general-purpose function for initiating an operation that affects a group.

```
DWORD WINAPI ClusterGroupControl(
  HGROUP hGroup,
  HNODE hHostNode,
  DWORD dwControlCode,
  LPVOID lpInBuffer,
  DWORD cbInBufferSize,
  LPVOID lpOutBuffer,
  DWORD cbOutBufferSize,
  LPDWORD lpcbBytesReturned
);
```

PARAMETERS

hGroup
> [in] Handle to the group to be affected.

hHostNode
> [in] If non-NULL, handle to the node to perform the operation represented by the control code. If NULL, the node that owns the group performs the operation. Specifying *hHostNode* is optional.

dwControlCode
> [in] Control code that defines the operation to be performed. Valid control codes are:
> CLUSCTL_GROUP_ENUM_COMMON_PROPERTIES
> CLUSCTL_GROUP_ENUM_PRIVATE_PROPERTIES
> CLUSCTL_GROUP_GET_CHARACTERISTICS
> CLUSCTL_GROUP_GET_COMMON_PROPERTIES

CLUSCTL_GROUP_GET_FLAGS
CLUSCTL_GROUP_GET_NAME
CLUSCTL_GROUP_GET_PRIVATE_PROPERTIES
CLUSCTL_GROUP_GET_RO_COMMON_PROPERTIES
CLUSCTL_GROUP_GET_RO_PRIVATE_PROPERTIES
CLUSCTL_GROUP_SET_COMMON_PROPERTIES
CLUSCTL_GROUP_SET_PRIVATE_PROPERTIES
CLUSCTL_GROUP_UNKNOWN
CLUSCTL_GROUP_VALIDATE_COMMON_PROPERTIES
CLUSCTL_GROUP_VALIDATE_PRIVATE_PROPERTIES

lpInBuffer
[in] Pointer to the input buffer with information needed for the operation, or NULL if no information is needed.

cbInBufferSize
[in] Number of bytes in the buffer pointed to by *lpInBuffer*.

lpOutBuffer
[out] Pointer to the output buffer with information resulting from the operation, or NULL if nothing need be returned.

cbOutBufferSize
[in] Number of bytes in the output buffer pointed to by *lpOutBuffer*.

lpcbBytesReturned
[in, out] Pointer to the number of bytes in the buffer pointed to by *lpOutBuffer* that were actually filled as a result of the operation. The caller can pass NULL for *lpcbBytesReturned* if **ClusterGroupControl** need not pass back the number of bytes in the output buffer.

ClusterGroupEnum

The **ClusterGroupEnum** function enumerates the resources in a group and/or the nodes that are possible owners of a group, returning the name of the resource or node with each call.

```
DWORD WINAPI ClusterGroupEnum(
  HGROUPENUM hGroupEnum,
  DWORD dwIndex,
  LPDWORD lpdwType,
  LPWSTR lpszResourceName,
  LPDWORD lpcbName
);
```

PARAMETERS

hGroupEnum
[in] Handle to a group enumerator object returned by the **ClusterGroupOpenEnum** function.

dwIndex

   [in] Index of the resource or node to return. This parameter should be zero for the first call to **ClusterGroupEnum** and then incremented for subsequent calls.

lpdwType

   [out] Pointer to the type of object returned by **ClusterGroupEnum**. Valid values are:

   CLUSTER_GROUP_ENUM_CONTAINS

   The object is one of the resources in the group.

   CLUSTER_GROUP_ENUM_NODES

   The object is one of the nodes that are in the possible owners list of the group.

lpszResourceName

   [out] Pointer to the name of the returned resource or node, including the terminating NULL character.

lpcbName

   [in, out] On input, pointer to the count of characters in the buffer pointed to by the *lpszResourceName* parameter. This size should include the terminating NULL character. On output, pointer to the count of characters stored in the buffer, excluding the terminating NULL character.

ClusterGroupOpenEnum

The **ClusterGroupOpenEnum** function opens an enumerator for iterating through a group's resources and/or the nodes that are included in its list of possible owners.

```
HGROUPENUM WINAPI ClusterGroupOpenEnum(
  HGROUP hGroup,
  DWORD dwType
);
```

PARAMETERS

hGroup

   [in] Handle to the group to be enumerated.

dwType

   [in] Bitmask describing the objects to be enumerated. Valid values are:

   CLUSTER_GROUP_ENUM_CONTAINS

   Enumerate all of the resources in the group identified by *hGroup*.

   CLUSTER_GROUP_ENUM_NODES

   Enumerate all of the nodes that are in the possible owners list of the group identified by *hGroup*.

CreateClusterGroup

The **CreateClusterGroup** function adds a group to a cluster and returns a handle to the newly added group.

```
HGROUP WINAPI CreateClusterGroup(
  HCLUSTER hCluster,
  LPCWSTR lpszGroupName
);
```

PARAMETERS

hCluster

[in] Handle to the target cluster.

lpszGroupName

[in] Pointer to the name of the group to be added to the cluster identified by *hCluster*. If there is not a group by this name, **CreateClusterGroup** creates it.

DeleteClusterGroup

The **DeleteClusterGroup** function removes a group from a cluster. Before a group can be deleted, all resources in the group must either be relocated or deleted.

```
DWORD WINAPI DeleteClusterGroup(
  HGROUP hGroup
);
```

PARAMETERS

hGroup

[in] Handle to the group to be removed.

GetClusterGroupState

The **GetClusterGroupState** function returns the current state of a group.

```
CLUSTER_GROUP_STATE WINAPI GetClusterGroupState(
  HGROUP hGroup,
  LPWSTR lpszNodeName,
  LPDWORD lpcbNodeName
);
```

PARAMETERS

hGroup

[in] Handle to the group for which state information should be returned.

lpszNodeName

[out] Optional pointer to the name of the node in the cluster where the group identified by *hGroup* is currently on-line or NULL.

lpcbNodeName

[in, out] On input, pointer to a count of characters in the buffer pointed to by *lpszNodeName*, including the terminating NULL character. On output, pointer to a count of characters in the name contained in the buffer pointed to by *lpszNodeName*, excluding the terminating NULL character.

If **GetClusterGroupState** is not successful, the value returned is ClusterGroupStateUnknown. If **GetClusterGroupState** is successful, it returns one of the following values:

State	Description
ClusterGroupFailed	The group is not operational but has not yet been taken off-line.
ClusterGroupOnline	The group is operational.
ClusterGroupOffline	The group is not operational.
ClusterGroupPartialOnline	One or more of the resources in the group have been brought on-line.

MoveClusterGroup

The **MoveClusterGroup** function moves a group and all of its resources from one node to another.

```
DWORD WINAPI MoveClusterGroup(
  HGROUP hGroup,
  HNODE hDestinationNode
);
```

PARAMETERS

hGroup

[in] Handle to the group to be moved.

hDestinationNode

[in] Optional handle to the node where the moved group should be brought back on-line or NULL.

OfflineClusterGroup

The **OfflineClusterGroup** function takes an on-line group off-line.

```
DWORD WINAPI OfflineClusterGroup(
  HGROUP hGroup
);
```

PARAMETERS

hGroup
> [in] Handle to the group to be taken off-line.

OnlineClusterGroup

The **OnlineClusterGroup** function brings an off-line group on-line.

```
DWORD WINAPI OnlineClusterGroup(
  HGROUP hGroup,
  HNODE hDestinationNode
);
```

PARAMETERS

hGroup
> [in] Handle to the group to be brought on-line.

hDestinationNode
> [in] Optional handle to the node where the group identified by *hGroup* should be brought on-line. A value of NULL signifies the current node.

> If the group cannot be brought on-line on the node identified by the *hDestinationNode* parameter, **OnlineClusterGroup** fails.

OpenClusterGroup

The **OpenClusterGroup** function opens a group and returns a handle to it.

```
HGROUP WINAPI OpenClusterGroup(
  HCLUSTER hCluster,
  LPCWSTR lpszGroupName
);
```

PARAMETERS

hCluster
> [in] Handle to a cluster that includes the group to open.

lpszGroupName
> [in] Name of the group to open.

SetClusterGroupName

The **SetClusterGroupName** function sets the name for a group.

```
DWORD WINAPI SetClusterGroupName(
  HGROUP hGroup,
  LPCWSTR lpszGroupName
);
```

PARAMETERS

hGroup
> [in] Handle to the group to name.

lpszGroupName
> [in] Pointer to the new name for the group identified by *hGroup*.

SetClusterGroupNodeList

The **SetClusterGroupNodeList** function sets the preferred node list for a group.

```
DWORD WINAPI SetClusterGroupNodeList(
  HGROUP hGroup,
  DWORD cNodeCount,
  HNODE phNodeList[]
);
```

PARAMETERS

hGroup
> [in] Handle to the group to be assigned the list of nodes.

cNodeCount
> [in] Count of nodes in the list identified by *phNodeList*.

phNodeList
> [in] Array of handles to nodes in order by preference, with the first node being the most preferred and the last node the least preferred.

Resource Management Functions

AddClusterResourceDependency

The **AddClusterResourceDependency** function creates a dependency relationship between two resources. A resource can only be dependent on another resource in the same group. Also, a resource cannot be brought on-line unless all dependent resources are already on-line.

```
DWORD WINAPI AddClusterResourceDependency(
   HRESOURCE hResource,
   HRESOURCE hDependsOn
);
```

PARAMETERS

hResource
  [in] Handle to the dependent resource.
hDependsOn
  [in] Handle to the resource that the resource identified by *hResource* should depend on.

AddClusterResourceNode

The **AddClusterResourceNode** function adds a node to the list of possible nodes that can bring a resource on-line.

```
DWORD WINAPI AddClusterResourceNode(
   HRESOURCE hResource,
   HNODE hNode
);
```

PARAMETERS

hResource
  [in] Handle to a resource that will add a node to its possible owners list.
hNode
  [in] Handle to the node to be added to the list of potential host nodes belonging to the resource identified by *hResource*.

CanResourceBeDependent

The **CanResourceBeDependent** function determines if one resource can be dependent on another resource. This function will return TRUE or FALSE. Situations in which FALSE would be returned inlude:

  ● The resources cannot be dependent on each other.
  ● The resources must be in the same group.

```
BOOL WINAPI CanResourceBeDependent(
   HRESOURCE hResource,
   HRESOURCE hResourceDependent
);
```

PARAMETERS

hResource

    [in] Handle to the resource in question.

hResourceDependent

    [in] Handle to the resource on which the resource identified by *hResource* may or may not depend.

ChangeClusterResourceGroup

The **ChangeClusterResourceGroup** function moves a resource from one group to another. The group the resource currently belongs to and the new group must be owned by the same node in order to be successful. Also, if the resource being moved has dependencies, all of the resources in its dependency tree will be moved to the new target group.

```
DWORD WINAPI ChangeClusterResourceGroup(
  HRESOURCE hResource,
  HGROUP hGroup
);
```

PARAMETERS

hResource

    [in] Handle of the resource to be moved.

hGroup

    [in] Handle of the group that should receive the resource identified by *hResource*.

CloseClusterResource

The **CloseClusterResource** function closes a resource by invalidating its handle, a handle returned from either **OpenClusterResource** or **CreateClusterResource**. **CloseClusterResource** returns TRUE or FALSE.

```
BOOL WINAPI CloseClusterResource(
  HRESOURCE hResource
);
```

PARAMETERS

hResource

    [in] Handle to the resource to be closed.

ClusterResourceCloseEnum

The **ClusterResourceCloseEnum** function closes a resource enumerator object by invalidating its handle, a handle returned from **ClusterResourceOpenEnum**.

```
DWORD WINAPI ClusterResourceCloseEnum(
  HRESENUM hResEnum
);
```

PARAMETERS

hResEnum
> [in] Handle to the resource enumerator to be closed.

ClusterResourceControl

The **ClusterResourceControl** function initiates an operation affecting a resource.

```
DWORD WINAPI ClusterResourceControl(
  HRESOURCE hResource,
  HNODE hHostNode,
  DWORD dwControlCode,
  LPVOID lpInBuffer,
  DWORD cbInBufferSize,
  LPVOID lpOutBuffer,
  DWORD cbOutBufferSize,
  LPDWORD lpcbBytesReturned
);
```

PARAMETERS

hResource
> [in] Handle to the resource to be controlled.

hHostNode
> [in] Optional handle to the node to perform the operation. If NULL, the node that owns the resource identified by *hResource* performs the operation.

dwControlCode
> [in] Resource control code that defines the operation to be performed.

lpInBuffer
> [in] Pointer to a buffer with information needed for the operation, or NULL if no information is needed.

cbInBufferSize
> [in] Number of bytes in the buffer pointed to by *lpInBuffer*.

lpOutBuffer
> [out] Pointer to a buffer with information resulting from the operation, or NULL if nothing need be returned.

cbOutBufferSize
> [in] Number of bytes in the buffer pointed to by *lpOutBuffer*.

lpcbBytesReturned
> [in, out] Pointer to the number of bytes of *lpOutBuffer* filled in as a result of the operation. The caller can pass NULL for *lpcbBytesReturned* if **ClusterResourceControl** need not pass back the number of bytes in the output buffer.

ClusterResourceEnum

The **ClusterResourceEnum** function enumerates a resource's dependent resources and/or nodes, returning the name of one object with each call. This is necessary when moving a resource to a new group, because all dependent resources must also be moved.

```
DWORD WINAPI ClusterResourceEnum(
  HRESENUM hResEnum,
  DWORD dwIndex,
  LPDWORD lpdwType,
  LPWSTR lpszName,
  LPDWORD lpcchName
);
```

PARAMETERS

hResEnum
> [in] Handle to a resource enumerator object—a handle returned from **ClusterResourceOpenEnum**.

dwIndex
> [in] Index of the resource or node object to return. This parameter should be zero for the first call to the **ClusterResourceEnum** function and then incremented for subsequent calls.

lpdwType
> [out] Type of object returned by **ClusterResourceEnum**. Valid types are:
> CLUSTER_RESOURCE_ENUM_DEPENDS
> The object is a resource that the resource identified by *hResource* directly depends on.
> CLUSTER_RESOURCE_ENUM_PROVIDES
> The object is a resource that depends on the resource identified by *hResource*.
> CLUSTER_RESOURCE_ENUM_NODES

The object is a node that can host the resource identified by *hResource*.

lpszName

[out] Pointer to the name of the returned object, including the terminating NULL character.

lpcchName

[in, out] Pointer to the count of characters in the buffer pointed to by the *lpszName* parameter. This size should include the terminating NULL character. On output, pointer to the count of characters stored in the buffer, excluding the terminating NULL character.

ClusterResourceOpenEnum

The **ClusterResourceOpenEnum** function opens an enumerator for iterating through a resource's dependencies and nodes.

```
HRESENUM WINAPI ClusterResourceOpenEnum(
  HRESOURCE hResource,
  DWORD dwType
);
```

PARAMETERS

hResource

[in] Handle to a resource.

dwType

[in] Bitmask describing the type of cluster objects to be enumerated. One or more of the following values are valid:

CLUSTER_RESOURCE_ENUM_DEPENDS

Enumerates resources that the resource identified by *hResource* directly depends on.

CLUSTER_RESOURCE_ENUM_PROVIDES

Enumerates resources that directly depend on the resource identified by *hResource*.

CLUSTER_RESOURCE_ENUM_NODES

Enumerates nodes that can host the resource identified by *hResource*.

CreateClusterResource

The **CreateClusterResource** function creates a resource in a cluster.

```
HRESOURCE WINAPI CreateClusterResource(
  HGROUP hGroup,
  LPCWSTR lpszResourceName,
  LPCWSTR lpszResourceType,
  DWORD dwFlags
);
```

PARAMETERS

hGroup
> [in] Handle to the group that should receive the resource.

lpszResourceName
> [in] Pointer to the name of the new resource. The specified name must be unique within the cluster.

lpszResourceType
> [in] Pointer to the type of new resource. The specified type must be installed in the cluster.

dwFlags
> [in] Bitmask describing how the resource should be added to the cluster. The *dwFlags* parameter is optional. If set, the following value is valid:
> CLUSTER_RESOURCE_SEPARATE_MONITOR
> This resource should be created using a separate resource monitor instead of a resource monitor that is shared.

DeleteClusterResource

The **DeleteClusterResource** function removes a resource from a cluster. The resource must be off-line to be successful.

```
DWORD WINAPI DeleteClusterResource(
  HRESOURCE hResource
);
```

PARAMETERS

hResource
> [in] Handle to an off-line resource.

FailClusterResource

The **FailClusterResource** function initiates a resource failure.

```
DWORD WINAPI FailClusterResource(
  HRESOURCE hResource
);
```

PARAMETERS

hResource
[in] Handle to the resource that is the target of the failure.

The resource identified by *hResource* is treated as inoperable, causing the cluster to initiate the same failover process that would result if the resource had actually failed. Applications call **FailClusterResource** to test their policies for restarting resources and groups.

GetClusterResourceNetworkName

The **GetClusterResourceNetworkName** function retrieves the network name from the Network Name resource on which a resource is dependent. Applications and resource DLLs call **GetClusterResourceNetworkName** to enumerate the dependencies of the resource identified by *hResource* in an attempt to find a Network Name resource on which the resource depends.

```
BOOL WINAPI GetClusterResourceNetworkName(
  HRESOURCE hResource,
  LPWSTR lpBuffer,
  LPDWORD nSize
);
```

PARAMETERS

hResource
[in] Handle to the dependent resource.
lpBuffer
[out] Pointer to a buffer containing a NULL-terminated character string containing the network name of the Network Name resource.
nSize
[in, out] On input, pointer to a count of characters in the buffer pointed to by *lpBuffer*. On output, pointer to a count of characters in the network name of the Network Name resource contained in the buffer pointed to by *lpBuffer*, excluding the terminating NULL character.

GetClusterResourceState

The **GetClusterResourceState** function returns the current state of a resource.

```
CLUSTER_RESOURCE_STATE WINAPI GetClusterResourceState(
  HRESOURCE hResource,
  LPWSTR lpszNodeName,
  LPDWORD lpcchNodeName,
```

```
  LPWSTR lpszGroupName,
  LPDWORD lpcchGroupName
);
```

PARAMETERS

hResource

> [in] Handle to the resource for which state information should be returned.

lpszNodeName

> [out] Pointer to the name of the node in the cluster where the group of the resource identified by *hResource* is currently on-line or NULL, if the node name is not required.

lpcchNodeName

> [in, out] On input, pointer to a count of characters in the buffer pointed to by *lpszNodeName*. On output, pointer to a count of characters in the name contained in the buffer pointed to by *lpszNodeName*, excluding the terminating NULL character.

lpszGroupName

> [out] Pointer to the name of the group that has as a member the resource identified by *hResource*. This parameter can be NULL if the group name is not required.

lpcchGroupName

> [in, out] On input, pointer to a count of characters in the buffer pointed to by *lpszGroupName*, including the terminating NULL character. On output, pointer to a count of characters stored in the buffer pointed to by *lpszGroupName*, excluding the terminating NULL character. If *lpsz-GroupName* is NULL, this parameter is ignored.

If the operation was successful, **GetClusterResourceState** returns the current state of the resource, which can be represented by one of the following values:

State	Description
ClusterResourceInitializing	The resource is performing initialization.
ClusterResourceOnline	The resource is operational and functioning normally.
ClusterResourceOffline	The resource is not operational.
ClusterResourceFailed	The resource has failed.
ClusterResourcePending	The resource is in the process of coming on-line or going off-line.
ClusterResourceOnlinePending	The resource is in the process of coming on-line.
ClusterResourceOfflinePending	The resource is in the process of going off-line.

OfflineClusterResource

The **OfflineClusterResource** function takes an on-line resource off-line.

```
DWORD WINAPI OfflineClusterResource(
  HRESOURCE hResource
);
```

PARAMETERS

hResource

> [in] Handle to the resource to be taken off-line.

OnlineClusterResource

The **OnlineClusterResource** function brings an off-line or failed resource on-line.

```
DWORD WINAPI OnlineClusterResource(
  HRESOURCE hResource
);
```

PARAMETERS

hResource

> [in] Handle to the resource to be brought on-line.

OpenClusterResource

The **OpenClusterResource** function opens a resource and returns a handle to it.

```
HRESOURCE WINAPI OpenClusterResource(
  HCLUSTER hCluster,
  LPCWSTR lpszResourceName
);
```

PARAMETERS

hCluster

> [in] Handle to a cluster.

lpszResourceName

> [in] Pointer to the name of the resource to be opened.

RemoveClusterResourceNode

The **RemoveClusterResourceNode** function removes a node from the list of nodes that can host a resource.

```
DWORD WINAPI RemoveClusterResourceNode(
  HRESOURCE hResource,
  HNODE hNode
);
```

PARAMETERS

hResource

[in] Handle to the target resource.

hNode

[in] Handle to the node that should be removed from the list of potential host nodes belonging to the resource identified by *hResource*.

RemoveClusterResourceDependency

The **RemoveClusterResourceDependency** function removes a dependency relationship between two resources.

```
DWORD WINAPI RemoveClusterResourceDependency(
  HRESOURCE hResource,
  HRESOURCE hDependsOn
);
```

PARAMETERS

hResource

[in] Handle to the dependent resource.

hDependsOn

[in] Handle to the resource that the resource identified by *hResource* currently depends on.

SetClusterResourceName

The **SetClusterResourceName** function sets the name for a resource.

```
DWORD WINAPI SetClusterResourceName(
  HRESOURCE hResource,
  LPCWSTR lpszResourceName
);
```

PARAMETERS

hResource
> [in] Handle to a resource to rename.

lpszResourceName
> [in] Pointer to the new name for the resource identified by *hResource*.

A Sample Application

The following sample program is located on the enclosed CD-rom. It demonstrates some of the resource management functions by:

- Creating a group
- Creating a resource that requires a dependency
- Bringing the resource online
- Taking the resource offline
- Deleting the resource
- Deleting the group

```
///////////////////////////////////////////////////////////////////////
//
// Cluster notification port example.
//
// Spawns a thread to create and monitor a notification port while
// main() produces events.
//
// NOTE:  In order to trigger event notifications, this example will:
//           1. Create a group named "EventDemoGroup"
//           2. Create a network share resource named "Application Server"
//              as part of "AppServer" network in the EventDemoGroup.
//           3. Bring the group online.
//           4. Take the group offline.
//           5. Delete the resource.
//           6. Delete the group.
//           All activity will take place on the local node and
//           that node's cluster.
//
///////////////////////////////////////////////////////////////////////
#include "ClusDocEx.h"
#include <process.h>   // for multithreading
#include <time.h>      // used to time stamp events


//
// Constants and global data
//
const DWORD MYAPP_GROUP_EVENTS = ( CLUSTER_CHANGE_GROUP_ADDED    |
                                   CLUSTER_CHANGE_GROUP_DELETED  |
```

```
                                CLUSTER_CHANGE_GROUP_STATE      );

const DWORD MYAPP_RES_EVENTS = ( CLUSTER_CHANGE_RESOURCE_ADDED   |
                                 CLUSTER_CHANGE_RESOURCE_DELETED |
                                 CLUSTER_CHANGE_RESOURCE_STATE      );


//---------------------------------------------------------------------
//
//  ClusDocEx_CreatePropertyListEntry.
//
//  Returns a buffer containing an entry for a property list,
//  formatted as a value list containing the following entries:
//      Property Name  (syntax, length, data, padding)
//      Property Value (syntax, length, data, padding)
//      CLUSPROP_SYNTAX_ENDMARK
//
//  Callers must call LocalFree on the returned pointer.
//
//  Arguments:
//      IN LPWSTR lpszPropName      Name of the property.
//      IN DWORD dwSyntax           Data syntax (see CLUSPROP_SYNTAX).
//      IN DWORD cbLength           Data length (see CLUSPROP_VALUE).
//      IN LPVOID lpData            Pointer to the data.
//      OUT LPDWORD lpcbEntrySize   Byte size of the resulting entry.
//
//  Return Value:
//      Pointer to a buffer containing a property list entry.
//
//---------------------------------------------------------------------
LPVOID
ClusDocEx_CreatePropertyListEntry(
    IN LPWSTR lpszPropName,
    IN DWORD dwSyntax,
    IN DWORD cbLength,
    IN LPVOID lpData,
    OUT LPDWORD lpcbEntrySize
)
{
    DWORD cbPropNameSize = ( lstrlenW( lpszPropName ) + 1 ) *
                          sizeof( WCHAR );
    DWORD cbNameEntrySize;
    DWORD cbValueEntrySize;

    CLUSPROP_BUFFER_HELPER cbh;
    LPVOID lpEntry = NULL;


// TBD:  Code that checks for bad parameters.
```

```
// Calculate sizes.
// ClusDocEx_ListEntrySize is defined in ClusDocEx.h.

    cbNameEntrySize = ClusDocEx_ListEntrySize( cbPropNameSize );

    cbValueEntrySize = ClusDocEx_ListEntrySize( cbLength );

    *lpcbEntrySize = cbNameEntrySize +
                     cbValueEntrySize +
                     sizeof( DWORD );

    lpEntry = LocalAlloc( LPTR, *lpcbEntrySize );

    if( lpEntry != NULL )
    {

// Position cbh.

        cbh.pb = (LPBYTE) lpEntry;

// Write the property name.

        cbh.pName->Syntax.dw = CLUSPROP_SYNTAX_NAME;

        cbh.pName->cbLength = cbPropNameSize;

        lstrcpy( cbh.pName->sz, lpszPropName );

// Advance cbh.

        cbh.pb += cbNameEntrySize;

// Write syntax and length

        cbh.pValue->Syntax.dw = dwSyntax;

        cbh.pValue->cbLength = cbLength;

// Position cbh.

        cbh.pb += sizeof( CLUSPROP_VALUE );

// Copy the data.

        memcpy( cbh.pb, lpData, cbLength );

// Position cbh.

        cbh.pb = (PBYTE) lpEntry + cbNameEntrySize + cbValueEntrySize;
```

```
    //  Set the endmark.

        *cbh.pdw = CLUSPROP_SYNTAX_ENDMARK;
    }


    cbh.pb = NULL;


    return lpEntry;

}
//  end ClusDocEx_CreatePropertyListEntry
//----------------------------
//------------------------------------------------------------------
//
//  ClusDocEx_GrpCreatePropertyList(
//
//  Returns a property list containing all of the read/write common
//  properties for a group.
//
//  Callers must call LocalFree on the returned pointer.
//
//  Arguments:
//      LPDWORD lpcbPropListSize      Byte size of the resulting
//                                    property list.
//      Use the remaining arguments to assign new values to the
//      read/write group common properties.
//
//  Return Value:
//      Pointer to a buffer containing a property list.
//------------------------------------------------------------------
LPVOID
ClusDocEx_GrpCreatePropertyList(
    LPDWORD lpcbPropListSize,
    DWORD dwAutoFailbackType,
    LPWSTR lpszDescription,
    DWORD dwFailbackWindowEnd,
    DWORD dwFailbackWindowStart,
    DWORD dwFailoverPeriod,
    DWORD dwFailoverThreshold,
    DWORD dwPersistentState
)
{
    LPVOID lpPropList;
    LPVOID lpAutoFailbackType;
    LPVOID lpDescription;
    LPVOID lpFailbackWindowEnd;
    LPVOID lpFailbackWindowStart;
    LPVOID lpFailoverPeriod;
```

```
       LPVOID lpFailoverThreshold;
       LPVOID lpPersistentState;

       DWORD dwPropCount = 7;
       DWORD cbPropEntrySize[7];
       DWORD cbPosition = 0;
       DWORD cb, dw;

       CLUSPROP_BUFFER_HELPER cbh_write, cbh_read;
//  Create the property list entries for each property.

       lpAutoFailbackType      = ClusDocEx_CreatePropertyListEntry(
                                     L"AutoFailbackType",
                                     CLUSPROP_SYNTAX_LIST_VALUE_DWORD,
                                     sizeof( DWORD ),
                                     (LPVOID) &dwAutoFailbackType,
                                     &cbPropEntrySize[0] );

       lpDescription           = ClusDocEx_CreatePropertyListEntry(
                                     L"Description",
                                     CLUSPROP_SYNTAX_LIST_VALUE_SZ,
                                     ( lstrlenW( lpszDescription) + 1 ) *
              sizeof( WCHAR ),
                                     (LPVOID) lpszDescription,
                                     &cbPropEntrySize[1] );

       lpFailbackWindowEnd     = ClusDocEx_CreatePropertyListEntry(
                                     L"FailbackWindowEnd",
                                     CLUSPROP_SYNTAX_LIST_VALUE_DWORD,
                                     sizeof( DWORD ),
                                     (LPVOID) &dwFailbackWindowEnd   ,
                                     &cbPropEntrySize[2] );

       lpFailbackWindowStart   = ClusDocEx_CreatePropertyListEntry(
                                     L"FailbackWindowStart",
                                     CLUSPROP_SYNTAX_LIST_VALUE_DWORD,
                                     sizeof( DWORD ),
                                     (LPVOID) &dwFailbackWindowStart,
                                     &cbPropEntrySize[3] );

       lpFailoverPeriod        = ClusDocEx_CreatePropertyListEntry(
                                     L"FailoverPeriod",
                                     CLUSPROP_SYNTAX_LIST_VALUE_DWORD,
                                     sizeof( DWORD ),
                                     (LPVOID) &dwFailoverPeriod,
                                     &cbPropEntrySize[4] );

       lpFailoverThreshold     = ClusDocEx_CreatePropertyListEntry(
                                     L"FailoverThreshold",
```

```
                              CLUSPROP_SYNTAX_LIST_VALUE_DWORD,
                              sizeof( DWORD ),
                              (LPVOID) &dwFailoverThreshold,
                              &cbPropEntrySize[5] );

    lpPersistentState      = ClusDocEx_CreatePropertyListEntry(
                              L"PersistentState",
                              CLUSPROP_SYNTAX_LIST_VALUE_DWORD,
                              sizeof( DWORD ),
                              (LPVOID) &dwPersistentState,
                              &cbPropEntrySize[6] );


//  Calculate the required size, which should be the sum of each entry
//  plus the size of the property count.

    *lpcbPropListSize = sizeof( DWORD );   // property count.

    for( cb = 0 ; cb < dwPropCount ; cb++ )
        *lpcbPropListSize += cbPropEntrySize[cb];

    lpPropList = LocalAlloc( LPTR, *lpcbPropListSize );


//  Position cbh and write the property count.

    cbh_write.pb = (PBYTE) lpPropList;

    *cbh_write.pdw = dwPropCount;

    cbPosition = sizeof( DWORD );


//  Iterate through the property list entries and copy each entry
//  to the property list buffer.

    for( dw = 0 ; dw < dwPropCount ; dw++ )
    {
        switch( dw )
        {
        case 0:  cbh_read.pb = (PBYTE) lpAutoFailbackType;    break;
        case 1:  cbh_read.pb = (PBYTE) lpDescription;         break;
        case 2:  cbh_read.pb = (PBYTE) lpFailbackWindowEnd;   break;
        case 3:  cbh_read.pb = (PBYTE) lpFailbackWindowStart; break;
        case 4:  cbh_read.pb = (PBYTE) lpFailoverPeriod;      break;
        case 5:  cbh_read.pb = (PBYTE) lpFailoverThreshold;   break;
        case 6:  cbh_read.pb = (PBYTE) lpPersistentState;     break;
        default: break;
        }
```

```
    //  cbPosition is the index into the property list buffer.
    //  cb is the index into the current entry buffer.
    //  dw iterates the entries.

        for( cb = 0 ; cb < cbPropEntrySize[dw] ; cb++, cbPosition++ )
            cbh_write.pb[cbPosition] = cbh_read.pb[cb];
    }

//  Free the memory allocated by ClusDocEx_CreatePropertyListEntry

    LocalFree( lpAutoFailbackType );
    LocalFree( lpDescription );
    LocalFree( lpFailbackWindowEnd );
    LocalFree( lpFailbackWindowStart );
    LocalFree( lpFailoverPeriod );
    LocalFree( lpFailoverThreshold );
    LocalFree( lpPersistentState );

    return lpPropList;


}
//  end ClusDocEx_GrpCreatePropertyList
//-----------------------------------------------------------------------


//-----------------------------------------------------------------------
//
//  ClusDocEx_ResCreateNetworkName
//
//  Creates a Network Name resource,
//  sets its required private properties,
//  and establishes a dependency on an IP Address resource.
//
//  Arguments:
//      IN HGROUP      hGroup           Group handle.
//      IN HRESOURCE   hIPDependency    Handle to the IP Address dependency.
//      IN LPWSTR      lpszResName      Name of the new Network Name
//                                      resource (the resource name).
//      IN LPWSTR      lpszNetName      Specifies the name of the network
//                                      for which the Network Name resource
//                                      is being created. This value will
//                                      be used to set the Name private
//                                      property.
//
//  Return Value:
//      Resource handle (if successful) or NULL (if unsuccessful)
//
//-----------------------------------------------------------------------
HRESOURCE ClusDocEx_ResCreateNetworkName(
```

```
        IN HGROUP    hGroup,
        IN HRESOURCE hIPDependency,
        IN LPWSTR    lpszResName,
        IN LPWSTR    lpszNetName )


    {

        HRESOURCE hNetNameRes = NULL;
        LPVOID lpPropList = NULL;
        LPVOID lpNameEntry = NULL;

        DWORD cb;
        DWORD cbPosition = 0;
        DWORD cbNameEntrySize = 0;
        DWORD cbPropListSize = 0;
        DWORD dwResult = ERROR_SUCCESS;

        CLUSPROP_BUFFER_HELPER cbh_read, cbh_write;

        hNetNameRes = CreateClusterResource(
                        hGroup,
                        lpszResName,
                        L"Network Name",
                        0 );

        if( hNetNameRes == NULL )
        {
            dwResult = GetLastError();
            goto endf;
        }


    //  Create a property list to set the Name private property.
    //  This example uses ClusDocEx_CreatePropertyListEntry, which
    //  is listed under "Creating Property Lists."

        lpNameEntry = ClusDocEx_CreatePropertyListEntry(
                        L"Name",
                        CLUSPROP_SYNTAX_LIST_VALUE_SZ,
                        (lstrlenW( lpszNetName ) + 1 ) * sizeof( WCHAR ),
                        (LPVOID) lpszNetName,
                        &cbNameEntrySize );


    //  This is a single-value property list, thus the size is just
    //  the size of the entry plus the size of the property count.

        cbPropListSize = sizeof( DWORD ) + cbNameEntrySize;

        lpPropList = LocalAlloc( LPTR, cbPropListSize );
```

```
// Use cbh to write the property count (1) and the single entry
// to the property list buffer.

    cbh_write.pb = (PBYTE) lpPropList;

    cbh_read.pb = (PBYTE) lpNameEntry;

    *cbh_write.pdw = 1;

    cbPosition = sizeof( DWORD );

    for( cb = 0 ; cb < cbNameEntrySize ; cb++, cbPosition++ )
        cbh_write.pb[cbPosition] = cbh_read.pb[cb];

    dwResult = ClusterResourceControl(
                    hNetNameRes,
                    NULL,
                    CLUSCTL_RESOURCE_SET_PRIVATE_PROPERTIES,
                    lpPropList,
                    cbPropListSize,
                    NULL,
                    0,
                    NULL );

    if( dwResult != ERROR_SUCCESS )
    {
        goto endf;
    }


// Establish the IP Address dependency.

    dwResult = AddClusterResourceDependency(
                    hNetNameRes,
                    hIPDependency );

endf:

    if( dwResult != ERROR_SUCCESS )
    {
        if( hNetNameRes != NULL )
        {
            DeleteClusterResource( hNetNameRes );
            CloseClusterResource( hNetNameRes );
            hNetNameRes = NULL;
        }
    }

    if( lpNameEntry != NULL ) LocalFree( lpNameEntry );
```

```
    if( lpPropList != NULL ) LocalFree( lpPropList );

    SetLastError( dwResult );

    return hNetNameRes;
}
//  end ClusDocEx_ResCreateNetworkName
//-------------------------------------------------------------------


BOOL g_bContinue; // controls thread's event retrieval loop

//
// Function Prototypes
//
void EventPort( void *dummy );

void EventMessage( HCLUSTER hCluster,
                   DWORD    dwNotifyKey,
                   DWORD    dwFilterType,
                   LPWSTR   lpszObjectName );

///////////////////////////////////////////////////////////////////////
// Main()
//
// Spawns a thread to create and monitor a notification port;
// then triggers event notifications.
//
// There can be only one console per process, so main()
// and the thread display to the same console.
//
// The Sleep statements are only there to slow down the output to
// a readable rate. They can be commented out if desired.
///////////////////////////////////////////////////////////////////////
int main()
{
    HCLUSTER   hCluster = NULL;
    HGROUP     hGroup   = NULL;
    HRESOURCE  hRes     = NULL, hResIP= NULL;
    DWORD      dwResult = 0;

    g_bContinue = TRUE;

    _beginthread( EventPort, 0, NULL );

    hCluster = OpenCluster( NULL );

    if ( hCluster )
    {
```

```
// Trigger add group event
wprintf( L"(main)     Create Group" );
hGroup = CreateClusterGroup( hCluster, L"EventDemoGroup" );


if( hGroup )
{
        hResIP = OpenClusterResource( hCluster, L"Cluster
    IP Address" );


    // Trigger add resource event
    wprintf( L"(main)     Create Resource" );
    hRes = ClusDocEx_ResCreateNetworkName( hGroup,
                            hResIP,
                            L"Application Server",
                            L"AppServer" );


    // Trigger group and resource state changes
    wprintf( L"(main)     Online Group" );
    dwResult = OnlineClusterGroup( hGroup, NULL );


    // Trigger group and resource state changes
    wprintf( L"(main)     Offline Group" );
    dwResult = OfflineClusterGroup( hGroup );


    if( hRes )
    {
        // Trigger remove resource event
        wprintf( L"(main)     Delete Resource" );
        dwResult = DeleteClusterResource( hRes );


        CloseClusterResource( hRes ); // always close after
     deleting
    }
    // Trigger remove group event
    wprintf( L"(main)     Delete Group" );
    dwResult = DeleteClusterGroup( hGroup );

    CloseClusterGroup( hGroup );
}

CloseCluster( hCluster );
}
```

```
    wprintf( L"(main)      End Thread" );
    g_bContinue = FALSE; // tells thread to break while loop

    return 0;
}


void EventPort( void *dummy )
{
    HCLUSTER  hCluster      = NULL;
    HCHANGE   hChange       = (HCHANGE)INVALID_HANDLE_VALUE ;
    LPWSTR    lpszObjectName = (LPWSTR)LocalAlloc( LPTR,
              ClusDocEx_DEFAULT_CB );
    DWORD     cbszObjectName;
    DWORD     dwFilterType;
    DWORD     dwNotifyKey;
    DWORD     dwStatus;
    DWORD     dwCount        = 0;

    hCluster = OpenCluster( NULL );

    if ( hCluster )
    {
        hChange = CreateClusterNotifyPort( hChange,
                                           hCluster,
                                           MYAPP_RES_EVENTS,    //
               dwFilter
                                           MYAPP_RES_EVENTS ); //
               dwNotifyKey

        hChange = CreateClusterNotifyPort( hChange,
                                           hCluster,
                                           MYAPP_GROUP_EVENTS,
                                           MYAPP_GROUP_EVENTS );

        hChange = CreateClusterNotifyPort( hChange,
                                           hCluster,
                                           CLUSTER_CHANGE_HANDLE_CLOSE,
                                           CLUSTER_CHANGE_HANDLE_CLOSE
            );

        if ( hChange == NULL )
        {
            dwStatus = GetLastError();
        }

        while( hChange )
        {
            // Reset name size descriptor
```

```
            cbszObjectName = ClusDocEx_DEFAULT_CB;

            dwStatus = GetClusterNotify( hChange,
                                         &dwNotifyKey,
                                         &dwFilterType,
                                         lpszObjectName,
                                         &cbszObjectName,
                                         2500); // = 2.5 seconds


            if( dwStatus == ERROR_SUCCESS )
            {
                EventMessage( hCluster,
                              dwNotifyKey,
                              dwFilterType,
                              lpszObjectName );
            }
            else if( dwStatus == WAIT_TIMEOUT )
            {
                // If any call to GetClusterNotify times out
                // (exceeds dwMilliseconds, which is 2500 in this case)
                // any code here will be executed.
                wprintf( L"(thread)   Waiting..." );
            }
            else
            {
                wprintf( L"(thread)   GetClusterNotify" );
                break ;
            }

            // main() sets this value to terminate thread
            if( g_bContinue == FALSE ) break;

        } //  end while( hChange )

        CloseClusterNotifyPort(hChange) ;

        CloseCluster(hCluster) ;
    }
    else // no cluster handle
    {
        dwStatus = GetLastError();
    }

    wprintf( L"(thread)   End" );
    LocalFree( lpszObjectName );
}

////////////////////////////////////////////////////////////////////
          /////////
```

```
// EventMessage()
//
// Generates event data.
//
// Arguments:
//   HCLUSTER hCluster        Cluster handle
//   DWORD    dwNotifyKey      Notification type
//   DWORD    dwFilterType     Event type
//   LPWSTR   lpszObjectName   Name of object affected by event
//
// Return Value:
//   None
///////////////////////////////////////////////////////////////////
          /////////
void EventMessage( HCLUSTER hCluster,
                   DWORD    dwNotifyKey,
                   DWORD    dwFilterType,
                   LPWSTR   lpszObjectName )
{
    HRESOURCE      hResource    = NULL;
    HGROUP         hGroup       = NULL;
    LPWSTR         lpszStatus   = (LPWSTR)LocalAlloc( LPTR,
            ClusDocEx_DEFAULT_CB );
    LPWSTR         lpszObject   = (LPWSTR)LocalAlloc( LPTR,
            ClusDocEx_DEFAULT_CB );
    DWORD          cbGroupName  = 0; // for GetClusterResourceState
    DWORD          cbNodeName   = 0; // for GetClusterResourceState
    DWORD          dwState;
    time_t         ptime;

    //
    // Specify object type.
    //
    switch( dwNotifyKey )
    {
    case MYAPP_RES_EVENTS:
        wcscpy( lpszObject, L"Resource" );
        break;
    case MYAPP_GROUP_EVENTS:
        wcscpy( lpszObject, L"Group" );
        break;
    case CLUSTER_CHANGE_HANDLE_CLOSE:
        wcscpy( lpszObject, L"Handle" );
        break;
    default:
        wcscpy( lpszObject, L"Unknown Object" );
        break;
    }

    //
```

```
// Get object status.
//
if( dwFilterType == CLUSTER_CHANGE_RESOURCE_STATE )
{
    hResource = OpenClusterResource( hCluster, lpszObjectName );
    if( hResource )
    {
        dwState = GetClusterResourceState( hResource,
                                           NULL,
                                           &cbNodeName,
                                           NULL,
                                           &cbGroupName );
        switch( dwState )
        {
        case ClusterResourceFailed:
            wcscpy( lpszStatus, L"Failed" );
            break;
        case ClusterResourceOnline:
            wcscpy( lpszStatus, L"Online" );
            break;
        case ClusterResourceOffline:
            wcscpy( lpszStatus, L"Offline" );
            break;
        case ClusterResourceInitializing:
            wcscpy( lpszStatus, L"Initializing" );
            break;
        case ClusterResourcePending:
            wcscpy( lpszStatus, L"Pending" );
            break;
        case ClusterResourceOnlinePending:
            wcscpy( lpszStatus, L"Online Pending" );
            break;
        case ClusterResourceOfflinePending:
            wcscpy( lpszStatus, L"Offline Pending" );
            break;
        }
        CloseClusterResource( hResource );
    }
    else // no resource handle
    {
        wcscpy( lpszStatus, L"Unknown State Change" );
    } //  end if( hResource )

}
else if( dwFilterType == CLUSTER_CHANGE_GROUP_STATE )
{
    hGroup = OpenClusterGroup( hCluster, lpszObjectName );

    if( hGroup )
    {
```

```
            dwState = GetClusterGroupState( hGroup, NULL, &cbNodeName
             );

            switch( dwState )
            {
            case ClusterGroupFailed:
                wcscpy( lpszStatus, L"Failed" );
                break;
            case ClusterGroupOnline:
                wcscpy( lpszStatus, L"Online" );
                break;
            case ClusterGroupOffline:
                wcscpy( lpszStatus, L"Offline" );
                break;
            case ClusterGroupPartialOnline:
                wcscpy( lpszStatus, L"Partially Online" );
                break;
            }
            CloseClusterGroup( hGroup );
        }
        else
        {
            wcscpy( lpszStatus, L"Unknown State Change" );
        }
        //  end if( hGroup )
    }
    else if( dwFilterType == CLUSTER_CHANGE_RESOURCE_ADDED ||
             dwFilterType == CLUSTER_CHANGE_GROUP_ADDED        )

    {
        wcscpy( lpszStatus, L"Added" );
    }
    else if( dwFilterType == CLUSTER_CHANGE_RESOURCE_DELETED ||
             dwFilterType == CLUSTER_CHANGE_GROUP_DELETED       )

    {
        wcscpy( lpszStatus, L"Deleted" );
    }
    else if( dwFilterType == CLUSTER_CHANGE_HANDLE_CLOSE )

    {
        wcscpy( lpszStatus, L"Closed" );
    }
    else
    {
        wcscpy( lpszStatus, L"Unknown Status" );
    }

    // Get time stamp
    time( &ptime );
```

```
    // Write event message to console; could also write to file
    wprintf( L"(thread)     " );
    wprintf( L"%ls %ls %ls = %ls \n\n", _wctime(&ptime), lpszObject,
             lpszObjectName, lpszStatus );

    LocalFree( lpszStatus );
    LocalFree( lpszObject );

} //  end EventMessage
```

APPENDIX A

Resource Dependency Table

The Cluster Servicer will not allow resources to be created unless the proper dependent resources have already been defined. In the shared nothing cluster model that Microsoft Cluster Server implements, group and resource planning are very critical because it is the method available to perform any load balancing of processing load between the cluster members. Table A.1 shows resource types and their associated dependencies. When reviewing the table and performing any preliminary planning, remember two basic rules:

1. A resource can only be a member of one group
2. A resource and all its dependent resources must reside in the same group

TABLE A.1

Cluster Resource	Required Dependencies
Distributed Transaction Coordinator	Physical disk and network name
Exchange Server	
File Share	None[*]
Generic Application	None
Generic Srevice	None
IIS Virtual Root	TCP/IP address
IP Address	None
Network Name	TCP/IP address
Message Queue Server	Physical disk, network name, SQL Server, and distributed transaction coordinator
Physical Disk	None
Print Spooler	Physical disk and network name
SQL Server	
Time Service	None

[*] The file share resource generally uses a physical disk resource, but it is not a required depenency.

System Performance

System performance, or lack thereof, probably generates more work and headaches for a system administrator than any other system support task. The four dreaded words to a system administrator's ears are, "The system is slow." What is the definition of "slow"? In my opinion, a good definition of the word is "Something is perceived to be moving at a rate that is less than expected." There are two key words here: "perceived" and "expected." When this definition is applied to computer system performance, the client base is generally the group stating that a system is running "slow." The first decision an administrator has to make is to determine whether the system is actually processing at a rate that is less than what it is capable of. If the answer is yes, then steps need to be taken to correct the problem. I call this reactive performance tuning. In a perfect world, administrators would be able to do proactive performance tuning, which is fixing potential performance issues before they really become an issue, but we all know how often the time is available to perform this task.

Before we delve into Windows 2000 and cluster performance, let's spend a few more minutes on the definition of "slow." As you all know, it is a difficult task to set client expectations on system and network response time. You cannot explain to a user that their screen display is actually an SQL query traveling over the routed network to a server that is supporting 30 other SQL users, all accessing the same disk. The client is concerned with how fast their data displays. In a previous career, I managed a data center that supported approximately 300 users. Getting the users to have a reasonable perception of response time was a difficult task. The problems generally arose when a new application was loaded or more clients were added to use the existing applications. The existing clients noticed degradation in their response time; therefore, the system was now "slow." How do you correct this? Of course, most systems will degrade, at least slightly, as more applications or clients are added. Along with the increased system load, now the network is supporting more traffic. I met a person once who had a very novel idea that he used, which I am *not* suggesting you implement. To address the above problem of clients experiencing degraded response times as new users or applications were added, this individual actually would configure a system so that it would not perform as well as it possibly could. He mistuned the system! As new users and applications were added, he would repair his tuning mistakes. It is sad to have to admit that this would correct users' perceptions of their systems being slower, as they would now generally experience response times similar to those they had always experienced. The client base would not know that the system was performing slower than was possible because they would have nothing else to compare the response time with.

Analyzing the performance of a cluster is an extension of analyzing the performance of any Windows 2000 computer. Notice I use the word "analyze" as opposed to "tune." I make this distinction because, for the most part, Windows 2000 is considered to be self tuning! For example, logic has been built into the operating system to allocate and reallocate memory to processes as they need it to minimize page faulting. Other operating systems I have worked with made the administrator define memory usage limits on a per-user basis. Over the next few pages, I will make suggestions on which system resources to examine to determine potential bottlenecks.

To properly determine bottlenecks and successfully correct them, it is important that the administrator know something about the applications that are running on the systems being analyzed. Are they CPU intensive applications such as a CAD application? Are they I/O intensive applications such as SQL Server? In addition, it may be necessary to have some knowledge of how those applications are being used. For example, SQL Server consumes a fair amount of memory and can generate numerous disk I/Os, but if users are issuing commands such as sorts on data, SQL Server will also consume more processor time. It is impractical to be familiar with every command your user base executes, but try to be familiar with the tasks that are performed regularly.

Analyzing System Performance

To analyze system performance, it is important to understand some of the basics of the operating system. I like to break down performance analysis into three or four categories that should be examined, and they should be examined in a specific order. The reason for the specific order will soon be clear. The categories I use are:

- memory utilization
- disk I/O
- CPU utilization
- network

Network is a very ambiguous term here. Do we mean throughput on the cable? If so, that is not system performance; it is network performance analysis. We can look at network traffic by protocol to and from a system. This can be useful in pinpointing some CPU and memory usage.

At first, it might seem important to know the types of the different components, such as "Are the disks SCSI or IDE?" or "How much memory is in the system?" I will agree that this is useful information to have, but the fact is, we want to determine the limiting resource. It will not change our performance analysis process whether we are examining an 8MB system or a 64MB system. Also, the method of analyzing disks I intend to show you does not concern itself with SCSI and IDE disk access times. When it *is* important to know the existing hardware is when the final outcome of the performance analysis is a hardware upgrade. This is not a cop-out. The last resort to alleviating bottlenecks is always to increase the hardware resource.

One more statement about the philosophy of performance analysis: There is always a bottleneck on a system. The definition of a bottleneck is the resource that limits the ability of other resources to perform at a faster rate. The question that needs to be asked is, "Are users content with their current level of response?" If so, performance analysis does not need to be performed at the present time.

Memory

WHAT IS VIRTUAL MEMORY?

To properly analyze memory and determine whether it is a bottleneck on a system, it is necessary to understand the concept of virtual memory. The word "virtual" means "not real." Virtual memory is therefore memory that is not "real." It is a method employed by the operating system to give processes the capability to utilize approximately 4GB of what appears to be memory. Virtual memory is not unique to Windows NT. It is a widely used method of allowing more programs to be running on a system than will fit into physical memory.

Windows 2000 is a 32-bit operating system. The largest number that can be represented using 32 bits worth of storage is approximately 4.3 billion. Since memory addresses are stored in 32 bits, 4.3 billion is also the total amount of memory in bytes that the operating system or an application program can reference. While this is an architectural limit, how many systems have 4.3GB of memory? To take advantage of the total range of addresses, regardless of the amount of physical memory on the system, the concept of a virtual address space is used. The virtual address space is the range of possible addresses. In the case of Windows NT, the size of the virtual address space is 4.3 billion. I stated earlier that an application program can reference the entire 4.3GB address range. Actually, one portion of the virtual address space is allocated to the application the user is running, and the rest is allocated to the operating system. See Figure B-1.

Virtual Address Space

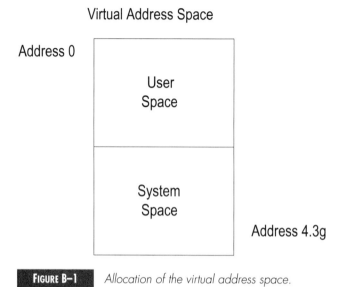

Address 0

User
Space

System
Space

Address 4.3g

FIGURE B–1   *Allocation of the virtual address space.*

In previous versions of Windows, the virtual address space had always allocated 2GB for the user and the other 2GB for the operating system. In Windows 2000, 3GB is allocated for the user space. This allows applications to become 50% larger, while taking away 50% from the operating system. This is not a performance penalty for the operating system, as it never uses all of the virtual memory allocated.

So, now we have a user space that can potentially address 2–3GB of memory, and this is on a per-user basis. Should we all run out and buy stock in memory chip manufacturers? The concept of virtual memory solves this problem. The next concept to discuss is a page table. A page table is actually a translation table that takes a virtual address space address and returns the actually memory location that the virtual address references. Every process running on the system will have its own virtual address space, and every virtual address space will have an address location 100. For the processes to be protected from each other, their address 100 needs to be a unique location in physical memory. It is the page table that stores this information. See Figure B-2.

The page table holds the actual memory address that corresponds to a virtual address. When a program is executed, it must be loaded into memory. As it is loaded, the page table is populated with the memory locations.

There are many advantages to a virtual memory model, such as the memory for a given program does not need to be contiguous. Also, the virtual memory model makes it simple to share memory. For example, every process has a system space where the operating system code is referenced. While

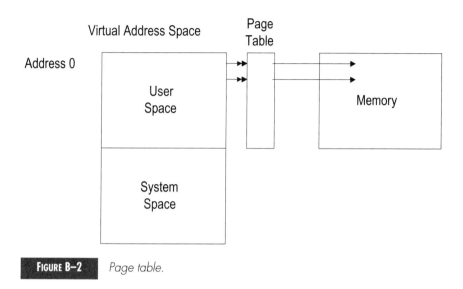

FIGURE B-2   *Page table.*

there is a separate page table for each user space, there is only one system space page table that all processes share. Every process now has the same pointers to physical memory in the system space. The memory is shared!

PAGING

Physical memory is divided into logical units called pages. The size of a page can vary with the hardware platform. Currently, the DEC Alpha uses 8192 bytes per page, whereas all other hardware platforms use 4096 bytes per page. Various events force data to be moved between disk and memory. This process is called paging. Paging is vital to the workings of a virtual memory operating system, even though extensive paging can overload the processor and disk resources.

Although a process may have access to 2–3GB of virtual address space, Windows 2000 will put a limit on how much physical memory a process can own. The amount of memory currently "owned" by a process is known as its working set. Depending on the activity of the process and the amount of free memory on the system, Windows 2000 will increase a process working set as necessary. Here is how it works. A user runs Excel. As the program is paged into memory, the page table for the process is updated with the proper memory locations. At this point, the user may have a working set size of 1MB. Next, the user creates a large spreadsheet. Windows 2000 starts allocating memory for the spreadsheet and updating the process page table. For this example, let's assume there is plenty of free memory, so the operating system just increases the size of the working set for the process. When the user closes the spreadsheet, the memory allocated to store it is released. When the user

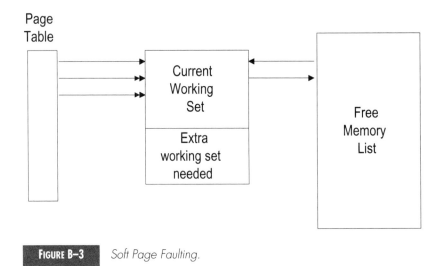

Page
Table

Current
Working
Set

Extra
working set
needed

Free
Memory
List

FIGURE B-3   *Soft Page Faulting.*

exits the Excel program, the memory used to store it is released. If we examined the user's working set at this time, we would have no idea of the load that had been put on memory earlier. One useful piece of information that can be retrieved from various monitoring tools is the peak working set for a process. This will tell us the largest demand that the process had placed on the system's memory resource.

PAGE FAULTING

For the next example, let's assume the same user has just loaded the Excel program, but this time, when the new spreadsheet is created, the system does not have sufficient free memory to increase the working set size of the process to the total amount necessary. For example, the operating system may allocate memory to store half of the spreadsheet but will not let the process have any more. Examine Figure B-3.

The operating system protects itself from running out of physical memory by restricting processes from allocating more memory when the amount of free memory is low. But what happens to the user running Excel that needs more memory? The operating system plays a juggling game. When the user process will not be allowed to extend its working set any further, for every page of memory that it receives from the operating system, it must give one back. The page of memory given up by the process goes on the end of the free page list. This sounds worse than it is. The process retains its pointer in the page table for the page that it gives back to the operating system; it just is not part of the process working set any longer. If the process requests access to that page at a future time, the operating system must return it to the working set. This is the definition of a page fault.

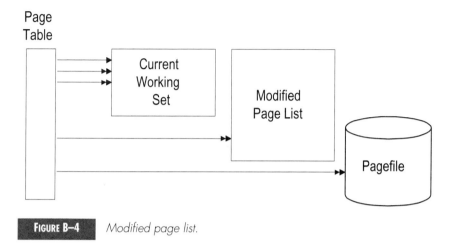

Page
Table

Current
Working
Set

Modified
Page List

Pagefile

FIGURE B–4 *Modified page list.*

There are a few different situations that could arise if a page given up by the process is needed again. For the first example, assume that the page released by the process is on the free page list. This is simple: The operating system gives the page back to the working set of the process but in turn may require another one to be released. Since the requested data was still in memory on the free page list, this is known as a soft page fault.

For our second example, assume the data in the page released by the process contains part of the Excel program. Before the process can request that the page be returned, there is a large demand on memory, and the page is allocated to another process. The free page list is a common pool of memory to be used for all processes. At this point, the operating system must retrieve the Excel program from disk. This is known as a hard page fault. Hard page faults have a larger impact on performance since they involve disk I/O, one of the slower hardware components.

For the last example, assume the page given up by the process does not contain a portion of the Excel executable; rather, it contains part of the spreadsheet the user is building. The danger here is that if this page is placed on the free page list, works its way to the top, and gets allocated to another process, the data is lost. If the user has modified the page of memory being released by the process, the page is stored in a special location called the modified page list. The modified page list is a portion of physical memory dedicated to storing this type of data. See Figure B-4. Since the modified page list is a set amount of memory, all of it could possibly be used. At this point, the data in the modified page list is copied to disk to a special file, known as a page file, named pagefile.sys. During this whole process, the page table for the process still has a pointer to the data, no matter where it is, and can always retrieve it. If the data is retrieved from the modified page list, it is a soft page fault. If it were retrieved from the page file, it would be a hard page fault. It is very important that the page file not fill up. If this happens, the modified page list will fill up next. Finally, processes will begin to hang when they need to place data in the modified page list.

MEMORY POOLS

The Windows 2000 operating system has reserved areas of memory called pools. These pools of memory are used to store critical operating system data structures. There are two types of pooled memory, referred to as paged and non-paged. The non-paged pool area is where the operating system stores its most critical information because the data will always be guaranteed to be in memory, since it cannot be paged out. The sizes of the paged and non-paged pool areas are defined by the operating system, but like most things, it can be overridden in the registry. In certain situations, the system may need to create something in a non-paged pool and not have sufficient memory to do so. When this happens, it is called a non-paged pool failure. Non-paged pool failures generally mean that an application will not be able to perform its requested task.

In many situations, non-paged pool failures can be associated with a misbehaving program with a "memory leak." A program with a memory leak is one that repetitively does something to allocate memory but never frees the memory when completed. Memory leaks can be hard to find, and worse, they will disappear, at least temporarily, if the system is rebooted. The Processes tab in Task Manager is a good place to start when examining memory problems.

ANALYZING MEMORY

From the previous discussion on virtual memory, page faulting occurs when a process requires more memory than its working set does. If the working set for a process is large enough, the process will never page fault. Remember, however, that the working set is the amount of physical memory that a process can own, so arbitrarily allocating large working sets would severely impact how many processes the operating system could support. In a virtual memory operating system, some page faulting is expected, the goal being to keep the number of page faults low.

Other operating systems I have worked with allow the system administrator to define working set values on a per-user basis. This can be beneficial to the administrator who will dedicate the time to monitoring each user and application to determine optimal working set values. The Windows 2000 operating system takes a different approach: It defines the working set values and then will increase or decrease the working sets of processes as they are running in an effort to minimize page faulting. For example, a process that is generating a high number of page faults will get an increase in its working set, whereas a process that is generating no page faults may get its working set size reduced. Since working set sizes will determine the amount of page faulting that occurs, by adjusting the working sets for processes, Windows NT is sometimes classified as self tuning. This is the reason for the earlier statement that in Windows NT, performance analysis is performed more than performance tuning is.

When analyzing memory, ask the following questions:

- Is the system generating too many page faults?
- If so, which process is generating the largest number of page faults?
- Can the amount of free memory be increased?

Performance Monitor

Windows 2000 comes standard with a monitoring tool called Performance Monitor. It is very useful for collecting all kinds of data, but it does not do any kind of analysis. The interpretation of the data collected by Performance Monitor is left to the administrator. There are some standard documented values that can be compared against the data supplied by Performance Monitor to determine whether the various components of the system, CPU, memory, and disk are performing within acceptable limits.

A key point to make about Performance Monitor is that it does not know anything about activity that occurred before it was started. For example, a user may call and say the system is sluggish. You decide to start Performance Monitor, and everything looks fine. The system could have had a page fault rate of 50 per second when the user noticed the system degradation, but if Performance Monitor was not running at that time, it did not collect that spike in page faults. So, should Performance Monitor be left running all the time? Some say that this in itself generates a system load. Performance Monitor has a sample interval that defines how often it should take a snapshot of the performance data. If there is a concern about Performance Monitor itself degrading the system, increase the sample interval. If you have ever taken a statistics course, you know that the more samples of data you have, the more accurate the result. Increase the sample interval and accept the less-accurate result.

Performance Monitor returns current, minimum, maximum, and average values for the data being collected. As a rule, be concerned about average numbers that are greater than acceptable limits. There will often be spikes, but if they are short, they will only have a slight impact on performance. Average numbers must be generated properly. For example, collecting data over a 24-hour period and looking at the average is useless information if the systems are only used 8 or 9 hours per day. The start and stop times for Performance Monitor data collection should parallel system usage.

VIEWS

Performance Monitor supports four different "views" of the data it collects. The first and most common view is the chart view, which is a graphical display of collected data.

The second is a log view. The log view is not actually a view of data at all but a mechanism by which to record data to a file to be examined at a later time, possibly in the form of a chart.

The third view is a report. This provides very simplistic reporting of either real-time data or data retrieved from a log. To generate more professional-looking reports, experiment with saving collected data as a comma-separated value (CSV) file or as a tab-separated value (TSV) file and then importing the data into Excel or Access.

The last view is an alert. This view can be very useful if implemented properly. An alert is a counter and a threshold value for that counter. As Performance Monitor runs, it compares the data collected with the threshold for defined alerts. If the data exceeds the threshold, Performance Monitor can be configured to send a message to another computer in reference to the problem counter. The messages appear as a pop-up window, similar to the "Send Message" utility. This is very handy for an administrator that manages many systems, as all systems could be configured to send alerts to the computer the administrator normally uses.

COUNTERS

Counters are the raw data collected by Performance Monitor. Most counters provide detail on the minimum, maximum, and average values collected for the counter since Performance Monitor was started. Average values will be the most important when looking for trends on system performance. Also, remember to get a large enough sample so that the average numbers show realistic data. For example, monitoring between 8:00 and 9:00 A.M. will give very different results than monitoring between the hours of noon and 1:00 P.M. (if your office follows any kind of normal lunch schedule).

There are a couple of counters that are not collected by default. For example, disk I/O counters are not automatically collected. The argument is that collecting performance data for disks can itself contribute to system degradation. Therefore, it is necessary to manually activate the collection of disk counters. It is done by issuing the command "Diskperf –Y." If the disk configuration includes disk RAID sets, the command is "Diskperf –YE." This enables the collecting of disk counters until manually disabled with the command "Diskperf –N."

Another component that is not configured for performance data collection by default is the TCP/IP protocol stack. To collect and view TCP/IP traffic, it is necessary to load the Simple Network Management Protocol (SNMP) software that ships with Windows 2000.

OBJECTS AND INSTANCES

When a system is monitored, it is actually monitoring the behavior of its objects such as processes, threads, and memory. In Windows 2000, an object is the standard mechanism for identifying and using system resources. There are object types and instances of objects. An example of an object type would be a process. When a process is created by the operating system, it is actually creating an instance of the process object.

In the Performance Monitor utility, an object can be loosely defined as a category of counters. For example, when the Process object is selected, all counters pertinent to analyzing the performance of a process will be made available.

Depending on the object selected, one or more instances may be available for monitoring purposes. For example, the process object will have an instance for every process currently running on the system. This is useful when it has already been determined that the system as a whole is overloaded, and the next step is to narrow down to a specific process. The administrator can simply select a process, such as SQL Server, and monitor various activities such as its page faulting rate and user time consumption.

Some objects contain an instance named Total. This provides an easy method to obtain theresource usage for all instances of the object. For example, an administrator might want to find out the total of all process working sets. This is easily obtained by selecting the process object, the total instance, and the working set counter.

Certain objects and their associated counters are present on all systems. Other counters, however, are application specific. For example, SQL Server and Exchange Server will install new objects and counters when the software is loaded.

Analyzing Disk Activity

The disk hardware is one of the slowest hardware components of the overall system. Because it is slow by nature, a bottleneck in the disk subsystem is magnified. Thankfully, faster disk configurations are appearing on a regular basis, but this does not help if money has already been invested in a disk configuration that cannot be replaced every 6–12 months. Disk hardware generally consists of two components, the disk and the controller. It is usually the disk that will be the source of a bottleneck, if there is one, but do not discount the possibility of the controller as a potential bottleneck. With the number of devices that can be connected to a SCSI bus, it deserves to be analyzed.

LAZY WRITES

Since the disk subsystem is one of the slower parts of the computer, the less time the operating system spends transferring data to or from the disk, the better the system will perform. The amount of data a program usually reads or writes is relatively small. Approximately 70–80% of the total time that a disk access takes is hardware related. The hardware time involved does not change significantly, based on the size of the disk I/O being performed. Therefore, if larger amounts of data could be transferred between memory and disk at one time, the average time per disk I/O would be reduced. This is the concept of a lazy write. An application program issues writes to the disk. The operating system lets the application think the disk write has completed, but actually the data is being saved in memory. At a later time, when there is enough data, or the system is less busy, the data is written to the disk. This mechanism limits the amount of times the disk hardware is accessed. Depending on the application, slight risks could arise from lazy writing. For example, suppose an application uses two files to store data. The application could issue two writes, one to each file; one may get written, and the other could be cached by the lazy write mechanism. Now suppose there is a power failure. The second file was never actually updated, and now the files are out of sync.

The action of lazy writing is the default for the Windows 2000 operating system. It is the responsibility of the application developer to disable lazy write support within the application.

The act of lazy writing can lead to some very confusing displays in Performance Monitor. For example, a program that is performing lazy writes will show little or no disk activity for a period of time, then show a large spike on disk data transfers. At first glance, this may seem to be a problem, but in reality it is not. One lengthy disk access will take less time overall than the same amount of data broken up into smaller disk I/Os.

Another misleading feature of lazy writing is that it makes the processor resource appear busier. This is because the operating system is not issuing a large number of disk I/Os that can cause the processor to wait for the I/O to complete before it can resume processing. For example, a processor running an application that is updating a file may appear 50% busy without lazy writing enabled, but it might appear 95% busy with lazy writing enabled. The information that is not available is that the application would complete much faster with lazy writing enabled because the processor was more efficient by saving the disk writes and performing a large number of writes at one time. For example, the application may run for 5 minutes without lazy writing enabled with processor time accounting for 50%, or 2.5 minutes. With lazy writing, the application may complete in 2 minutes, with the application accounting for 95% of the time. So, the question arises, has a processor bottleneck been introduced to alleviate a disk bottleneck? No, because lazy writing will make better use of the processor because the waiting by the processor for disk I/Os to complete has been minimized. The application still consumes the same amount of processor time; it just does it over a smaller elapsed time period. Since applications will use the processor at a greater rate with lazy writing enabled, application response times could be impacted in unforeseen ways. But the main idea is that more of the potential processor time is available to applications, which should increase throughput.

This is not always possible, but it is useful to know whether an application supports lazy writing, especially when evaluating the disk subsystem in Performance Monitor.

DISK QUEUES

All of the different types of disk hardware can make evaluations confusing. For example, which is closer to being a bottleneck, a disk with a 12-millisecond access time performing 25 I/Os per second or a disk with a 15-millisecond access time performing 20 I/Os per second? There are all kinds of algorithms to calculate the average response time for a disk and then compare that value with acceptable ranges. It is not necessary to perform those calculations. It is possible to determine how busy any disk is by examining its queue length. A disk queue is the number of outstanding I/Os that have been issued to a disk but are in a waiting state because the disk is busy serving another I/O request. The nice feature about the disk queue length is that it becomes unnecessary to know the relative speed of the disks being analyzed. A disk with a 10-millisecond access time and a queue length of 1 is just as overloaded as a disk with a 15-millisecond access time and a queue length of 1.

Disk queues can be examined at the physical disk and logical disk level. To determine whether a disk is a bottleneck, examine the physical disk queue length. Once it is determined that a specific disk is overloaded, examine the queue length of each logical drive on the disk. This may help in determining which application is the cause of the excessive I/O requests.

Object: Physical disk or logical disk

Counter: Current disk queue length

What to look for: The average queue length should be less than 2 for the physical disk.

FILE SYSTEM CACHES

The file system cache is a portion of physical memory reserved for frequently used file system data. File system data is any information that would be necessary to retrieve a file from disk. The directory entry for a file would be an example of data that could be stored in the file system cache. The NT file system is a B-tree directory structure. Think of it as an inverted tree with many branches, with files being at the very end of the smallest branches, like leaves. To locate a file on a disk, it is necessary to traverse the entire tree from top to bottom, eventually reaching the file entry. Every branch is a possible disk I/O. It is possible for one file access to generate three or more disk I/Os. The file system cache stores recently and frequently used portions of the tree. Any time that file system, or "tree" data, can be located in memory instead of reading the data from the disk, performance will be better. Again, this is because the disk is one of the slowest, if not the slowest, hardware component.

The memory resource is critical to file system caching. If the amount of free memory on a Windows NT system drops below 4MB, the memory allocated for file system caching is reclaimed by the operating system to solve the shortage of available memory.

Object: Memory
Counter: Cache bytes
What to look for: This is the size of the file system cache; it should not be zero.

Object: Cache
Counter: MDL read hits %
What to look for: This is the percentage of time that data is found in the cache. Anything over 70% is good.

Analyzing Processor Activity

The processor is probably the easiest of the major components of the hardware to analyze. Every process running on the system is competing for processor time. There is an operating system component called the scheduler that decides which process can use the processor. A process uses the CPU for a period of time known as a time slice. When a process has used its time slice, the scheduler will move another process into the CPU. The scheduler makes its decision based on the priority of any processes waiting to use the CPU.

The main focus when examining the CPU resource as a potential bottleneck is, "How busy is the processor?" This is represented as a percentage value, such as 60%. If your processor shows 100% busy, you may feel you are getting your money's worth from the system, but this is not the case. As a general rule, a processor should not average more than 70–80% busy.

When analyzing processor performance, ask the following questions:

- Is the processor averaging more than 70% busy?
- Is there a processor queue? If not, the CPU is probably not a bottleneck at this time.
- If yes, is the majority user time or privileged time?
- If privileged time, is there a memory or disk resource bottleneck?
- If user time, what process is consuming the majority of the CPU resource?
- Can the amount of CPU activity be reduced?

USER TIME

Processor usage is divided into two categories, user time and privileged time. User time is generally considered to be running application code, not operating system code. For example, the amount of processor time spent executing instructions from a program such as Excel is classified as user time. This should be the majority of processor usage.

Object: Processor
Counter: User time
What to look for: Should be 60% or more of total processor time in use. If it is less, this is a sign of excessive operating system overhead, such as paging, disk activity, or interrupts.

PRIVILEGED TIME

Privileged time is processor time that is consumed running operating system code instead of user application code. Examples of privileged time include performing disk I/O and handling page faults generated by a user process. It is easy to get led down the wrong path here. Overloaded memory and disk resources can generate what appear to be processor bottlenecks by generating a lot of privileged mode activity. This is the reason that the memory and disk resources should be analyzed before the processor resource is analyzed. Problems that are discovered with the disk and memory components should be resolved before doing a thorough analysis of the processor.

Object: Processor
Counter: Privileged time
What to look for: The average queue length should be less than .2.

PROCESSOR QUEUE

A processor queue is the list of threads waiting to use the processor but cannot use it because it is occupied. The processor queue length is the best measure of whether the CPU is a bottleneck, even better than processor utilization is. Here is why. A program that performs no I/O and only does calculations can make the processor appear to be between 90 and 100% busy, especially if it is the only process that currently needs the CPU. To the untrained observer, a processor bottleneck may be declared, but there isn't one necessarily. What if the processor queue length is zero? This means there are no jobs waiting to use the CPU. Can there really be a bottleneck if no processes are getting blocked from using the processor? In the situation where a processor does show 90–100% busy but the processor queue length is low, the CPU is not currently a bottleneck, but adding new applications or users could lead to creating a processor bottleneck.

The one situation where the processor could be considered a bottleneck with no processor queue is when one extremely intensive CPU application is running, such as a CAD application. The response time of the application in this case will correlate directly with the speed of the processor.

Object: System
Counter: Processor queue length
What to look for: The average queue length should be less than .2.

Analyzing Network Activity

It does not matter how well the cluster nodes are running if the network between the client and the server is experiencing performance problems. Network performance can be impacted by numerous factors. The network could be busy because of large print jobs being transmitted or numerous file transfers. Malfunctioning devices introducing "noise" to the cable can also impact the network. Since Ethernet is single channel, meaning only one device can be transmitting successfully at any point in time, a faulty network device can slow an entire network segment.

NETWORK MONITOR

The Network Monitor utility has functionality similar to a network sniffer. It can collect network traffic and do some basic analysis, such as which node is sending the most data or which node is the destination for the majority of the network traffic. The Network Monitor utility does not take the place of components such as sniffers. There is information necessary to network administrators that Network Monitor does not provide, such as the rate of collisions on the cable. A collision is when two systems attempt to use an Ethernet cable at the same time. If this is the case, there is no guarantee that either packet will reach its destination. The sending systems will detect a collision and will resend the packet in question. The number, or rate, of collision is useful in determining what kind of true throughput is being achieved on an Ethernet segment. Believe it or not, on a 10MB Ethernet segment, 3–4MB of throughput can normally be expected.

Network Monitor has two distinct components. First is the Network Monitor agent. The function of the agent is to collect the data from the network. The second piece of the software is the Network Monitor tool. The Network Monitor tool accepts information from the Network Monitor agent and displays it graphically.

There are two versions of the Network Monitor utility. The first one ships with Windows NT. This version of Network Monitor only has the capability to examine and analyze the network traffic to or from the node that it is installed on. This is useful for examining whether the network for a given server is busy, but it does not give any information regarding the overall load on the network cable.

The second version of Network Monitor is bundled in with Microsoft's Systems Management Server product, which is part of the BackOffice suite of products. This version of Network Monitor is a more complete solution in that it monitors all traffic on a network segment. It also has the capability to monitor remote network segments by attaching to remote Network Monitor agents. This can be useful in a support desk situation where clients are on various network segments.

Cluster Performance

The first step in analyzing a cluster's performance is to view each cluster member independently. The Windows NT environment on each node is totally separate. The only normal communications that occur between nodes are the heartbeat packets used to determine whether cluster members are on-line or off-line. The amount of network traffic is minimal. Recall that the Cluster Server software can use a separate cable for cluster communications. This includes the heartbeat messages and any cluster group movement between members due to a failure or a request initiated by the Cluster Administrator utility.

To achieve the best performance, the approach should be to balance the load between cluster members. Let's briefly review each primary system component and discuss possible balancing techniques.

MEMORY

The primary clue that a memory bottleneck exists is page faulting. If both cluster members are similar in hardware configurations, the first thought may be to split the load of four applications by placing two on each processor. However, this does not take into account the memory consumption and processing characteristics of the individual applications. One poorly written application can generate as many page faults as three or more efficiently designed programs. By using Task Manager and Performance Monitor, the amount of page faulting for each application can be determined.

Should applications be allocated between cluster members to minimize page faulting or to balance the amount of free memory? There is a performance penalty when the amount of free memory drops below 4MB. Memory that is normally used for file system caching is reclaimed, disabling caching for the most part. It should be a high priority to guarantee that both cluster members have at least 4–6MB of free memory.

Realize that if a resource is moved between cluster nodes to relocate a portion of the page faulting activity, there is the potential for an increase in disk I/O. This will occur if the page faults incurred by the cluster member are hard page faults. If the cluster member is already incurring waits on disk I/Os, reconsider moving the cluster resource. Processor activity will increase with the number of page faults because a page fault is an operating system routine. If the processor is already recording a high percentage of privileged time, again reconsider moving the application.

DISK I/O

The main idea to keep in mind when analyzing disk I/O performance is, "Less is more." The fewer disk I/Os that are performed, the better the system performance will be. Since a disk can only be accessed by one cluster member, balancing the I/Os between cluster members is not an option. Even if it were an option, splitting I/Os to a single disk between two or more computers does not make the disk hardware work any less. Actually, it would most likely make it work harder because the various computers would probably be reading data at different locations on the disk!

The goal should be to spread the I/Os across the different physical disk resources to achieve the lowest possible I/O wait times, not to balance the number of I/Os. Balancing the number of I/Os across the different disk resources does not take into account variables such as the relative speed of each disk or the size of the disk I/O being performed. To accomplish this, first monitor the disk queue length of each of the disk resources. If disk queues are out of balance, the way to even them out is to move applications between disks. One of the problems with a tool such as Performance Monitor is that it does not supply information on what are sometimes called "hot" files. These are the files that are the target of the majority of disk I/Os. There is no clean way to determine which application is generating the disk I/Os, since I/O rates cannot be monitored by process. If the physical disk resource is divided into multiple logical drives, the counter Logical Disk in Performance Monitor will display the amount of disk I/O to each logical drive. This should help to determine which applications are generating the most disk I/Os.

If possible, attempt to take advantage of file system caching to alleviate any disk I/O problems. Experiment with locating the more I/O-intensive applications on the cluster member that has more memory available. The cluster member should have a larger file system cache, which may in turn reduce disk I/Os.

PROCESSOR

You may recall that processor time consists of user time and privileged time. Privileged time occurs when the operating system is performing work outside the applications that are currently running. Page faulting and disk I/O are good examples of events that consume privileged time. If the memory and disk I/O resources have already been analyzed and the load allocated between the cluster members, the processor privileged time is inherently balanced between processors.

Privileged time is not generally the largest consumer of processor time. If it is, this is a problem that needs to be analyzed. Generally, the majority of processor time should be in user mode. This is the time spent actually executing the code of the applications that are currently running.

The goal is to allocate cluster resources between the cluster members and balance the amount of processor time used. This will give the best possible response times to clients of all applications.

There may be a situation where one application is considered to have a higher degree of importance. If this is the case, an arbitrary decision will need to be made regarding how much more of the processing load will be shifted to one of the cluster members. As a rule, a processor should never be loaded to the point where it continually runs 70% busy or higher.

GLOSSARY

ARP   Address resolution protocol. The method by which TCP/IP converts TCP/IP addresses to MAC addresses to properly address a network packet.

Bottleneck   In system performance terms, the hardware component, usually disk, memory, or processor, which hinders performance of a system from being better. It is sometimes referred to as "the limiting resource."

Client/server   An application design method that divides its processing into a front end (client) and a back end (server).

Cluster   A group of two or more independent computers that are addressed and used as a single system.

Cluster API   A set of program routines that allow application developers to interface with the Cluster Service and perform tasks such as creating new resources and initiating a failure on a resource.

Cluster-aware application   An application that includes Cluster API routines to be capable of interfacing with the Cluster Service.

Cluster.exe   A command lines program that allows an administrator to perform cluster administration. The Cluster.exe program is useful in situations where a series of similar commands are going to be issued.

Cluster log   A log file of important cluster events and errors. To implement cluster logging, it is necessary to define the environment variable CLUSTERLOG to the path where the log file should be stored.

Cluster member   A computer running Windows NT Server, Enterprise Edition, or Windows 2000 Advanced Server and the Cluster Service.

Cluster service   A component of the Cluster software that is implemented as a Windows 2000 service. The Cluster Service manages all aspects of the cluster's operation and manages the configuration database. Each node in a cluster runs an instance of the Cluster Service.

Cluster transition   The time necessary to relocate resources and groups to the proper cluster members when a cluster member exits or rejoins the cluster. Depending on the number of resources that need to be moved, cluster transition can range from 5 to 30 seconds. During this time, all user processing is suspended.

Dependency   The requirement of one resource needing another resource in order to function properly. A resource does not contain all of its configuration information. For example, a network name resource logically represents a computer name on the network, but a computer name is really a representation of a TCP/IP address. The network name resource does not have a TCP/IP address as part of its properties. What it does have is a dependency on an IP address resource to fulfill the address requirement.

Disk mirroring   A disk fault-tolerant method that writes data simultaneously to two disks using the same disk controller. The disks operate in parallel, storing and updating the same files. Disk mirroring protects against a disk failure and file corruption generated by a hardware malfunction. It does not protect against a software-generated corruption such as a file being opened and modified with the incorrect tool such as Notepad.

Disk striping   A disk configuration where multiple disks are treated as one logical disk. Data is written across the disks as opposed to filling one disk and moving to the next as with a volume set. Disk striping provides no fault tolerance.

Disk striping with parity   Similar to disk striping except that one disk in the set will store parity information. If a member disk of a stripe set with parity fails, the parity information in conjunction with the data available from the remaining disks can be used to regenerate the data that was stored on the failed disk.

Distributed lock manager   Software used in a shared resource cluster model to coordinate user activity on multiple cluster members to concurrent access to a file.

Distributed transaction coordinator resource   A cluster resource capable of functioning as a coordinator in a Microsoft Transaction Server environment. The Transaction Server product allows for guaranteed transaction processing in chronological order.

DNS   Domain Name Server. In industry-standard method of providing name resolution. A static database of computer names and TCP/IP addresses is maintained on one or more DNS servers. For a client to use DNS for resolution, it must contain a software component referred to as a DNS resolver. This is included in most TCP/IP implementations.

Domain   There are two definitions. In Windows 2000, a domain is logical group of computers that share a security account database. In TCP/IP, a domain is a logical group of computers for naming purposes, such as ucicorp.com.

Domain Controller   A computer running Windows 2000 Advanced Server that holds a copy of the domain account database. The backup domain controller can validate logon requests against its read-only copy of the user account information.

Dynamic Link Library (DLL)   A file that is a library of functions that one or more programs can share. The addition of new resource types to the cluster is generally implemented by providing a DLL with the program routines necessary to support a resource type.

Dynamic load balancing   A method of allocating the application load between cluster members based on the current processing load of the members. As the processing activity on cluster members changes, application resources can be dynamically relocated to the lesser used processor to provide the best possible client response times.

Failback   The action of moving a resource back to the cluster member designated to be the resource's preferred owner. By default, resources are owned by their preferred owners, so a failback will only occur if the resource has been moved from its preferred owner. This would most likely be the result of a failover.

Failover   The process of taking one or more resources off-line on one cluster member and bringing them on-line on another cluster member.

Failover threshold   The number of times a resource failure will be allowed before the resource is moved to another cluster member.

Failure   When a resource stops functioning properly. Cluster resource failure is detected by either the *IsAlive* or *LooksAlive* timers.

Fault tolerant   The capability to offer uninterrupted availability in the event of a hardware or software failure.

Fiber channel   Fibre Channel is an ANSI standard gigabit networking technology that maps IP and SCSI for native connection of servers and storage devices.

File share resource   A standard shared directory that is accessible via the normal NetBIOS naming convention, or UNC name, such as \\server\share. Implemented by the Cluster Server as a resource.

File system cache   A portion of physical memory that the operating system uses to store file system data such as directory and file header information. The goal of the cache is to reduce the amount of actual disk I/O the operating system performs.

Generic application resource   A standard batch file or executable file that is supported by the Cluster Server software as a resource.

Generic service resource   A Windows 2000 service that is supported by the Cluster Service as a resource. Not all Windows 2000 services are capable of running as a generic service resource.

Group   A logical organization of resources. A resource is not failed from one cluster member to another, groups are. Allows the administrator to place dependent resources into one unit to guarantee that the same cluster member will always own a resource and all its dependent resources.

Heartbeat   A message sent between cluster members to notify each other of their existence. If heartbeat messages are not received from a cluster member, it is considered to have gone off-line, and all resources that it owned are failed over to the remaining cluster members.

Host name   An alphanumeric representation of a TCP/IP address. Host names are used by TCP/IP utilities such as ftp, telnet, and, Ping.

IIS virtual root resource   A cluster resource to be used with Internet Information Server that supports a unique WWW or FTP service. Cluster software does not support virtual roots containing access information.

IP address resource   A valid TCP/IP address that is supported as a cluster resource.

IsAlive timer   Compared with the *LooksAlive* timer, this check is a more thorough check of a resource.

Lazy write   An operating system method of minimizing physical disk access. When an application issues a disk write, the data is held in memory, but the application is notified that the write has completed. The operating system then performs the physical disk I/O at a time when the system is less busy.

LPR   A method by which printing is supported over a TCP/IP network. Consists of a server, or daemon, and a TCP/IP addressable printer.

LooksAlive timer   A timer that triggers a quick check by the Cluster Service to determine if resources that are considered to be on-line are actually available.

Message queue server resource   A cluster resource capable of performing the role of server in a Microsoft Message Queue Server environment. Message Queue Server is a message delivery mechanism that can be used by programmers to transport application-independent messages across a network, with guaranteed delivery, even if the target computer is not currently available.

NetBIOS name   An alphanumeric name that is used by clients to reference a computer on the network. NetBIOS names are used as the server in a UNC name.

Network name resource   A cluster resource that offers a valid host or NetBIOS name on the network.

NTFS-NT File System   A file system supported by Windows 2000 that supports user-level security with access control lists.

Off-line   The state of a resource or group that classifies it as unavailable. When used in context with a cluster member, off-line implies the cluster member may not be booted or the Cluster Service on the node in question may not be functioning properly.

On-line   The state of a resource or group that classifies it as available. When used in context with a cluster member, on-line implies the other cluster members are receiving heartbeats from the cluster member in question.

Page fault   The function performed by the operating system when data needs to be mapped into memory. Excessive page faulting is a sign that the system does not have enough memory to support its current workload.

Paging   An operating system event where data is moved between disk and memory.

Paused   A cluster member state where it does not accept any new connections. Administrators can place a cluster member in this state before shutting it down to minimize the effect of cluster transition on the client base.

Physical disk resource   A disk attached to the shared SCSI bus to store shared directories and applications that are to be implemented as cluster resources.

Possible owners   A list of cluster members that are capable of supporting a specific resource. A resource can only be failed over to a cluster member that appears in this list.

Preferred owner   The cluster member that should own a group when both the group and cluster member are on-line. A preferred owner is the cluster member a resource will be failed back to if and when the cluster member returns to an on-line state. Static load balancing of resources is accomplished by having one group per cluster member and defining a different preferred owner for each group.

Print spooler resource   A print spooler that is supported as a cluster resource. The print spooler resource can support one or more print queues. Printers typically shared in this manner will be network printers (lpr) as opposed to local attached printers, since the print server function can move between cluster members.

Private network   A network segment used by cluster members strictly for cluster communications traffic such as heartbeat packets and resource failover.

Process   The object used by the operating system to execute a program. A process is allocated system resources, such as memory, and is therefore a common focus of performance analysis. A process has one or more threads.

Public network   The network segment used by clients to gain access to the cluster and its related resources.

Quorum   Means "majority." Guarantees that all cluster members participate in a single cluster. This is accomplished by allowing only the cluster member that owns the quorum resource to create the cluster. A cluster member that does not own the quorum resource can only join an existing cluster. Avoids what is known as a "partitioned cluster," where two cluster members that boot at the same time both create a cluster because they do not detect one already in existence.

Quorum resource   The disk that signals to a booting cluster member whether the cluster already exists and it should join the cluster or whether the cluster needs to be created.

RAID   Redundant Array of Independent Disks. RAID is a storage mechanism that uses two or more disks to provide one logical disk that supports varying levels of performance improvement and fault tolerance. RAID can be implemented at the hardware or software levels. The Microsoft Cluster Service only supports hardware RAID on the shared SCSI bus.

Registry   The set of files that Windows 2000 uses to store all configuration information. Can only be viewed and modified with a registry editor such as the regedt32.exe utility.

Resource   A physical or logical entity managed by a cluster member. A resource offers a service to clients in a client/server application.

Resource DLL   A set of routines that facilitates communication between a resource and the Cluster Service.

Resoure monitor   A cluster software component that provides communication between one or more resources and the Cluster Service. The resource monitor is also used to determine whether a resource has failed by using the *IsAlive* and *LooksAlive* timers to poll the resource.

Restart   The action performed by the cluster software when it is determined that a resource has failed due to a lack of response from the *IsAlive* and *LooksAlive* timers. The cluster will reexecute the command used to originally bring the resource on-line.

Scalability   The capability to incrementally add one or more systems to an existing cluster when the cluster reaches its processing capacity.

SCSI bus   The connection medium used to daisy-chain SCSI devices that are serviced by the same controller. There are various SCSI specifications, such as SCSI-2 and Wide SCSI. Each specification uses a different hardware bus.

SCSI device   A device connected to a SCSI bus. Each device requires a unique SCSI id. Examples of SCSI devices include disks, CD-ROMs, tape drives, and scanners.

SCSI id   The logical address assigned to every device on a SCSI bus. The basic rule is that every device on a SCSI bus requires a unique SCSI id, thus limiting the number of devices that can be supported on one bus.

SCSI termination   The mechanism of dissipating an electronic signal to prevent bounce back on a cable. Termination is used on various busses, including SCSI and Ethernet.

Service   An application that runs on a Windows 2000 system that is not associated with the desktop or the currently logged-in user. A service is the equivalent of a daemon from the UNIX environment.

Service pack   An update to the operating system that corrects documented problems. Whenever files are loaded from the operating system distribution media, the service pack needs to be reapplied, since files the service pack had repaired could be overwritten.

Shared nothing cluster model   An implementation of a cluster that does not allow resources to be accessed simultaneously by multiple cluster members. This is the cluster model implemented by Microsoft Cluster Server.

Shared resource cluster model   An implementation of a cluster that supports multiple cluster members accessing the same resource, such as a file, simultaneously. While this implementation allows for more dynamic load balancing, the overhead involved in supporting the resource access is high.

Static load balancing   A method of load balancing processing activity between computers where the administrator is required to manually assign the applications that should execute on each processor. This method does not automatically move applications between processors based on current processing loads.

Thread   An execution context of a process. A process that is multithreaded has multiple, independent execution contexts at one time.

Time service   A resource supported by the Cluster Service that maintains consistent time settings between cluster members.

UNC   A standard naming convention for referencing computers and file shares on a network. The format is \\computer_name\share_name.

Virtual memory   The mechanism by which operating systems allow processes to address more memory than is possibly available on the system.

Virtual server   A collection of resources that supply the appearance of a Windows 2000 Server to clients. A virtual server generally refers to all the resources, such as an IP address and network name resource, necessary to run a specific application.

WINS   Windows Internet Naming Service. A WINS Server is a name-resolution server that supports dynamic registration of information from application servers. To use a WINS Server for name resolution, the host must be capable of being a WINS client. Currently, only Microsoft operating systems support WINS client functionality.

Working set   The amount of physical memory that a process is allowed to reserve for ownership. Process working sets may be adjusted by the operating system depending on current available memory on the system.

INDEX

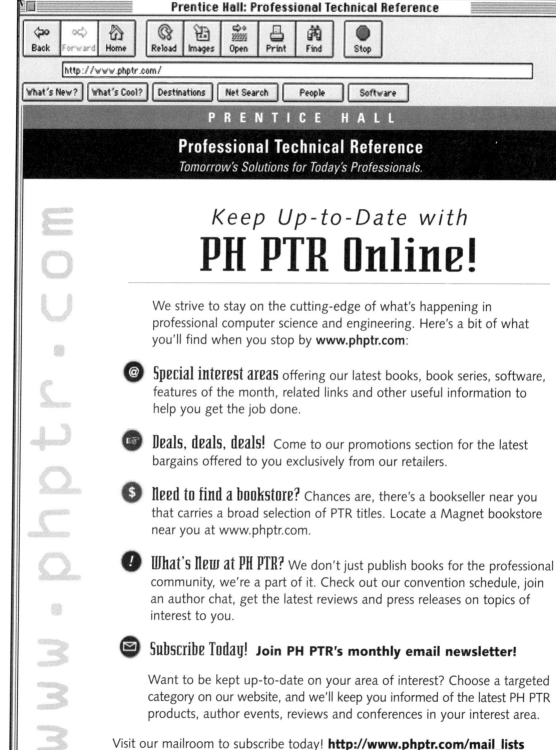

LICENSE AGREEMENT AND LIMITED WARRANTY

READ THE FOLLOWING TERMS AND CONDITIONS CAREFULLY BEFORE OPENING THIS SOFTWARE MEDIA PACKAGE. THIS LEGAL DOCUMENT IS AN AGREEMENT BETWEEN YOU AND PRENTICE-HALL, INC. (THE "COMPANY"). BY OPENING THIS SEALED SOFTWARE MEDIA PACKAGE, YOU ARE AGREEING TO BE BOUND BY THESE TERMS AND CONDITIONS. IF YOU DO NOT AGREE WITH THESE TERMS AND CONDITIONS, DO NOT OPEN THE SOFTWARE MEDIA PACKAGE. PROMPTLY RETURN THE UNOPENED SOFTWARE MEDIA PACKAGE AND ALL ACCOMPANYING ITEMS TO THE PLACE YOU OBTAINED THEM FOR A FULL REFUND OF ANY SUMS YOU HAVE PAID.

1.   **GRANT OF LICENSE:** In consideration of your payment of the license fee, which is part of the price you paid for this product, and your agreement to abide by the terms and conditions of this Agreement, the Company grants to you a nonexclusive right to use and display the copy of the enclosed software program (hereinafter the "SOFTWARE") on a single computer (i.e., with a single CPU) at a single location so long as you comply with the terms of this Agreement. The Company reserves all rights not expressly granted to you under this Agreement.

2.   **OWNERSHIP OF SOFTWARE:** You own only the magnetic or physical media (the enclosed software media) on which the SOFTWARE is recorded or fixed, but the Company retains all the rights, title, and ownership to the SOFTWARE recorded on the original software media copy(ies) and all subsequent copies of the SOFTWARE, regardless of the form or media on which the original or other copies may exist. This license is not a sale of the original SOFTWARE or any copy to you.

3.   **COPY RESTRICTIONS:** This SOFTWARE and the accompanying printed materials and user manual (the "Documentation") are the subject of copyright. You may not copy the Documentation or the SOFTWARE, except that you may make a single copy of the SOFTWARE for backup or archival purposes only. You may be held legally responsible for any copying or copyright infringement which is caused or encouraged by your failure to abide by the terms of this restriction.

4.   **USE RESTRICTIONS:** You may not network the SOFTWARE or otherwise use it on more than one computer or computer terminal at the same time. You may physically transfer the SOFTWARE from one computer to another provided that the SOFTWARE is used on only one computer at a time. You may not distribute copies of the SOFTWARE or Documentation to others. You may not reverse engineer, disassemble, decompile, modify, adapt, translate, or create derivative works based on the SOFTWARE or the Documentation without the prior written consent of the Company.

5.   **TRANSFER RESTRICTIONS:** The enclosed SOFTWARE is licensed only to you and may not be transferred to any one else without the prior written consent of the Company. Any unauthorized transfer of the SOFTWARE shall result in the immediate termination of this Agreement.

6.   **TERMINATION:** This license is effective until terminated. This license will terminate automatically without notice from the Company and become null and void if you fail to comply with any provisions or limitations of this license. Upon termination, you shall destroy the Documentation and all copies of the SOFTWARE. All provisions of this Agreement as to warranties, limitation of liability, remedies or damages, and our ownership rights shall survive termination.

7.   **MISCELLANEOUS:** This Agreement shall be construed in accordance with the laws of the United States of America and the State of New York and shall benefit the Company, its affiliates, and assignees.

8.   **LIMITED WARRANTY AND DISCLAIMER OF WARRANTY:** The Company warrants that the SOFTWARE, when properly used in accordance with the Documentation, will operate in substantial conformity with the description of the SOFTWARE set forth in the Documentation. The Company does not

warrant that the SOFTWARE will meet your requirements or that the operation of the SOFTWARE will be uninterrupted or error-free. The Company warrants that the media on which the SOFTWARE is delivered shall be free from defects in materials and workmanship under normal use for a period of thirty (30) days from the date of your purchase. Your only remedy and the Company's only obligation under these limited warranties is, at the Company's option, return of the warranted item for a refund of any amounts paid by you or replacement of the item. Any replacement of SOFTWARE or media under the warranties shall not extend the original warranty period. The limited warranty set forth above shall not apply to any SOFTWARE which the Company determines in good faith has been subject to misuse, neglect, improper installation, repair, alteration, or damage by you. EXCEPT FOR THE EXPRESSED WARRANTIES SET FORTH ABOVE, THE COMPANY DISCLAIMS ALL WARRANTIES, EXPRESS OR IMPLIED, INCLUDING WITHOUT LIMITATION, THE IMPLIED WARRANTIES OF MERCHANTABILITY AND FITNESS FOR A PARTICULAR PURPOSE. EXCEPT FOR THE EXPRESS WARRANTY SET FORTH ABOVE, THE COMPANY DOES NOT WARRANT, GUARANTEE, OR MAKE ANY REPRESENTATION REGARDING THE USE OR THE RESULTS OF THE USE OF THE SOFTWARE IN TERMS OF ITS CORRECTNESS, ACCURACY, RELIABILITY, CURRENTNESS, OR OTHERWISE.

IN NO EVENT, SHALL THE COMPANY OR ITS EMPLOYEES, AGENTS, SUPPLIERS, OR CONTRACTORS BE LIABLE FOR ANY INCIDENTAL, INDIRECT, SPECIAL, OR CONSEQUENTIAL DAMAGES ARISING OUT OF OR IN CONNECTION WITH THE LICENSE GRANTED UNDER THIS AGREEMENT, OR FOR LOSS OF USE, LOSS OF DATA, LOSS OF INCOME OR PROFIT, OR OTHER LOSSES, SUSTAINED AS A RESULT OF INJURY TO ANY PERSON, OR LOSS OF OR DAMAGE TO PROPERTY, OR CLAIMS OF THIRD PARTIES, EVEN IF THE COMPANY OR AN AUTHORIZED REPRESENTATIVE OF THE COMPANY HAS BEEN ADVISED OF THE POSSIBILITY OF SUCH DAMAGES. IN NO EVENT SHALL LIABILITY OF THE COMPANY FOR DAMAGES WITH RESPECT TO THE SOFTWARE EXCEED THE AMOUNTS ACTUALLY PAID BY YOU, IF ANY, FOR THE SOFTWARE.

SOME JURISDICTIONS DO NOT ALLOW THE LIMITATION OF IMPLIED WARRANTIES OR LIABILITY FOR INCIDENTAL, INDIRECT, SPECIAL, OR CONSEQUENTIAL DAMAGES, SO THE ABOVE LIMITATIONS MAY NOT ALWAYS APPLY. THE WARRANTIES IN THIS AGREEMENT GIVE YOU SPECIFIC LEGAL RIGHTS AND YOU MAY ALSO HAVE OTHER RIGHTS WHICH VARY IN ACCORDANCE WITH LOCAL LAW.

ACKNOWLEDGMENT

YOU ACKNOWLEDGE THAT YOU HAVE READ THIS AGREEMENT, UNDERSTAND IT, AND AGREE TO BE BOUND BY ITS TERMS AND CONDITIONS. YOU ALSO AGREE THAT THIS AGREEMENT IS THE COMPLETE AND EXCLUSIVE STATEMENT OF THE AGREEMENT BETWEEN YOU AND THE COMPANY AND SUPERSEDES ALL PROPOSALS OR PRIOR AGREEMENTS, ORAL, OR WRITTEN, AND ANY OTHER COMMUNICATIONS BETWEEN YOU AND THE COMPANY OR ANY REPRESENTATIVE OF THE COMPANY RELATING TO THE SUBJECT MATTER OF THIS AGREEMENT.

Should you have any questions concerning this Agreement or if you wish to contact the Company for any reason, please contact in writing at the address below.

Robin Short
Prentice Hall PTR
One Lake Street
Upper Saddle River, New Jersey 07458

The CD contains three directories. Each is a Visual C++ project. The projects were built with Visual C++ Version 6.0. You will find a separate readme file for the projects NewResource and NewResourceEx in their own project directory that has a more complete desription of what the project does. The first and second projects were created the Cluster Resource wizard found in Visual Studio. The three projects included are:

1. **ClusterApp** This program spawns a thread to create and monitor a notification port. The program then sends the following messages to the port to produce events:

- Create a group named "EventDemoGroup"
- Create a network share resource named as part of EventDemoGroup.
- Bring the group online.
- Take the group offline.
- Delete the resource.
- Delete the group.

This project must be built using the multithreaded runtime library.

2. **NewResource** This projects implements a new cluster resourcetype via a DLL.

3. **NewResourceEx** This project implements extensions to the Cluster Administrator tool. It will be necessary to modify the administration tool to support the new resourcetype created in the first project.

TECHNICAL SUPPORT

Prentice Hall does not offer technical support for this CD-ROM. However, if there is a problem with the media, you may obtain a replacement copy by emailing us with your problem at:

disc_exchange@prenhall.com